DECONSTRUCTIVE CRITICISM

DECONSTRUCTIVE
CRITICISM,

An Advanced Introduction

VINCENT B. LEITCH

1983
Columbia University Press
New York

Library of Congress Cataloging in Publication Data

Leitch, Vincent B., 1944–
Deconstructive criticism.

Includes bibliographical references and
index.
1. Deconstruction.   I. Title.
PN98.D43L4   808'.00141   82-4269
ISBN 0-231-05472-6   AACR2

Columbia University Press
New York

Clothbound editions of Columbia University Press books are Smyth-sewn
and printed on permanent and durable acid-free paper.

10 9 8 7 6 5 4

For all lost brothers and sisters

Contents

Preface

I lean back and begin to write about the book.
I write that I wish to move beyond the book . . .
      —Mark Strand, "The Story of Our Lives," *Selected Poems*

This book deals with two perennial questions: what is a text? and what is interpretation? Traditionally, the process of interpretation reconstructs themes from the rich, sometimes cryptic, substance of a text, producing as much sense and meaning as the flow of words and images permits. Interpretation resolves textual difficulties through careful comparison and combination of scattered passages. Yet, however saturated a text is with meaning, its enigmas often endure repression through omission, forgetfulness, and elision. At the end of the interpretive activity, the text is more or less intelligible because all elements appear tied together and unified. As a mode of textual theory and analysis, contemporary *deconstruction* subverts almost everything in the tradition, putting in question received ideas of the sign and language, the text, the context, the author, the reader, the role of history, the work of interpretation, and the forms of critical writing. In this project a past crumbles and something monstrous emerges: a future.

Deconstructive Criticism: An Advanced Introduction aims to portray deconstruction clearly, concisely, and comprehensively, using a prudent selection of interesting and important source materials. Such selectivity should offend someone. Patterned like a history of ideas, the book approximates a spiral as it regularly returns to significant concepts, texts, and figures. Yet reading it should produce the sense of a straightforward progress, though not a smooth narrative. Each Part follows particular directions of inspiration, tracks clusters of related concerns, and reflects recurring modes of thought and style. Occasionally, the text mimics the production of Penelope's tapestry, weaving a series of passages only to unstitch them later.

Part One focuses on modern theories of language, especially formulations of the *sign,* as they relate to the activity of textual interpretation. An initial reading of the *Iliad* briefly previews the

central problematics of the "sign in interpretation." Thereafter the
discussion reviews, in order, fundamental semiological theories
developed by Ferdinand de Saussure, Jacques Lacan, and Claude
Lévi-Strauss. Then the text summarizes Jacques Derrida's canonical critiques of each of these thinkers, highlighting initial deconstructive responses to linguistics, psychoanalysis, and anthropology. To balance the opening discussion, Derrida's early
critique of phenomenology and his attendant development of the
essential theory of *differance* receive preliminary consideration, followed by explanations of Paul de Man's and J. Hillis Miller's
related theories of language. While Part One centers on notions
of the sign, it regularly considers issues connected with interpretation and matters concerning the general style of each thinker.

Part Two opens with a manifesto concocted to preview up-
coming topics and to encapsulate the program of deconstruction.
After this short introduction, Part Two investigates theories of
literature and tradition, which usually assume or announce ac-
companying notions about language and interpretation. Such secondary matters regularly elicit serious, yet subordinate, attention.
At the outset, materials from the *destructive* phenomenologists
Martin Heidegger and William V. Spanos undergo careful exposition so as to balance further the discussion in Part One of
semiology and to situate deconstruction within its modern tradition. At this point the text considers Joseph N. Riddel's deconstructive work in its confrontation with Yale-school deconstruction, then examines Roland Barthes' later works in their striking
presentations of various unstable versions of deconstruction. To
clarify and dramatize Derrida's decisive formulations on textuality
and intertextuality, the book stages a short review of theories of
language, calling on everyone from Saussure to Barthes for an
appearance. Toward the end, Part Two surveys three separate
influential theories concerning history and tradition developed by
Hayden White, Harold Bloom, and Michel Foucault, culminating
in a discussion of various contemporary strategies designed to
subvert traditional ideas about historical contextualization.

Part Two considers formulations of literature and textuality and
of tradition and intertextuality, invoking at suitable moments discussions of language and sign theory and of theories of criticism

and interpretation. Like Part One, Part Two sets deconstructors amid nondeconstructors in order to articulate fine, though significant, points of dispute and in order to promote a productive historical understanding of deconstruction. In addition, Part Two also comments on the general style of each thinker, aiming to continue the series of swiftly etched portraits begun in Part One.

Part Three changes the focus and surveys various influential contemporary practices of critical reading and writing. It begins by reviewing Derrida's famous deconstructive reading in *Of Grammatology,* and goes on to articulate a general method of such reading. Thereafter the critical practices of de Man and Miller come under renewed consideration, leading to broad characterizations. To shift from the general to the specific, the text next considers the ground-breaking work carried out in Barthes' *S/Z,* Derrida's *Glas* and Gilles Deleuze's and Félix Guattari's *Anti-Oedipus.* Near the end a discussion of metacriticism sketches some issues and directions in current criticism, focusing on the work of Geoffrey Hartman. To conclude, Part Three offers the reader a review and summary of the previously discussed interpretive modes and styles of all the central figures considered throughout the book. Like Parts One and Two, Part Three brings in important nondeconstructors to highlight significant issues of contention surrounding deconstruction and to distinguish deconstruction from other related projects. Throughout Part Three matters of critical reading and writing dominate the discussions, though topics examined in earlier Parts are always more or less near at hand.

Discussed on scholarly panels and television talk shows and written up in professional journals and mass-circulation magazines, deconstruction since the mid-1970s has provoked widespread astonishment and condemnation. Often the press on deconstruction pushes its points without benefit of preliminary readings or familiarity with fundamentals. Rather than argue merits, *Deconstructive Criticism* explains deconstruction—disinclined to take particular sides, uninterested in advancing "original" knowledge, and uncommitted to converting the wary or reluctant reader. A certain "neutrality" characterizes the book's strategy, which is designed to suit the general state of current knowledge and information about deconstruction. More introduction and survey than polemic or manifesto, *Deconstructive Criticism*, nevertheless, inevitably assumes a sympathetic stance toward deconstruction.

Infectious, corrosive, and irrepressible, deconstruction regularly threatens all forms of convention. In particular, it undermines the very notion *book,* offering in its place a radical form nicknamed *text*. Caught between these two, *Deconstructive Criticism* continuously imitates the book. Strictly speaking, to write a *book* on deconstruction should not be possible. Our present vantage and aim, however, compel us to repeat the book and to delay the move beyond it.

Acknowledgments

Bits and pieces of this book first appeared in *Studies in the Literary Imagination* (Spring 1979), 12, *Critical Inquiry* (Summer 1980), 6, and a Finnish *Festschrift* entitled *Mitat ja puntit: Tutkielmia kirjallisuudesta Pekka Mattilalle* (Weights and Measures: Studies in Literature for Pekka Mattila), ed. I. Tiitinen et al. (Tampere, Finland: University of Tampere Publications, 1980). I am grateful to the editors and publishers for permission to reprint.

Several stanzas from "The Thinker as Poet" are printed with the permission of Harper & Row Publishers from Martin Heidegger's *Poetry, Language, Thought,* translated by Albert Hofstadter, © 1971 by Martin Heidegger. A few lines from "The Widow" are printed with the permission of Atheneum Publishers from W. S. Merwin's *The Lice,* © 1967 by W. S. Merwin. And some lines from Homer's *Iliad,* translated by Richmond Lattimore, are printed with the permission of the University of Chicago Press, © 1951.

Deconstructive Criticism was a long time in planning. It started in 1976 at Princeton University when I was studying in a seminar with Earl Miner, and continued in earnest at the School of Criticism and Theory in 1978 where, as a Fellow, I worked with Geoffrey Hartman and Murray Krieger. It approached fruition in 1980 with the aid of a grant from the National Endowment for the Humanities. I am grateful to the Endowment, the School of Criticism and Theory, and to Professors Miner, Hartman, and Krieger. Mercer University provided released time from teaching duties and financial support for which I am thankful.

Some of my material was initially assembled for classroom presentations, conference speeches, and book reviews. Particularly helpful in this process was a course of lectures I delivered in 1979 at the University of Tampere in Finland where I served as a Fulbright-Hays Lecturer. I am grateful to my students and colleagues abroad.

Of people who have aided my thinking and assisted in this endeavor I want to mention my generous colleague John Dunaway. I thank Jill, Kristin, and Rory for love and patience.

I

SEMIOLOGY AND DECONSTRUCTION: MODERN THEORIES OF THE SIGN

Prologue: The Greek Edge

Readers of the *Iliad* remember well the valor of Hector, yet often forget his striking lack of luck, dramatically manifested by his failures with interpretation. When Hector converses with Poly-damas, who was "born on the same night with him," he four times exhibits the dangers and difficulties of interpretation. At the exact center of the *Iliad*, to take one telling instance, these Trojan doubles stand precariously before the Greek camp near a ditch's edge:

> As they were urgent to cross a bird sign had appeared to them,
> an eagle, flying high and holding to the left of the people
> and carrying in its talons a gigantic snake, blood-coloured,
> alive still and breathing, it had not forgotten its warcraft
> yet, for writhing back it struck the eagle that held it
> by chest and neck, so that the eagle let it drop groundward
> in pain of the bite, and dashed it down in the midst of the battle
> and itself, screaming high, winged away down the wind's blast.[1]

(12. 200–7)

Seeing this sign, the Trojan soldiers shiver with fear. The text tells us the sign is "a portent of Zeus of the aegis." (The "aegis" is itself an elaborate sign.) Venturing his interpretation, Polydamas employs an analogy: just as the eagle harmed its prey yet failed to return home in triumph, so the Trojans will hurt the Greeks yet face eventual disaster in crossing over the ditch. He concludes: "'hōdé ke hupokrínaito theoprópos, hòs sápha thumō̄/ eideíei teráon kaí hoi peithoíato laoí'" ("'So an interpreter of the gods would answer, one who knew in his mind the truth of portents, and whom the people believed in'"—12. 228–29).[2] Presump-tuously, Polydamas casts himself as a double for the absent prophet—the man with special interpretive powers and the trust of the community. To be sure, Polydamas begins carefully enough, prefacing his interpretation with "'if the bird sign . . . was a true one,'" yet he is soon enmeshed in his reading. In spite of discretion, the interpreter quickly becomes a rhetorician and soothsayer, believing firmly in the truth of reading. What about his double?

Hector's impatient response to the other's interpretation is, we recognize, typical: his colleague isn't serious; his friend can "'contrive a saying better than this one'"; his double's brains are addled. Past the emotion, Hector counters "'you tell me to put my trust in birds, who spread wide their wings, I care nothing for these, I think nothing of them. . . .'" Thus he calls into doubt the status of the sign itself, not the validity of Polydamas' reading. Here erupts a crisis in interpretation. For Polydamas the bird clearly signifies something: in this case the message of an absent god (Zeus of the aegis). While he initially expresses some doubt of this certainty, he quickly forgets his reservation, grounding his interpretation in an elaborate analogy and authorizing it in the guise of a seer. For Hector the bird signifies "nothing"; there is no reserve. Hector refuses interpretation. Yet this refusal is a reading.

Hector directly undermines the interpretation of Polydamas by claiming special status. His knowledge surpasses the would-be soothsayer's; he possesses a guarantee from Zeus: "'Zeus guarantees power to you to kill men, till you make your way to the strong-benched vessels, until the sun goes down and the blessed darkness comes over'" (11. 207–9). With this prior pledge from Zeus, delivered personally by the goddess Iris, Hector confidently refutes the venturesome rhetoric and prophetic posturing of Polydamas. The basis of Hector's interpretation is faith in Iris' message. Clearly, the contrived reading of Polydamas is wrong. Thus Hector can enact an ironic reversal of Polydamas: "'let us put our trust in the counsel of great Zeus, he who is lord over all mortal men and all the immortals'" (12. 241–42). The man of faith here tells the worried prophet to trust in the god—which, of course, is exactly what the new seer first professed to do. This drama of two people reading differently the messages of the god is familiar enough.

But is it so? This epic demonstrates that neither Hector nor Polydamas actually reads the discourse of Zeus. Significantly, the guarantee of Zeus ends when the "sun goes down," which both fail to remember. (We may forgive Polydamas since the messenger of Zeus did not visit him.) Because of the oversight, Hector refuses interpretation of the bird sign and Polydamas relents from his initial reading. The Trojans cross the edge and attack the Greeks' defenses "in the confidence of the portents shown," meaning in the (interpreted) assurance that Zeus is with them. Still, just a few minutes earlier they were shivering at "a portent of Zeus." The community here invests Hector with the power to read divine portents. In an obvious reversal, Hector without discretion plays the prophet, who believes firmly in the truth of his interpretation. He practices rhetoric when he urges "'let us put our trust in the counsel of great Zeus,'" for this is the counsel of Hector—this is his reading substituted for the mediated and forgotten text of Zeus. The truth slips away. The original text is irretrievable. Two soothsayers vie for authority. Forgetfulness grounds their enterprise. Just as the bird sign is a colorful substitute for the absent word of the god, so the trusted interpretation of the hero takes the place of the unrecoverable text of Zeus. Everywhere the discourse is doubled; all now labor in the same night of darkness.

In one reading the "sign" enjoys divine status, receiving the inspired rhetoric and visionary interpretation of a clear-headed and prudent leader. (Commentators appear unanimous on this assessment of Polydamas.) In another, the sign means nothing: it is a nonsignifying natural phenomenon in the mind of a courageous and blessed hero. The community awaits the outcome of the crisis. This outcome rests in the interpretation of an unreachable prior text.

Yet the conception of "sign" is the key factor in any elucidation of the crisis. Both interpreters tacitly agree that the sign may be meaningless. Thus any eventual meaning must be, to some extent, arbitrated and arbitrary. Polydamas admits his reservations. The sign need not make reference to Zeus, or to ephemeral victory, or to eventual disaster. A space exists between the sign and its potential meaning. And another space opens between an assigned meaning—whatever it may be—and the actual reality. These two openings constitute the spaces of interpretation—the conditions under which any and all interpretation is possible. To close these gaps, to perform an interpretation, is necessarily to play the rhetorician and the prophet. Polydamas and Hector demonstrate the process.

As it happens, the venturesome reading of Polydamas is indeed prophetic: the Trojans suffer eventual disaster. Yet this outcome

involves luck, despite the fact that birds in the conventions of
Greek culture are invariably signs from the gods (see, e.g., 24.
281–322; and *Oedipus the King*, 964–72). Any particular bird may
or may not be a divine messenger. Again, luck is with Polydamas
on this occasion. The conclusion is clear: the interpreter appears
generically as soothsayer, who must contrive readings from signs,
who must always cover over the spaces of interpretation. So it
is with Hector. To decide the status of the bird sign he has recourse
to an earlier text (to prior signs), which allows him to refute the
assigned meaning of Polydamas' reading: disaster is impossible;
Zeus (-Iris) pledged victory; Polydamas is wrong. Like Polydamas, Hector finds himself playing seer and rhetor. In an act of
faith, he negates the reality of Polydamas' assigned meaning. For
his part, Polydamas, in an act of faith, assigns and then asserts the
meaning of the sign—only after repressing his reservations. (Hector represses the text of Iris through forgetfulness.) The spaces
of interpretation are silently covered over. Swiftly the crisis is
resolved. Unluckily, disaster comes on apace.

In the Homeric text only the Olympian narrator receives im-
munity from the crisis of interpretation. But does he really? The
narrator wants us to believe that the gods create the text—not he.
Thus the gods are invoked at the very outset and occasionally
thereafter as reminders:

> Tell me now, you Muses who have your homes on Olympos.
> For you, who are goddesses, are there, and you know all things,
> and we have heard only the rumour of it and know nothing.
>
> (2. 484–86)

Since the gods tell the story, the text is true. Here the narrator
joins Hector and Polydamas: he too is seer and rhetor, covering
over the treacherous spaces of interpretation and truth in the name
of the divine. (Given the transmission of the *Iliad* from ancient to
contemporary times, we may think of this narrator as "plural"
and the text as permanently "mediated.")

Is anyone surprised that all readers must join this visionary
company of prophets and rhetoricians? The structure of interpretation repeats itself ceaselessly. We all stand precariously before
the edge of the Greek encampment, fronting the spaces of error
under the sign.

I

Foundations: Linguistics, Psychoanalysis, and Anthropology

A Modern Adamic Enterprise

A science that studies the life of signs within society is conceivable; . . . I shall call it *semiology* (from Greek *sēmeîon* 'sign'). Semiology would show what constitutes signs, what laws govern them. Since the science does not yet exist, no one can say what it would be. . . .

Here Ferdinand de Saussure, the twentieth-century father of the science of *signs*, stakes out a virgin territory and confers a Greek name.[1] This Adamic enterprise, first made public during the ravenous trench-warfare of World War I, has dramatically affected most discussions of the sign and of interpretation since its inauguration. Unpredictably, Saussure constructed the groundwork for intellectual crisis in our time.

Here is Saussure's theory of the sign. All signs conjoin a form and a concept, a signifier and a signified, as when the packet of six English phonemes in "eraser" [ɪresər] summons up in the mind the simple idea "eraser." Significantly, the relationship of the signifier and the signified, the two components of the sign, is arbitrary. For example, the phonemes in "pyyhekumi" suggest to Finnish ears and eyes the concept "eraser." Say [ɪresər] to a Finn and you will get no response, for this pattern of English sounds is meaningless. The signifier is arbitrary. (The only minor exception is onomatopoeia, where the signifier's sound image is "motivated" by imitation.) Not only the signifier but the signified is arbitrary: "relay" in Chaucer's time meant "a set of fresh hounds or horses posted to take up a chase" and in our time "an electromagnetic device for remote control of other devices in a circuit." Concepts change often. A leisurely glance at the *Oxford English Dictionary* convinces the wary. No necessary or natural or essential meaning—no intrinsic property—exists to determine or fix the signified of a signifier: the concept connected with a signifier may assume any shape. The arbitrary nature of both components of the sign renders the relationship between signifier and signified as differential or, let's say, relational. In every case, it's a matter, not of simple identity, but of *difference.*

What is the import of *difference?* In order for any signifier to express meaning, it must differ from the other signifiers in a language. So too, each signified in a linguistic system must be different—however minimal the contrast—from all others. For signs to work in language differences are essential. (While cast as linguistic rules, these observations endure empirical testing.) The point is made succinctly by Saussure: "A linguistic system is a series of differences of sound combined with a series of differences of ideas . . ." (120). The sign in a language is constituted by the differences that separate its acoustic image and its core idea from those of all other signs: the sign is always distinct—different. Put in other terms, "a segment of language can never in the final analysis be based on anything except its noncoincidence with the rest" (118). Any sign is what all the others are not.

Saussure insists on the linguistic *system* as the place of the sign. Signs don't exist outside a system. And it is always a system of differences. "Whether we take the signified or the signifier, language has neither ideas nor sounds that existed before the linguistic system, but only conceptual and phonic differences that have issued from the system" (120). To accept the theory of the sign is to accede the primary place of the linguistic system. Language (as system) provides the very possibility of the sign. There is no "before" or "outside" language.

Inevitably, the theory of signs leads Saussure to the theory of language as system. It is so because signs are differential and arbitrary, which compels him to envision and situate the linguistic system as primary ground. Making a distinction between *langue* (language) and *parole* (speech), he presents the overall linguistic system as two-sided: language/speech, institution/event, system/realization, society/individual, grammar/usage, rules/expressions, synchrony/diachrony, model/data. . . . One could go on. The point is that Saussure focuses almost exclusively on *langue*—on the structural rather than the empirical side of language. As such, he is the forerunner of modern theorists of structuralism: for Saussure, language is a largely unconscious system of hierarchical elements and forces defined always by their differences from and relations to one another within a system.

In semiology there are three types of signs so classified by the different relations of their signifiers and signifieds.[2] With the *index* the relationship is causal: dark clouds mean rain; smoke denotes fire; sobbing signifies sorrow. With the *icon* the relation is one of resemblance: a portrait bust depicts a particular person. With the *symbol* (or *sign* proper) the relationship is arbitrary: nodding the head signifies "yes"; [ɪresər] connotes "eraser." Saussure focuses mostly on the *sign* (*symbol*)—on the *arbitrary* signifier and signified.

A thorough semiological interpretation, for instance, of the structure of alchemy or astrology would yield a map of the rules and conventions that operate in these fields of knowledge. Since we no longer believe in these sciences, the analysis would focus on signs, not indices. It doesn't matter, though, whether we believe or not. The result is the same. To chart rules and conventions (structures) is not to uncover truth. Semiology doesn't seek truth. Focusing on the operations of the signifier, rather than the fortunes of truth, semiology lays bare the grounds of signifying practices—the codes or sign systems used in the production of meaning. Accordingly, astrology and, say, meteorology are framed as "systems of discourse," not sciences of true statements. With such semiological analysis Saussure opened for meticulous inspection the spaces in the activity of all human interpretation.

Toward the end of his life Saussure expended vast energies in collecting concealed anagrams of proper names from poetry. He worked here to uncover a systematic signifying code used in the production of poetic meaning.[3] In fact, he endeavored to create a new type of reading, moving from the sign itself to the isolated syllable. He suffered doubts, however, for he realized that he could never decide the actual status of anagrams. Did the poets intend such signifying codes? Were these devices accidental or designed? Guiltily, Saussure continued to interpret this poetry creatively, compiling massive notes, yet always on edge in the role of interpretive seer. "L' 'anagramme' n'est pas à définir comme une dislocation réglée en mal de complétude, mais comme une multiplicité infixable, indécidabilité radicale qui défait tous les codes" (The "anagram" should not be defined as a regulated dislocation lacking completeness, but as an indeterminable multiplicity, a radical undecidability, which undoes all codes).[4]

Perhaps fancifully, the Saussurean life-work can serve as an allegory of our time. We can envision the history of the contemporary critical or interpretive project as moving always between a rigorous science seeking structural rules and an indiscreet art celebrating creative readings. In the flight from postwar structuralism to space-age poststructuralism, we may trace shifts from the object of analysis to the reader, from a generative theory of the work to a textual or rhetorical theory of discourse, from codification of signs to explosion of all chains of (isolated) signifiers, from law to anarchy, from exacting science to extreme art, from seriousness to play. (However, Saussure's Adamic guilt is now invariably absent.) One could go on multiplying these oppositions. Too simply put, the career of Saussure suggests the outer boundaries of the contemporary hermeneutic enterprise. His theory of the sign typically serves as a beginning. And as his work on anagrams comes more completely into view, one detects an outline of end-point. Or at least traces of what an end might look like. But this is fancy.

The Language of Dreams

the slightest alteration in the relation between man and the signifier, in this case in the procedures of exegesis, changes the whole course of history by modifying the lines which anchor his being.[5]

—Jacques Lacan

Insofar as Saussure altered the relation between man and the signifier, he precipitated crises in the sciences and arts of interpretation. Jacques Lacan, the contemporary French psychoanalyst, early recognized Saussure's distinction, and he set about reformulating traditional Freudian theory using linguistic and semiological insights. In this dramatic postwar recasting of Saussure and Freud, Lacan called for renewed attention to the Freudian texts and the revision of psychoanalysis along structuralist lines. Essentially, Lacan perceived that "the unconscious is the whole structure of language" and that "the dream-work follows the laws of the signifier" (147, 161). Meticulously working out the implications of these striking insights, Lacan fathered a contemporary psychoanalysis, all the while seeming more and more to be a second Adam for semiology.

The rupture between the old and the new psychoanalysis appears most prominently in Lacan's *Discourse of Rome*, delivered in Italy at a divisive congress of analysts in the fall of 1953 and printed up three years later. In this lengthy manifesto, Lacan castigates the traditionalists and instigates the new directions.[6] Here and in "The Insistence [or Agency] of the Letter" (1957) he initiates his revisionary project mainly through several significant extensions of Saussure's sign theory. According to Lacan, the formula,

$$\frac{\text{Signifier} \quad S}{\text{signified} \quad s}$$

establishes "the primordial position of the signifier and the signified as being distinct orders separated initially by a barrier resisting signification" (149). This opening strategic fracture of a simple harmony between signifier and signified, between spoken word and its intended concept, allows Lacan to hold to one side of the dividing edge and to dwell on the signifier. Ultimately, Lacan will warn us not to "cling to the illusion that the signifier answers to the function of representing the signified, or better, that the signifier has to answer for its existence in the name of any signification whatever" (150). In this crucial moment, Lacan sets the signifier free of the signified. Henceforth we encounter a "sliding signified" and "floating signifier."

At this point Lacan breaks up an old heroic affair, bows before the barrier, and celebrates primordial *difference* as impassable. Ever more intensely his signifier doesn't represent the signified. The Lacanian signifier need not signify at all; it may float free.

To situate this pure signifier in practice, let us pursue a psychological perspective. Constituted before we are born, linguistic and cultural systems impose orders and structures upon us *as* we come into language. We enter into a network of preexistent signifiers. For any single signifier to operate, as Saussure teaches us, it must be enmeshed in a language system. This network is the very condition of language. Accordingly, the relationship of signifier to signified (or $\frac{S}{s}$) is continually mediated for us through the whole body of signs in a language. In this instance, *the* formulaic line or "barrier" or difference marks out the structural detour of the signifier in its quest for the signified—for meaning.

Between immediate experience and use of signifiers there lies an obvious gap. When we explain and envision our selves and our world to our selves in discourse, we undermine any possibility of immediate relation between self and experience. Further rupture. We construct "self" in language—as we wish it to be or want it to appear. Seeking to organize and mold experience, our reflection diverges from that experience: our signifiers deflect our reflection. (Experiences of reality are mediated through signifiers, as is experience of self.) Thus the barrier at the core of the sign, the fraction in sign, designates the wandering space of the signifier as it cuts away from and toward any signified.

Extending Freudian theories, Lacan suggests some provocative ratios—

$$\frac{S}{s} :: \frac{\text{Consciousness}}{\text{Unconscious}}$$

—in which the Unconscious is the whole structure of language and its dreamwork follows the laws of the signifier. In this scheme psycho*analysis* becomes rhetorical exegesis of the Unconscious through the signifier. So where Freud sees psychic "distortion," Lacan sights the *floating signifier*. Moreover, Freud's dream "displacement" shows up in Lacan as *metonymy* and "condensation" becomes *metaphor*. The range of "defense mechanisms" is glimpsed as a stock of *tropes and figures*: "Periphrasis, hyperbaton, ellipsis, suspension, anticipation, retraction, negation, disgression, irony, these are the figures of style (Quintilian's *figurae sententiarum*); as catachresis, litotes, antonomasia, hypotyposis are the tropes, whose terms suggest themselves as the most proper for the labeling of these mechanisms" (169). To sum up, the Freudian processes of dream formation become operative tropes and figures of rhetoric in Lacan. The Unconscious is a writing system. From the verbal report of the dream by the dreamer down to the production of the dream in the Unconscious, rhetorical processes structure all operations. Necessarily, psychoanalysis is rhetorical exegesis.

Where Freud sees the general dynamic of psychic "distortion," Lacan observes the *floating signifier*. Examples for Freud of such distortions formed in the Unconscious include dream substitutions, reversals, inversions, associations, and identifications.[7] According to Freud, these distortions ultimately disguise the signified beyond recognition. In other words, the formative processes of the dreamwork in the Unconscious distort and thereby create floating signifiers. Just here Lacan revises Freud, observing that all signifiers float since they are always already productions of the human psyche. To the extent that signifiers have psychological values and associations, they have undergone some degree of distortion. All signifiers are distorted from the start. While Freud implies an originally undistorted signifier that, unfortunately, undergoes later distortion, Lacan posits distortion at the source so that no uncontaminated signifier exists to start with.

For Lacan dream "displacement" manifests itself as *metonymy*. To characterize this phenomenon, he constructs a formula (164):

$$f (S \ldots S') \ S \cong S \ (\text{---}) \ s$$

(Here $\cong$ means "equivalence" and (---) means *the* "barrier.") Metonymy S functions f by the displacement from one signifier to another (S . . . S'). The first signifier S is equivalent $\cong$ to the second one S: just as the first signifier hides a displaced original term and thereby resists revealing the complete signified, so the

second signifier retains the line of resistance—the "barrier" (—)
s. Metonymy suppresses one term. But this is a rhetorical decoding only. From a psychoanalytic perspective, the formula describes
the classic machinations of the psychic Censor, in which the force
of censorship displaces a significant term by calling on a contiguous one as substitute for disguise. Further, the formula depicts
the conventional psychic displacement of desire from a "true"
object to an insignificant "false" one, revealing the "lack of being"
inherent in repressed desire (164). In general, Lacan's formula
displays psycho*analysis* as a scientific rhetoric of the Unconscious
while it demonstrates how the dreamwork follows the basic laws
of the signifier. It provides a scientific illustration of his theory
of the "unconscious as the structure of language." And it shows
that the signifier doesn't represent the signified. Finally, it portrays
the psyche as a system of discourse—a writing machine.

In an early seminal essay, "The Mirror Stage as Formative of
the Function of the I" (*Écrits*, 1–7), first written in 1936 and later
revised in 1949, Lacan outlines a prelinguistic stage of psychological development that occurs in infancy sometime during the first
six to eighteen months. Recognizing her own image in a mirror,
the infant identifies and assumes an image—an "Ideal-I" or fictional *Ego*—prior to broad social determination, before contact
with the Other, earlier than entry into language. This "specular
I" soon engages the Other, society, and language whereupon the
pure subject encounters the whole human world of mediated
knowledge and experience: the world of signifiers quickly comes
into play. Still, the imaginary "I" created in infancy remains important life-long psychic material for psychoanalysis. Fascinating
in itself, the *stade du miroir* modifies, however minimally, the thoroughgoing linguistic determinism first apparent in Lacanian
psychoanalysis.[8]

What are the methods of interpretation in Lacan's psychoanalysis? Passing through the "defiles of the signifier," the psychoanalyst tries to track the flights and conversions of reality and fantasy
in the subject so as to let him see "to what signifier—to what
irreducible, traumatic, non-meaning—he is, as a subject, subjected."[9] Strictly speaking, the analyst doesn't search for meaning.

Working at the level of the signifier in the Unconscious, the Lacanian exegete seeks the signification of irreducible, nonsensical signifying elements. The "effect of interpretation is to isolate in the subject a kernel, a *kern*, to use Freud's own term, of *non-sense*, [which] does not mean that interpretation is in itself nonsense" (250). The disabling nonmeaning embedded in a primary signifier is approximated as signification by the analyst and revealed to the subject. In this procedure, "it is false to say, as has been said, that interpretation is open to all meanings under the pretext that it is a question only of the connection of a signifier to a signifier, and consequently of an uncontrollable connection. Interpretation is not open to any meaning" (249–50). The kernel of non-sense, the primary signifier lodged in the Unconscious, destroys meaning for the subject, which interpretation reveals for him. Not surprisingly, the interpretation itself may appear as nonsense to anyone uninformed. There are, quite clearly, several ways to read Lacan's "Interpretation is not open to any meaning."

The dissemination of Lacanian psychoanalytic theory through the intellectual environment creates a second phase for semiology as well as a renewal of Freudian studies. As it enters into literary criticism, Lacanian psychoanalysis, dragging along its commentators, opens new territory and affirms the structuralism already at work. It helps to confirm further the postwar model of the text as a system of discourse composed of floating signifiers. Exposing the mimetic fallacy from a new angle, Lacan assists in subverting any naive belief in the referential function of language and, in doing so, he further insures the growing prominence of linguistic determinism. As a playful, sometimes elegant, yet often opaque prose stylist, he legitimates the allusive and surreal critical writing style much in favor among avant-garde literary critics. Where Lacan fashions memorable epigrams and amusing, yet telling puns, his followers too often imitate the master with a dreary difference. All of Lacan's printed work consists of public addresses, speeches, seminars, and other occasional pieces, lending an abiding sense of performance to his work. Unmistakably, Lacan plays, like some latter-day gingerbread man, the elusive visionary, refusing with much refinement and rarity to be caught, systematized, stopped, signified. Jacques Lacan is emperor of the exquisite and alluring ellipsis. With his language of dreams, he courts the uncanny; it beckons as cure, as final fetish for literary criticism.

The Ways of the Shaman

Whatever emendations the original formulation may now call for, everybody will agree that the Saussurean principle of the *arbitrary character of linguistic signs* was a prerequisite for the accession of linguistics to the scientific level.[10]

We conceive anthropology as the *bona fide* occupant of that domain of semiology which linguistics has not already claimed for its own. . . .[11]

—Claude Lévi-Strauss

Here in two of the most important and influential essays written during a world-famous, forty-year career, Claude Lévi-Strauss situates his project and that of anthropology under the sign of Saussure. To be sure, he had effected this as early as 1945 with the publication of a programmatic inaugural essay in *Word: Journal of the Linguistic Circle of New York.*[12] Yet, as a colleague of Roman Jakobson at the École Libre des Hautes Études in New York, where both were teaching during the war years, Lévi-Strauss from the outset actually favored a Jakobsonian or Eastern European version of Saussurean linguistics. In fact, he has always followed the emended Saussure of R. Jakobson and N. S. Troubetzkoy.

What are the basic emendations? Going beyond Saussure, Troubetzkoy details the rules for determining, classifying, and combining phonemes. Then Jakobson provides a further refinement, demonstrating that phonemic oppositions are systematically binary, begetting ternary structural patterns through the presence of gradational or mediating phonemes. This theory of dichotomous relations deployed with systematic mediations is the machine that powers all of Lévi-Strauss' structuralist studies: his anthropological data regularly reduce to mediated binary oppostions. Just as basic linguistic units like phonemes necessarily operate within systems of binary/ternary relations, so elementary cultural units function through demonstrable patterns of two- and three-way oppositions.

The influence of Eastern European linguistics on Lévi-Strauss is broader, though less singular or crucial, than the continuous and rigorous application of binary analytics. When he comes to stipulate the four key operations of structuralism in the inaugural program set up during the war, Lévi-Strauss relies completely on a Troubetzkoy article of 1933. Here the Russian phonologist outlines the basic procedures for structural analysis. First, structural inquiry investigates unconscious infrastructures of phenomena—not their observable or conscious layers; second, it treats terms "in relation"—not as independent entities; third, it focuses always on systems; and fourth, it founds general laws, using either induction or deduction to establish the absolute character of such laws. Not surprisingly, Lévi-Strauss here nominates Troubetzkoy as "the illustrious founder of structural linguistics" (*SA*, 33).

Following Jakobson, Lévi-Strauss seeks the smallest constituent units in his anthropological analyses of mythological and kinship systems. Like phonemes, his *mythemes* embody the most basic "relations" in a system of myth. To uncover these mythemes, the analyst works through a myth aiming to connect a subject and a function in a minimal formulation of one sentence only. For instance, "Oedipus marries his mother, Jocasta" (see *SA*, 213–19). Once all such mythemes are isolated, a chart is constructed in which homologous mythemes are aligned vertically in respective columns. To the Oedipus-Jocasta column we can add these homologous constituent units (mythemes): (1) "Antigone buries her brother, Polynices, despite prohibition" and (2) "Cadmos seeks his sister Europa, ravished by Zeus." Thereafter each column of homologies is interpreted. The illustrative Oedipus column, for instance, signifies an "overrating of blood relations." Finally, relations—that is ratios and proportions—between and among all columns of homologies are examined. In the end, the four columns of the Oedipus myth form a compact proportion: "[1] the overrating of blood relations is to [2] the underrating of blood relations as [3] the attempt to escape autochthony is to [4] the impossibility to succeed in it" (my brackets). Here we read the "structural law" of the Oedipus myth. Glancing back over this sketch, we can detect the fourfold operation of Troubetzkoy. In addition, we can spot Lévi-Strauss' preference for synchronic or homologous relations over diachronic or narrative successions; he values the underlying system over actual narrative realization—Saussurean *langue* over *parole*. Most revealing, Lévi-Strauss formulates the structural law of myth as a system of binary oppositions. He insists that "mythical thought always progresses from the awareness of oppositions . . ." and that "two opposite terms with no intermediary always tend to be replaced by two equivalent terms which admit of a third one as mediator . . ." (*SA*, 224).[13] Characteristically, binary oppositions tend toward mediations in a manner faithful to Jakobson's ternary structural patterns.

Taking inspiration and direction from structural linguists, Lévi-Strauss institutes the mytheme as an elementary constituent unit, which serves functions comparable to that of the phoneme in linguistics. Very rarely does he employ the "sign," a larger unit, in the manner of Saussure or the fashion of Lacan.[14] Just as the overall progression in modern science is toward ever smaller units of analysis (atoms → neutrons/protons/electrons → quarks; cells → organelles → membranes/proteins), so the general direction of structuralism is from the word to the signifier/signified to the phoneme. (Eventually, we shall exceed all distinctive features and arrive at the imperceptible "trace.") Actually, though, Lévi-Strauss conceives of the mytheme as a unit qualitatively different from the sign or the phoneme; it is not, in fact, an issue of magnitude. "It is a different matter with mythemes, since they result from a play of binary or ternary oppositions (which makes them comparable to phonemes). But they do so among elements which are already full of signification at the level of the language . . ." (*SA* 2: 143). Unlike the phoneme or (floating) signifier, mythemes, like words, signify, appearing to contradict the general semiological trend toward ever more minimal and *non*signifying elements for analysis. Yet, mythemes "operate simultaneously on two levels: that of language, where they keep on having their own meaning, and that of metalanguage, where they participate as elements of a supersignification that can come only from their union" (*SA* 2: 143). What Lévi-Strauss stresses is the insignificance of mythemes as "words on the level of language" and the importance of these constituent elements as future supersignifiers in the metalanguage of synchronic structuralist analyses. This transvaluation of sign value effects a devaluation of the sign similar to Lacan's. When Lévi-Strauss institutes the mytheme, he establishes a minimal unit of potential signification which functions in the unconscious infrastructures of language. Like Saussure's arbitrary signifier and Lacan's floating signifier, Lévi-Strauss' mytheme resists signification, except through structuralist analysis. Mythemes, as Lévi-Strauss revealingly insists, "are, to use the formula applied by Jakobson to phonemes, 'purely differential and contentless signs.'"[15] The mytheme as such possesses no content.

The domain of signification is the Unconscious. Hence, Lévi-Strauss conceives of structuralism as an investigator of unconscious rules and structures. But the Unconscious itself ceases to operate as the traditional distinctive repository of individual experiences and memories; it is not a specific place—a crypt; rather it serves a general function. "It is reducible to a function—the symbolic function . . . which is carried out according to the same laws among all men. . . . As the organ of a specific function, the unconscious merely imposes structural laws upon inarticulated elements which originate elsewhere—impulses, emotions, representations, and memories" (SA, 203). The results of structuralist analyses often appear unpredictable and surprising since they articulate *hidden* infrastructures of experience. Framed as general laws or universal truths, these secrets precede the individual and consciousness. In the Overture to the four magisterial volumes of *Mythologiques* (1964–1971), which inventories more than eight hundred myths, Lévi-Strauss states: "I therefore claim to show, not how men think in myths, but how myths operate in men's minds without their being aware of the fact."[16] The structuring operations in the Unconscious, primordial forces of nature, underlie culture and consciousness. Unlike Freud's Unconscious, Lévi-Strauss' precedes the thinking subject and provides order for his subjectivity. Thus the ultimate dream of Lévi-Strauss is to chart the Adamic laws of all life. Not surprisingly, he journeys to the primeval gardens of primitive societies to restore the lost gods of myth and to reveal the hidden rules of human community.

Like Lacan, Lévi-Strauss sees the Unconscious as language system. But he is less forward and systematic and seems more careful, sometimes secretive, in this matter, proceeding often on the level of implication and intuition. Written in English for a conference at Indiana University, the following statement reveals his characteristic tone and care: "Language, from this point of view, may appear as laying a kind of foundation for the more complex structures which correspond to the different aspects of culture" (*SA*, 69).[17] Language is foundation for culture. Or is it? Kind of. Cultural mechanisms "correspond" to linguistic operations, yet the nature of the correspondence remains unexplored; we never get a rigorous rhetoric of culture.

Lévi-Strauss' method of interpretation is not rhetorical but scientific. It values trial and error, economy of explanation, and unity of solution. And it courts the power to predict (*SA*, 211). Detailed charts, graphs, and mathematical formulas proliferate to bring copious data to precise order. Computers are praised and coveted. More than Roland Barthes' catechismal *Elements of Semiology* (1964), the work of Lévi-Strauss serves as the testament of scientific semiology and structuralism. Yet the texts of the master invite another view. In the Overture to the *Mythologiques*, for instance, he confides: "It follows that this book on myths is itself a kind of myth" (*RC*, 6). When he proffers the exemplary analysis of the Oedipus myth, he warns: "The 'demonstration' should therefore be conceived, not in terms of what the scientist means by this term, but at best in terms of what is meant by the street peddler, whose aim is not to achieve a concrete result, but to explain, as succinctly as possible, the functioning of the mechanical toy which he is trying to sell to the onlookers" (*SA*, 213). Not scientific demonstration, but "at best" a sales pitch from a street peddler—Lévi-Strauss as huckster offers us a beguiling portrait of structuralism. Structural models are mechanical toys. Explanations are sidewalk hustles. All is admitted. Using for a moment the often repeated terms of his *The Savage Mind*, we can easily oppose Lévi-Strauss' methods here as a kind of *bricoleur* (handyman) to those of the "engineer." As *bricoleur*, he employs everything at hand to create structures for past events, unlike the scientist who changes the world and creates events by means of his refined structures. Is Lévi-Strauss peddler, odd-job man, engineer, or scientist? Perhaps the appropriate figure for him is neither salesman nor man of science but shaman.

Attracted to this mysterious figure in more than one study, Lévi-Strauss early exhibits special sympathy for the shaman. Is it merely whimsical to see the master as a double for the magician?

When he examines an exemplary South American shaman's ritual song cure, administered to a native woman during a difficult childbirth, Lévi-Strauss comes to a special understanding:

> From our brief synopsis, the song appears to be rather commonplace. The sick woman suffers because she has lost her spiritual double or, more correctly, one of the specific doubles which together constitute her vital strength. . . . The shaman, assisted by his tutelary spirits, undertakes a journey to the supernatural world in order to snatch the double from the malevolent spirit who has captured it; by restoring it to its owner, he achieves the cure. The exceptional interest of this text does not lie in this formal framework, but, rather, in the discovery . . . that *Mu-Igala*, that is, "Muu's way" [Muu is the feminine power forming the fetus in the uterus] and the abode of Muu are not, to the native mind, simply a mythical itinerary and dwelling-place. They represent, literally, the vagina and uterus of the pregnant woman, which are explored by the shaman and *nuchu* [protective spirits embodied in figurines] and in whose depths they wage their victorious combat. (*SA*, 188)

On the one hand, this shamanistic cure is unexceptional: the virtuoso magician restores vital strength by making a symbolic journey in song to retrieve a lost soul from an evil underworld spirit. On the other hand, the cure of the shaman is exceptional: the gifted doctor journeys after the underworld spirit through a literal voyage into the birth canal where some strong power blocks delivery. The symbolic mode, conventionally employed as a necessary and sufficient substitution in figurative form, surprisingly introduces a literal mode in which dramatic physical enactment occurs. The shaman's roles here as magician manipulator of myth and as master physician of physical phenomena mark out the undeclared extremes that Lévi-Strauss himself incessantly plays amidst. Within this polarity he sometimes appears in the guise of *bricoleur*, peddler, huckster, engineer, or scientist, yet he is the wily shaman, prophet with music, seeking man's secret double, his lost soul, now encrypted in indecipherable myth and opaque ritual, the sealed Unconscious of humanity, whose restoration renews vital strength and effects cultural cure. Without the return of this lost element of humanity, stolen away by time, yet protected by mythical discourse, modern man, man without myth, awaits cure.

The search of the authentic magician and master goes beyond any merely symbolic epic itinerary; it calls for actual examination of the real, a mathematics of the mytheme, a science of the concrete, aided by the computer and digital algebra (modern *nuchu*). With the new science—semiology—the "entire process of human knowledge thus assumes the character of a closed system. And we therefore remain faithful to the inspiration of the savage mind when we recognize that . . . the scientific spirit in its most modern form will have contributed to legitimize the principles of savage thought and to re-establish it in its rightful place" (*SM*, 269). Back into hidden wisdom, a closed system, the shaman, a prophet and scientist for the savage tribe, crosses over precarious edges and ominous inner spaces, chanting and computing cure. His gadgets and scores appear preposterous props, yet, when they work, these marvellous machines constitute tools of a science. Maybe Lévi-Strauss is the closest thing we have in the human sciences to a shaman, for in this whimsy he exceeds the individual ranges of either the peddler, *bricoleur*, engineer, or scientist.

Fronting the sign, the interpreter, whether great warrior or famous anthropologist, whether linguist or psychoanalyst, whether ancient precursor or fellow contemporary, finds an arbitrary signifier; undergoing interpretation, the sign forces the interpreter to confront one or another form of uncanny emptiness: the sign means nothing to Hector; it functions through disembodying difference for Saussure; it floats free before Lacan; it shows up contentless in Lévi-Strauss. And, remarkably, the sign requires, nay, demands that the interpreter fill emptiness in a prophetic gesture through the agency and insistence of rhetoric: careful Polydamas is the ancient model; wily Lévi-Strauss a recent incarnation. As medium of meaning, sign, trumped-up, transports truth then, allowing the interpreter to act, to comprehend, to cure, to explain, to err, to fall sick, to lie, to talk, to invoke gods—to write. Shrinking, the sign, whether fleeing bird and falling snake, or acoustic form and ideal concept, or floating signifier and sliding signified, or differential and contentless mytheme, begets always and everywhere presumptuous soothsaying and bold rhetoric.

2

The Subversion of Foundations

Adam's Expulsion or Stalking the Trace

A full historical investigation of deconstruction would necessarily include numerous precursors and forerunners: Freud, Hegel, Heidegger, Husserl, Lacan, Lévi-Strauss, Marx, Nietzsche, Saussure. . . . Let's say provisionally that the history of *contemporary* deconstruction opens with Jacques Derrida's *De la grammatologie* (1967), which opens with a critique of Saussure. The semiology of Saussure is here framed as a final gasp of Western philosophy, that is, of a metaphysical system that spans from Plato and Aristotle to Heidegger and Lévi-Strauss. By Derrida this system is called "logocentric," meant as a critical and unkind epithet. Saussure marks a closing of the long logocentric epoch. In his prefatory "Exergue," Derrida complains that logocentrism imposed itself upon the world and controlled the concept of writing, the history of metaphysics, and the forms of science. Now this epoch is ending. Future beckons. In the role of seer, Derrida concludes his "Exergue" and begins his project: "The future can only be anticipated in the form of an absolute danger. It is that which breaks absolutely with constituted normality and can only be proclaimed, *presented*, as a sort of monstrosity. For that future world and for that within it which will have put into question the values of sign, word, and writing, for that which guides our future anterior, there is as yet no exergue."[1] The principal aim in *Of Grammatology* is to put in question the traditional values of sign, word, and writing; its speculative mode, perhaps inevitably, partakes of danger, abnormality, and monstrosity; its most utopian impulse is to proclaim and present future; and its tone throughout is prophetic and uncomfortably sure.

As portrayed by Derrida, the logocentric system always assigns the origin of truth to the *logos*—to the spoken word, to the voice of reason, or to the Word of God. Moreover, the being of any entity is always determined as *presence*: the "object" of science and metaphysics is characteristically the "present entity." In these circumstances, the full presence of the voice is valued over the mute signs of writing. Writing, in fact, is conceived by the tradition as secondary speech, as a device to convey the voice, as an instrumental substitute for full presence. It is belated—secondary. Writing represents a fall from full speech.

The general debasement of writing and the singular preference for phonetic writing (writing as imitated speech) characterize the logocentric epoch. When it translates full speech, writing serves its proper technical function: it transports voice, which is fully present to itself, to its signified and to the other(s). Insistently, logocentrism collapses writing into speech; it is phonocentric through and through. The dynamics of the logocentric era generate an entire historical and cultural matrix of axiological oppositions: voice/writing, *phonè* (spoken word)/*graphie* (written mark), sound/silence, being/nonbeing, phonetic script/nonphonetic writing, consciousness/Unconscious, originary speech/secondary marks, inside (interiority)/outside (exteriority), thing/sign, reality/image, essence/appearance, signified/signifier, truth/lie, presence/absence. . . . (The logocentric tradition confers privileged status on the first term of each pair.) Significantly, Saussure's semiology is situated squarely within this epistemological system or matrix—this *epistémè*.

Derrida reveals the logocentric dynamic in Saussure's new science. Quoting the father of structural linguistics and semiology at length and incisively, Derrida's commentary nudges us beyond Saussure toward a poststructuralist future. "It is this logocentrism which, limiting the internal system of language in general by a bad abstraction, prevents Saussure and the majority of his successors from determining fully and explicitly that which is called 'the integral and concrete object of linguistics'" (43). (Not surprisingly, Derrida's footnote on Saussure's "successors" lists the central contributions of Troubetzkoy and Jakobson.) In effect, Derrida criticizes structural linguistics because it is consciously and thoroughly constructed upon phonological foundations; it always studies the *phonè* and *logos*, never the outlawed *graphie* or *trace*. Speech is celebrated; writing condemned. "For it is indeed within a sort of intralinguistic leper colony that Saussure wants to contain and concentrate the problem of deformations through writing" (42). Even Saussure's *signifier*, which one initially imagines as written, is an "*acoustic* image." Written signifiers are derived from or doubled forms of "spoken" signifiers. In writing we get the signifier, but this signifier "represents" the prior primary signifier—the *phonè*. Here as everywhere, phonocentrism, part and parcel of the logocentric network, controls the science of structural linguistics and orders its field of study. Nevertheless, Saussure's text unwittingly opens the possibility that the *graphie*, and not the *phonè*, is the proper element of language for analysis. "Then one realizes that what was chased off limits, the wandering outcast of linguistics, has indeed never ceased to haunt language as its primary and most intimate possibility. Then . . . writing itself as the origin of language writes itself within Saussure's discourse" (44).

Writing (*écriture*) is the origin of language; the origin is not the voice (*phonè*) transporting the spoken word (*logos*). Thus the values of the logocentric *epistémè* require extensive reordering. *Grammatology* displaces semiology. The *text* supersedes the book. The *trace* or *arche-trace*, a formation of *writing* and *difference*, takes the place of the sign. But here we anticipate the whole deconstructive project. For now *writing* begets language.

What is this *writing*? Let's admit, it appears as abnormal. At first. Fundamentally, *writing* exceeds, precedes, and comprehends language. It serves as ground of language rather than as belated secondary elaboration. *Écriture* is not a vehicle for already constituted units, but the mode of production that constitutes such units. *Writing*, in this new and extended sense, signifies any practice of differentiation, articulation, and spacing. Consequently, we must hereafter distinguish between (1) logocentric "writing," which names an instrument, a phonetic-alphabetic script, that conveys the spoken word, and (2) grammatological or poststructuralist *writing* (*écriture*), which designates the primary processes that produce language. This new meaning intends to force a break with normality.

No longer may we think of writing in the old way. We shall have to recast all the guiding polarities as such: writing/voice, *graphie/phonè*, silence/sound, nonbeing/being, *écriture*/phonetic script, Unconscious/consciousness. . . . Yet each such reversal creates enigmas. How, for example, do we construe "nonbeing/ being"? When we try to think "nonbeing precedes, grounds, is being," we experience the dizziness, feel the danger, and sense the monstrosity which characterize deconstruction as Derrida warns us at the outset. Re-forming "being/nonbeing," Derrida demonstrates the break with the normal that typifies deconstructive vision; it is a difficult passage:

What writing itself, in its nonphonetic moment, betrays, is life. It menaces at once the breath, the spirit, and history as the spirit's relationship with itself. It is their end, their finitude, their paralysis. Cutting breath short, sterilizing or immobilizing spiritual creation in the repetition of the letter . . . it is the principle of death and of difference in the becoming of being. (25)

Here *écriture* is depicted as the end of breath (voice), of spirit (the inner self as fully present), and of history (truth as self-present). These differences between breath and the letter, between the inner spirit and the text, and between present events and written history introduce not only the powers of *écriture* (paralysis and nonbeing), but the operations and very principle of *difference* (the becoming of being). At bottom *difference* provides the force that allows Derrida to reformulate the relationship of "being" and "nonbeing" in the context of *écriture*. Writing, the nonbeing of the voice, begets being, the entry into (differentiating) language. Does the dizziness return? No longer may we think of writing in the old way. Writing is the most primordial "activity" of differentiation. As this prevocal process operates, it inaugurates language, bestows consciousness, institutes being. These three emerge out of silence, the Unconscious, nonbeing, writing. Thus nonbeing precedes being and writing comes before language. In the end, the disruptive powers of writing and difference (will) effect and authorize the reversal of all logocentric polarities.[2]

Reversing the traditional crucial pair, "signified/signifier," Derrida produces a new concept. In place of Saussure's *sign*, Derrida installs the *trace*. Mysterious and imperceptible, the *trace* arises as a force and formation of writing. Like the *quark* in physics, the *trace* is a theoretical unit in grammatology that, though imperceptible—more nothing than something—operates amidst the innermost reaches of writing, permeating and energizing its entire activity, affecting omnipresence, yet remaining out of hand. Just as the *quark*, posited by Gell-Mann and Zweig during the early 1960s, accounted for the strange activities of particles within subatomic spheres, so Derrida's *trace* explains the peculiar effects of writing detected at microlevels of the sign. Neither a free *quark* nor a pure *trace* can be dislodged or isolated because they are functions of relations—mirage "effects" of primordial differentiation in process. The *trace* is the sum of all possible relations, whether isolated or not, which inhabit and constitute the sign. And, similar to the *quark* that so soon showed up with other guises and with different charges in the *up quark, down quark, strange quark, charmed quark* and *anti quark*, the *trace* almost immediately appears in other roles and with different values in *arche-trace, grapheme, grammè*, difference, and writing. "Writing is [just] one of the representatives of the trace in general, it is not the trace itself. *The [pure] trace itself does not exist.* (To exist is to be, to be an entity, a being-present . . .)" (167). Without doubt the general trend in semiological-grammatological theory, as in modern science, points toward ever more minimal units: word → sign (signified/signifier) → phoneme (mytheme) → distinctive features → trace → arche-trace. . . . Beyond structuralism and semiology and so past the signifier and mytheme, deconstructive analysis tracks the trace in, of, through, and with writing.

While he is displacing the sign, Derrida registers his complaints. The sign, understood as traditional signifier-signified, rests firmly within the phonocentric-logocentric *epistémè*, marking there the proximity of voice and truth, of voice and being, of voice and meaning. In this tradition, the signified is constituted as a "presence" near to or the same as *logos*; the signifier, arbitrary yet transparent, always an instrument transporting truth, remains within the reaches of consciousness and speech. Significantly, the

silent and unconscious (differentiating) operations of the trace—
of writing—undergo repression and censorship during the logocentric epoch so that all the formative differences and absences
produced in the production of the sign stay hidden by this history.
It is unthinkable in the logocentric tradition that the signified itself
is originarily a writing, a trace, and that this signified always
already partakes of the signifier. Derrida announces "there is no
linguistic sign before writing" (14). The sign is a production of
writing or, to put it another way, the trace institutes the possibility
of the sign: writing and trace precede and permit the appearance
of sign.

What then is the project of grammatology? As a new science
of writing, it resists "the historico-metaphysical reduction of writing to the rank of an instrument enslaved to a full and originarily
spoken language" (29).[3] It never subordinates writing to speech,
but examines and analyzes writing before and in speech—in texts.
"On what conditions is a grammatology possible? Its fundamental
condition is certainly the undoing of logocentrism" (74). An immense and interminable enterprise: the dangerous and monstrous
burden of deconstruction. As a critique of Saussure, grammatology seeks to replace semiology:

I shall call it [grammatology]. . . . Since the science does not yet exist,
no one can say what it would be; but it has a right to existence, a place
staked out in advance. Linguistics is only a part of [that] general science. . . . (51)

Rewriting Saussure's famous words, Derrida here inaugurates
grammatology by boldly overturning and displacing the project
of semiology. In the new science, the old voice–sign–writing
complex yields to writing–trace–difference. Thus is Adam ex-
pelled; and we set out to stalk the trace.

The Dream of the Transcendental Signifier Revoked

When Jacques Derrida, the major source of deconstructive wisdom in our time, the father of the school, criticized the psychoanalytic theory of Jacques Lacan in an interview published in 1971,[4]

he promised, too breezily for some, to substantiate his rough critique on a later occasion. He did so in 1975.[5] Actually, Derrida from the outset in the early 1960s and throughout the next two decades evidenced a growing and meticulous concern with psychoanalytic materials, particularly the work of Sigmund Freud and later that of Nicolas Abraham.[6] From the start the main strand of contemporary deconstructive thinking intertwines with the patterned threads of thought constituting psychoanalysis. Lacan's work, however, assumes only a minor, though important, position in this general configuration. Why? Significantly, Derrida lodges several revealing complaints against Lacan's psychoanalytic theory during his interview: Lacan works within the logocentric system; he succumbs to phonocentrism; he relies on traditional phenomenological concepts (revived from Hegel, Husserl, and Heidegger); he simplifies the Freudian texts; he practices an evasive and anachronistic style of ellipsis; and he utilizes Saussure's sign and thereby reduces *écriture*. Nevertheless, the Lacanian problematic is, in Derrida's assessment, historically important in the domain of psychoanalysis (*Pos*, 107–13).

When in 1975 he takes on the "Seminar on 'The Purloined Letter,'" the lead study of Lacan's *Écrits*, Derrida quickly underscores the position of priority that Lacan assigns this work, implying that a thorough exposé of the "Seminar" amounts to an extensive critique of Lacan's whole enterprise.[7] Again, the charges enunciated earlier in the interview surface, yet they are now prefaced with earnest appreciation of Lacan's work. In particular, Derrida notes with approval Lacan's tempering of naive interpretive semanticism in his attention to the enigmatic textual activity of the signifier. And he isolates for admiration Lacan's refusal to refer the text back to the author, whose life and history invariably license traditional criticism to limit any free flight of the signifier. Lastly, he singles out for reserved praise Lacan's elaboration of a logic of the signifier, in which the autonomy of the signifier emerges as a result of the fraction, the barrier, in the sign ("PT," 39–45).

Derrida examines the "Seminar" apparently because it takes up the seminal problematic of "truth" and "fiction." Traditionally, psychoanalytic textual interpretation, using refined techniques

first advanced by Freud, aims to uncover the content of a discourse—the truth in fiction. Lacan, of course, inherits this logocentric tradition. In his analysis of Poe's famous tale, Lacan
swiftly omits the narrative frame, the scene of writing, and fixes
immediately upon two triangular relationships. From then on
Lacan's reading displays "an analytical fascination with a content"
(48). Even though the stolen letter, whose content remains un-
revealed in Poe's story, functions as floating signifier, Lacan analyzes it as a signified. The initial omission of the narrator forces
him to estimate and specify the truth of the letter and to ignore
the full textual activity of this mobile signifier. Thus writing turns
into the written, the text into message, process into product,
signifier into signified. Lacan exhibits not just a "rush to truth"
but a "demand for the truth" (57); he is the classical "decoder,
the purveyor of truth" (65). In general, "all the [Lacanian] texts
situated, more accurately, published, between 1953 (the so-called
Rome Speech) and 1960 seem to belong to the same system of the
truth. That is, quantitatively, almost the totality of the *Écrits*
. . ." (82). As Derrida construes it, Lacan's major work enacts the
old logocentric idolatry for unveiling truth. The "Seminar" is
representative.

The logocentrism of Lacan is most apparent in his phonological
orientation. In Lacanian analysis the truth (*logos*) systematically
shines forth as spoken or voiced (as *phonè*). In fact, "he always
resorts ultimately to a writing sublated by the voice" (82) and
"the law of the signifier unfolds only in vocalizable letters" (83).
While Lacan's works after *Écrits* mute the logocentric-phonocentric orientation, nonetheless the worship of truth and the practice
of oral exchange endure. With Lacan, early and late, psychoanalysis remains "talking cure" founded on spoken truth. Even when
the analysand's voice truly misleads, the truth of the decoy
emerges from the unveiling in the oral-aural analysis.

The entire Lacanian project points toward the phallus as the
grandest signifier of all. That is to say, a pervasive possibility, a
continuous implication, persists that every and any signifier partakes of this most peerless signifier. Thus the phallus in Lacan's
psychoanalysis occupies a transcendental position. "We are always
led back, step by step, to this contract of contracts which guar-

antees the unity of the signifier to the signified through all the points of stability, thanks to the 'presence'. . . . of the *same* signifier (the phallus), of the 'signifier of signifiers' underneath all the signified-effects. This transcendental signifier is therefore also the signifier of all signifieds . . ." (85). The singular effect of the transcendental signifier is to center and regulate systematically the processes of interpretation, the unveilings of truth, the imports of the voice, and the flights of the signifier. (The unity and stability of the "signifier-signified" complex are stipulated as in a legal contract.) As transcendental signifier, the Lacanian phallus makes possible chains of signification at the same time that it belongs to such chains.[8] The phallus is *logos* revealed in the speech of cure. Ultimately, Derrida's critique finds in Lacan's work "the complicity of structure between the motif of the veil and that of the voice, between the truth and phonocentrism, phallocentrism and logocentrism" (97).

Essentially, Lacan overlooks or represses the scene of writing, the activity of the trace, the production of the written, the functioning of narration. As always, such grammatological matters are ruled out by the imperious logic and secret necessity of the logocentric systematics. Thus triumph voice, *phonè*, speech, presence, truth . . . in the transcendental signifier. Derrida revokes this dream.[9]

Defrocking the Shaman or Centers of Play

When he delivered his notorious critique of structuralism at the Johns Hopkins University Conference in the fall of 1966, Jacques Derrida opened the era of contemporary deconstruction for an American audience, boldly exposing the logocentric limitations permeating the structuralist work of Claude Lévi-Strauss.[10] This assault on Lévi-Strauss continued in *Of Grammatology*.[11] Basically, Derrida situates the overall project of Lévi-Strauss, like that of Saussure and that of Lacan, on the edges of the passing *epistémè*: "At once conserving and annulling inherited conceptual oppositions, this thought, like Saussure's, stands on a borderline: sometimes within an uncriticized conceptuality, sometimes putting a strain on the boundaries, and working toward deconstruction" (OG, 105). Derrida praises yet subverts the texts of Lévi-Strauss, turning their issues and discussions over more fully toward deconstruction.

Studying the central problem of anthropology, the passage from nature to culture, Lévi-Strauss regularly and symptomatically ends up "privileging" the state of nature over that of culture. He appears sentimental and nostalgic, trapped in a Rousseauistic dream of innocent and natural primitive societies. Of the often studied and much admired Nambikwara indians of South America, Lévi-Strauss proclaims: "In one and all there may be glimpsed a great sweetness of nature, a profound nonchalance, an animal satisfaction as ingenuous as it is charming, and, beneath all this, something that can be recognized as one of the most moving and authentic manifestations of human tenderness" (OG, 117). All this original innocence and goodness, sweetness of nature and charming animality, human tenderness and authenticity brings out in Lévi-Strauss' text an impulse and longing to escape culture, to return to nature, to flee degradation and violence, to find an isle of purity and peace, to secure a time to relive the lost childhood of our race. Beneath the guilt and nostalgia, endemic to the field of anthropology, lies an ethnocentrism masking itself as liberal and humane anti-ethnocentrism. This whole system of thought, undergirding the reflection of Lévi-Strauss, comes to the fore most revealingly on the matter of writing. Of his charming indians Lévi-Strauss casually observes: "That the Nambikwara could not write goes without saying" (OG, 122). The absence of writing and the presence of speech characterize the society of these noble savages. When writing does come to the Nambikwara, it brings forth evil: "It seems to favor rather the exploitation than the enlightenment of mankind. . . . Writing, on this its first appearance in their midst, had allied itself with falsehood" (OG, 101).

Underneath this anthropology of the Nambikwara indians runs a logocentric systematics. Derrida turns it up, as he does with the texts of Saussure and Lacan:

I have earlier emphasized the ambiguity of the ideology which governs the Saussurian exclusion of writing: a profound ethnocentrism privileging the model of phonetic writing, a model that makes the exclusion of the *graphie* easier and more legitimate. . . . By radically separating language from writing, by placing the latter below and outside, believing at least that it is possible to do so . . . one thinks in fact to restore the status of authentic language, human and fully signifying language, to all languages practiced by *peoples whom one nevertheless continues to describe as "without writing."* It is not fortuitous that the same ambiguity affects Lévi-Strauss's intentions. (*OG,* 120)

This indictment is not ambiguous. Like Saussure, Lévi-Strauss conceptualizes writing as a late cultural arrival, a supplement to speech, an external instrument; writing does not inhere in language; it can easily be excluded. (If we must have writing, it should be phonetic, that is, it should mimic and incarnate speech.) Authentic language, fully signifying language, shows up prominently in primitive societies without writing, as, for example, in Nambikwara society. (Writing, when it does appear, produces falsehood, exploitation, oppression.) "The ideal profoundly underlying this [logocentric] philosophy of writing is therefore the image of a community immediately present to itself, without difference, a community of speech where all the members are within earshot" (*OG,* 136). Assembled in the self-presence of its speech, this innocent and charming community, a community of freedom and nonviolence, endures the intrusion from outside of writing, an instrument of evil.

Speech versus writing. "Lévi-Strauss is never suspicious of the value of such a distinction" (*OG,* 120). Once again, as in the critique of Saussure, Derrida argues that "writing appears well before writing in the narrow sense; already in the differance or the arche-writing that opens speech itself" (*OG,* 128). Introducing *écriture* into the polemic, Derrida presents a provocative *koan* in direct response to the information that across the territory of the Nambikwara, bush terrain, runs an almost imperceptible track. He asks us to meditate:

one should meditate upon all of the following together: writing as the possibility of the road and of difference, the history of writing and the history of the road, of the rupture, of the *via rupta,* of the path that is broken, beaten, *fracta,* of the space of reversibility and of repetition traced by the opening, the divergence from, and the violent spacing, of nature, of the natural, savage, salvage, forest. The *silva* is savage, the *via rupta* is written, discerned, and inscribed violently as difference . . . ; it is difficult to imagine that access to the possibility of a road-map is not at the same time access to writing. (*OG*, 107–8)

Scene of meditation: cuts, ruptures, fractures, and spaces in nature offer instances of primordial differences, of omnipresent lines of differentiation. In the forest, the road or track, carved out and inscribed, appears as rupture, as opening, as space, as difference, as writing. Across the terrain of the Nambikwara the track testifies to the presence of *spacing*, of difference, of writing. That writing is present in Nambikwara culture goes without saying. Everyone in the community, for instance, has a proper name; that is to say, everyone is differentiated in a classification system. Lévi-Strauss knows this, but his ethnocentric concept of writing blinds him to such pervasive writing. He is naive.

Yet Lévi-Strauss is "working toward deconstruction." A borderline case, he relies on inherited conceptual oppositions, as, for example, nature/culture, speech/writing, interiority/exteriority, innocence/corruption, and truth/falsehood, but he annuls traditional oppositions often enough. Caught in this boundary situation, between a logocentric structuralism and an emerging poststructuralism, Lévi-Strauss points toward a new critical discourse—a deconstructive "hermeneutic." "In effect," summarizes Derrida, "what appears most fascinating in this critical search for a new status of discourse is the stated abandonment of all reference to a *center*, to a *subject*, to a privileged *reference*, to an origin, or to an absolute *archia* [a founding and controlling first principle]" (*WD*, 286). In short, the decentering operations of Lévi-Strauss exceed the project of structuralism and prefigure the work of deconstruction. Fascinated, Derrida marks the difficult turn.

Throughout the logocentric epoch the concept of structure requires and depends upon the concept of center. In any particular structure, whether anthropological, political, economic, psychological, scientific, theological, or metaphysical, the center functions to stabilize the panoply of elements in the system. Taken together, all traditional centers, fulfilling the same structural function though named differently, possess the common determination of *Being* as "presence." (Here we come upon a crucial point in Derrida's critique.) This ontological ground, a stabilizing factor affording reassurance and certitude, keeps the center, the structural matrix, out of play. However vast and complicated a particular logocentric system, the center of its structure insures balance, coherence, and organization, all deployed around a controlled point. Glancing from one structural center to another throughout history, we can conceive of this observable chain of stable elements as a series of metaphors or metonymies serving a similar function. When a new name enters the chain, it appears as a fresh substitution. Rather than conceptualize the center as a locus or a particular site or a present entity, we may regard center as a systemic function whose purpose is to orient and balance structure and whose history consists of a series of sign substitutions. To isolate this string of substitutions is to uncover a play of names at the center. In other words, the historical set of central signifieds or transcendental signifieds ultimately collapses into a play of privileged signifiers, which we may characterize, on the one hand, as structural necessities and, on the other, as floating signifiers at play.

What Derrida admires in Lévi-Strauss is the deliberate abandonment of the center, the origin, the fixed subject, the absolute *archia*. With approval Derrida cites Lévi-Strauss' telling statement in the Overture to the *Mythologiques*: "the unity of the myth is never more than tendential and projective and cannot reflect a state or a particular moment of the myth. It is a phenomenon of the imagination, resulting from the attempt at interpretation; and its function is to endow the myth with synthetic form and to prevent its disintegration into a confusion of opposites" (*WD*, 287). The purpose of centered structure in interpretation is to limit the disintegrating play of opposing elements. Structure, a production of interpretation, appears here as tendential, projective, imaginary, synthetic. An ounce of prevention and a pound of cure, structure staves off the disintegrations of the free play of elements in a system. The center is protection.

Interpretation imposes structures to delimit and arrest *play*. The center, one transcendental signified or another, orders and regulates the structure, serving as self-present primary ground for interpretation. *Play* is ruled out. Nevertheless, *play* precedes the operations of structuration; in fact, it allows the very structurality of structure and the imposition of a center. Before the alternative of presence or absence and prior to the possibility of center or structure, *play* operates. It then disrupts presence, producing chains of substitutions at the center, undermining the solidifications of structure and subverting the stability of the origin. The repetitions of *play* disintegrate the ground and insure a *play* of repetitions through a network of differences—of substitutions. "If Lévi-Strauss, better than any other, has brought to light the play of repetition and the repetition of play, one no less perceives in his work a sort of ethic of presence, an ethic of nostalgia for origins, an ethic of archaic and natural innocence, of a purity of presence and self-presence in speech . . ." (*WD*, 292). Lévi-Strauss, in Derrida's critique, occupies the boundary: while the transcendental signifier, as central function of structure, is subverted, the disintegrations of play are checked and, guiltily, structures appear finally as centered.

Defrocking the wily shaman, Derrida opens to view the monstrous future. Delivered in America in 1966, this vision takes us finally beyond the confident reign of semiological structuralism and the logocentric tradition. We may read this passage as the historic charter of contemporary deconstruction:

> Turned towards the lost or impossible presence of the absent origin, this structuralist thematic of broken immediacy is therefore the saddened, *negative*, nostalgic, guilty, Rousseauistic side of the thinking of play whose other side would be the Nietzschean *affirmation*, that is the joyous affirmation of the play of the world and of the innocence of becoming, the affirmation of a world of signs without fault, without truth, and without origin which is offered to an active interpretation. . . .
>
> There are thus two interpretations of interpretation, of structure, of sign, of play. The one seeks to decipher, dreams of deciphering a truth or an origin which escapes play and the order of the sign, and which lives the necessity of interpretation as an exile. The other, which is no longer turned toward the origin, affirms play and tries to pass beyond man and humanism, the name of man being the name of that being who, throughout the history of metaphysics or of ontotheology—in other words, throughout his entire history—has dreamed of full presence, the reassuring foundation, the origin and the end of play. (*WD*, 292)

Culminating in Lévi-Strauss, the ancient logocentric tradition long ago set humanistic man up to search for a truth, an origin, a foundation, a reassuring presence. Equipped with this dream, man deciphered the world's truths as transcendental *archia*. The endeavor required the repression of play and the suppression of the sign. Now sad, nostalgic, guilty, the last shaman practices, as an exile, the ancient search after the lost origin and the reassuring truth. He writes of primitives and misunderstands these disruptive road builders, as logocentric man must.

As prophet, Derrida presents to us deconstructive man—who accepts in joy and affirmation the play of the world and the innocence of becoming, who affirms the world of signs and the activity of interpretation, who neither pesters the world for truth nor indulges the dream of origins, who traces around the center the free play of signifiers and the tendential productions of structure, who writes off man and humanism, who denounces the old logocentric wizardry and passes joyously beyond. Cold and remorseless, deconstructive man assaults the old sensibility and subverts traditional foundations. Semiology, a recent formation of the logocentric era, is savaged: deconstruction offers us an affront of joy and affirmation.[12]

3

Extensions of Subversion

Presence, Being, and Differance
or the Sign Undone Again

The year 1967 is the *annus mirabilis* of deconstruction, for Jacques
Derrida brings to print three deconstructive books, including *De
la grammatologie, L'Écriture et la différence* and, as yet unmentioned,
La Voix et le phénomène, subtitled *Introduction au problème du signe
dans la phénoménologie de Husserl*.[1] When asked about the proper
order of these texts, in an interview published in December 1967,
Derrida playfully offers a number of different and complicated
plans of organization, all pressing toward the implication that
these texts constitute one project. *Speech and Phenomena*, in particular, *may* be read first since it poses "the question of the privilege
of the voice and of phonetic writing in their relationship to the
entire history of the West, such as this history can be represented
by the history of metaphysics, and metaphysics in its most modern, critical, and vigilant form: Husserl's transcendental phenomenology" (*Pos*, 5). Although this book receives priority, because
it puts in question the most vigilant logocentric conception of
writing, it nevertheless can serve "as a long note to one or the
other of the other two works" (*Pos*, 4). Essential introduction or
long note? In the development of deconstruction after 1967, *Speech
and Phenomena* invariably gets handled as a note.[2]

At the outset, in the early 1960s, Derrida attends carefully to
the phenomenology of Husserl and then to that of Heidegger.
While less renowned than his critiques of structuralism, particularly those of works by Saussure, Lacan, and Lévi-Strauss, Der-

rida's deconstructions of Husserl and Heidegger form the indispensable groundwork for his passage "beyond" logocentric metaphysics. In fact, throughout his entire enterprise, Derrida makes frequent references to Husserl and Heidegger. Here his general strategy produces deconstructive counterreadings of their refined metaphysics of "presence" and exquisite ontologies of "being." Examining their texts, he extrapolates *difference, trace,* and *writing* out of presence, being, and voice. Often the route seems tortuous. We shall take brief note of Husserl now and Heidegger more fully later.

Although phenomenology criticizes traditional metaphysics, it aims to reawaken and restore metaphysics to its most authentic and original purpose: the determination of being as presence. Not surprisingly, Husserl founds his entire project upon the *lebendige Gegenwart* (living present), the universal and ultimate ground of all experience. Upon this ground the perception or intuition of self by self in presence functions as a principle of principles. Husserl insists that this primordial constitution of self-presence occurs without the agency of signs or the operations of any signification. This pre-expressive experience of pure or ideal self-present identity takes place in silence. The sign is secondary. Husserl's whole enterprise "confirms the underlying limitation of language to a secondary stratum of experience and, in the consideration of this secondary stratum, confirms the traditional phonologism of metaphysics. If writing brings the constitution of ideal objects to completion, it does so through phonetic writing: it proceeds to fix, inscribe, record, and incarnate an already prepared utterance" (*SP,* 80–81). Self-present being, pure being, precedes language. Following the primordial silence of pure being, language expresses and embodies, yet buries in secondary sedimentations, the self-presence of pure being. Language appears, yet again, as belated, instrumental, and phonetic. In the beginning is being—determined in presence and prior to language.

Working within the logocentric tradition, Husserl situates language in a secondary stratum, after the determination of being as presence. Necessarily, this operation proceeds, as a possible metaphysics, through the initial suppression of primordial difference.

In other words, "pure difference, which constitutes the self-presence of the living present, introduces into self-presence from the beginning all the impurity putatively excluded from it. The living present springs forth out of its nonidentity with itself and from the possibility of a retentional trace. It is always already a trace" (*SP*, 85). Where Husserl envisions self-presence, Derrida sights difference and the trace. Writing invades ontology. Derrida's point is that the expressive energies of primordial differentiation animate and produce being and presence. Husserl has it backwards. The living present is for Derrida an effect of difference, of spacing, of the trace. Husserl himself senses this. For "although he had not made a theme of 'articulation,' of the 'diacritical' work of difference in the constitution of sense and signs, he at bottom recognized its necessity. And yet, the whole phenomenological discourse is . . . caught up within the schema of a metaphysics of presence which relentlessly exhausts itself in trying to make difference derivative" (*SP*, 101). Difference opens and sets going the phenomena of presence, being, and signification. Phenomenology, a philosophy of presence, exhausts itself in denial, making difference a belated phenomenon.

To follow Derrida we move beyond *Speech and Phenomena* to the seminal essay on *differance*, where the conceptualization of primordial difference receives its fullest articulation. To begin with, Derrida's neologism *differance* captures three significations: (1) "to differ"—to be unlike or dissimilar in nature, quality, or form; (2) "differre" (Latin)—to scatter, disperse; and (3) "to defer"—to delay, postpone. The first two significations mark out spatial distinctions, while the third makes reference to differences in temporality. In French, the "a" in *differance* passes unheard; the word registers as *différence*. This undetected difference shows up only in writing.

As a first approximation, a set of refined extracts from Derrida's essay shall channel our attention. (Efficiency rather than lassitude prompts this severe distillation; so too does the idea that, in this case, an adequate exposition might best emerge from an imploded chain of citations free of diluting commentary.) The topic of this assemblage is *differance*:

differance could be said to designate the productive and primordial constituting causality, the process of scission and division whose differings and differences would be the constituted products or effects. (*SP*, 137)

[Differance refers to] the origin or production of differences and the differences between differences, the *play* of differences. (130)

What we note as *differance* will thus be the movement of play that "produces" (and not by something that is simply an activity) these differences, these effects of difference. This does not mean that the differance which produces differences is before them in a simple and in itself unmodified and indifferent present. Differance is the nonfull, nonsimple "origin"; it is the structured and differing origin of differences. (141)

it denotes not only the activity of primordial difference but also the temporalizing detour of deferring. (144–45)

It is not a being-present, however excellent, unique, principal, or transcendent one makes it. It commands nothing, rules over nothing, and nowhere does it exercise any authority. It is not marked by a capital letter. Not only is there no realm of differance, but differance is even the subversion of every realm. This is obviously what makes it threatening and necessarily dreaded by everything in us that desires a realm, the past or future presence of a realm. (153)

[Differance is not] capable of being something, a force, a state, or power in the world, to which we could give all kinds of names. . . . (145)

it has neither existence nor essence. It belongs to no category of being, present or absent. (134)

there is no *name* for this, not even essence or Being—not even the name "differance," which is not a name, which is not a pure nominal unity, and continually breaks up in a chain of different substitutions. (159)

Differance is neither a *word* nor a *concept*. (130)

It is clear that it cannot be *exposed*. We can expose only what, at a certain moment, can become *present*, manifest; what can be shown, presented as present, a being-present in its truth, the truth of a present or the presence of a present. (134)

At a certain moment differance appears to us as an omnipresent cosmic *force*, the operative primordial power of proto-differentiation, invading every entity and concept in the universe. Clearly, this force functions negatively because it manifests itself mainly through the silent disruption and division of everything. Nothing comes before it. Nothing escapes it. Oddly enough, it even permits sameness, repetition, and identity to emerge as such. (When, for instance, we proclaim twins are identical, we necessarily first assume their difference.) Yet differance is not ultra-differentiation. Why not? It cannot be thought of as an event; it does not spring from a prior moment of unity or undisturbed harmony. The fundamental detour or delay implicit in differance disappears unacceptably if we make differance show up in our thinking as event—as a particular activity preceded by nonaction and followed by stasis or stability. The qualities of play and detour characteristic of differance keep it from appearing as origin, as being-present, as production, as master concept or word. Neither process nor product, differance is nothing.

Beyond all logocentric thinking, unthinkable as such, differance, as it comes into view, begets substitutions: spacing, trace, and writing, for instance. These "nonsynonymic names" surface everywhere in the work of deconstruction. (Derrida himself produces roughly three dozen new names by the early 1980s. We shall have more to say about such *undecidables* later.) Once they emerge, these sightings fade swiftly. "For us, differance remains a metaphysical name; and all the names that it receives from our language are still, so far as they are names, metaphysical" (158). Imprisoned within the closure of metaphysical thinking and locked into the necessity of naming, we reduce differance to a word or a concept; or, perhaps worse, we celebrate differance as a master name, a unique word, a founding concept. No such words or concepts exist. "There is nothing kerygmatic about this 'word' so long as we can perceive its reduction to a lower-case letter" (159).

For now, we can conceptualize differance as the structured and differing "origin" of difference.

As he uncovers movements of differance in the work of semiology as well as phenomenology, Derrida subverts the logocentric theory of the sign. To be sure, Saussure himself proclaims the differential character of the language system and the arbitrariness of signs, yet he succumbs ultimately, as does Husserl, to the metaphysics of presence. Classically formulated, the semiological signifier refers to a signified, that is, an acoustic image signifies an ideal concept—both of which are *present to consciousness*. The sound cluster "chair," for instance, indicates the idea *chair*. The real chair, the *referent*, is not present. The sign marks an absent presence. Rather than present the object, we employ the sign. We postpone or defer producing the referent. Just here the structure of delay and the configuration of difference (between signifier and signifed and signifed and referent), characteristic of differance, comes into view, disrupting the ethic of presence. In other words, when we use signs, the being-present of the referent and signified, incarnated in the self-present signifier, appears to us immediately, but it is delusion, misperception, dream. There is neither substance nor presence in the sign, but only the play of differences. Differance invades the sign, allowing its operation as *trace*—not self-present sign. Reformulating semiology, Derrida writes "we shall designate by the term *differance* the movement by which language, or any code, any system of reference in general, becomes 'historically' constituted as a fabric of differences" (141).

The logocentric-phonocentric tradition, exemplified in the work of Saussure, Husserl, Lacan, Lévi-Strauss, and many others, privileges the spoken self-present word without seemingly questioning voice, presence, or sign. Derrida counters with *writing, differance*, and *trace*. First and foremost, the tradition determines being as presence and, consequently, all structures and systems are grounded in self-present centers available to consciousness. Derrida then foregrounds the disintegrating *play* of differences, which disrupts sites of origination and centers of transcendental signification. In the tradition, acts of interpretation always produce the truth as a stable and present entity. The hidden spaces in the activity of interpretation, however, are opened wide and dwelled upon by Derrida so that *spacing* itself counters and disrupts stability, presence, and truth. Here *spacing* designates the divisive intervals between things, the unsettling operations of setting aside, and the fragmenting forces of temporalization—all of which interrupt every homogeneous and self-present assemblage. We are put on edge.

As he exceeds logocentrism, Derrida extends the texts of the tradition. We enjoy new versions of forerunners. We encounter other ways of reading. We examine over and over the problematics of reading as activity. We experience revisionary energy in full force. We endure tortuous writing and extremes of play. Soon we may crave a center, a truth, a final place of rest. Such death comes quietly: quietly we elevate *differance* or *écriture* or *trace* to the status of transcendental signifier. We get Derrida; we comprehend him; we capture his text and truth. As trained readers we grind the play of traces into smooth patterns of signifiers with stable and transcendental values. The burden of deconstruction is to refuse such ground-up transcendence.

Rhetoric on the American Exchange

During the late 1960s and early 1970s deconstruction as a mode of textual "interpretation" appeared in the works of Paul de Man, J. Hillis Miller, Joseph N. Riddel and, to a lesser extent, Harold Bloom. These first American practitioners of deconstruction, however, displayed little doctrinaire Derrideanism, though at the outset all deconstructors were regarded as elite troops in Derrida's revolutionary new division. Lecturing at Yale University from the early 1970s into the 1980s, Derrida, de Man, Miller, Bloom, and Geoffrey Hartman (who exhibits a minimal deconstructive orientation) seemed in the public mind a centered movement—a new school. As leading spokesman, Miller especially encouraged this view. By the middle and late 1970s, however, deconstruction as a theory and practice of literary criticism spread so widely and swiftly throughout the continent that, in the early 1980s, it appeared impossible any longer to envision the many practitioners as a localized cadre, a unified front, or a harmonious movement. Yet vociferous hostile criticism and seemingly instinctive antipathy, increasingly in evidence from the late 1970s onward, created the enduring impression of unity. To opponents, new and old, deconstruction shows itself as an autonomous system of thought, entrenched unfortunately in growing numbers of university literature departments throughout the land. To the early practitioners, Miller in particular, the success and dissemination of deconstruction are, ironically, saddening and, perhaps, vaguely threatening.

Paul de Man is the leading American deconstructor for insiders, and for outsiders J. Hillis Miller fills this role. Influential and imitated, de Man's unique form of deconstruction varies markedly from Derrida's. For his part, Miller, receptive to both Derrida and de Man, practices a more derivative variety of deconstructive criticism. We shall consider Miller in the next section and also in subsequent discussions. De Man will figure here and in later sections.

While Derrida writes early and often about semiology and grammatology, about the sign and differance, about logocentrism and phonocentrism, about writing, spacing, and the trace, about structure, center, and play, about Freud, Saussure, and Husserl, de Man almost never mentions any of these topics, concepts, or people. The recurrent and dominant words in his critical lexicon are *language* and *rhetoric*. The one crucial forerunner is evidently Nietzsche. De Man eschews overt theorizing about theories of criticism, ontology, metaphysics, semiology, anthropology, psychoanalysis or hermeneutics. He prefers to practice close textual exegesis, punctuated now and then with theoretical generalizations. "My tentative generalizations," proclaims de Man in the Foreword to *Blindness and Insight* (1971), "are not aimed toward a theory of criticism but toward literary language in general."[3] And he confirms his preoccupation with language and rhetoric, which frustrate ontology and hermeneutics, in the concluding analysis of *Allegories of Reading* (1979): "The main point of the reading has been to show that the resulting predicament is linguistic rather than ontological or hermeneutic," and indeed the specific aim of the reading is ultimately to demonstrate a profound "discontinuity between two rhetorical codes."[4]

De Man's most revealing expression of his fundamental notions about language and rhetoric occurs in 1973 during a conference presentation on Nietzsche's theory of rhetoric. This exposition is important, for de Man's theory of the sign comes clearly to the fore. Here we learn that Nietzsche shifts the study of rhetoric from methods of persuasion and eloquence to the prior theory of figures and tropes. About Nietzsche's formulation that "Tropes are not something that can be added or subtracted from language at will; they are its truest nature," de Man generalizes:

the straightforward affirmation that *the paradigmatic structure of language is rhetorical* rather than representational or expressive of a referential, proper meaning . . . marks *a full reversal of the established priorities* which traditionally root the authority of the language in its adequation to an extralinguistic referent or meaning, rather than in the intralinguistic resources of figures. (*AR*, 106; my italics)

Nietzsche, the decisive forerunner, presents a categorical rupture in the theory of language, starting a new historical epoch in which language is first consciously conceived of as always, at once and originarily, figural or rhetorical, rather than referential or representational. No primordial unrhetorical language exists. As the distinctive feature of language, rhetoricity necessarily undermines truth and "opens up vertiginous possibilities of referential aberration" (*AR*, 10). *Thus the linguistic sign is the site of an ambivalent and problematic relation between referential and figural meaning.*

(This problematic of the sign brings into question thematic interpretation and encourages rhetorical reading. For de Man the revisionary project of criticism, therefore, is to create a nonthematic figural criticism—deconstructive rhetoric.)

The later elaborations of *rhetoricity* lead to the incorporation of enriching materials from contemporary speech-act and grammatical theory. De Man aligns "constative language" with rhetorical persuasion and referentiality, and he correlates "performative language" with rhetorical devices and figurality (*AR*, 130–31). The chain of oppositions underlying his enterprise now becomes clearer: typical polarities include action/substance, figure/reference, (vertiginous) aberration/meaning, trope/persuasion, performative/constative, rhetoricity/referentiality. When he first introduces grammar into this chain in 1973, de Man frankly observes: "To distinguish the epistemology of grammar from the epistemology of rhetoric is a redoubtable task" (*AR*, 7). Indeed, the

later work bears out this point. Although nowhere explicitly ac-
commodated to the theory of rhetoricity, grammar in more recent
reading experiences reaches a provocative formulation. Significantly, grammar interrupts the reference/rhetoric polarity and
creates the very possibility of figurality: "The divergence between
grammar and referential meaning is what we call the figural dimension of language" (*AR*, 270; see 298–301). Rather than a displacement of rhetoric by grammar in the chain of oppositions, a
triad composed of grammar/rhetoric/reference enters the chain;
the point is that "the logic of grammar generates texts only in the
absence of referential meaning . . ." (*AR*, 269). Thus the addition
of grammar to the theory of rhetoric is all important because it
brings about an altered conception of the sign: all signs now necessarily consist of *grammatical*, rhetorical, and referential strata.
Since each stratum may and frequently does have divisions within
itself, the stability and unity of sign more than ever come undone.
The sign as such produces extravagant effects of referential aberration approaching the limits of vertigo.

Although he doesn't use Derrida's terminology, de Man's sign,
composed of unstable and divisive grammatical, rhetorical, and
referential strata, demonstrates effects parallel to the movements
of differance and the play of spacing. The machinelike forces of
grammar and rhetoric, manufacturing the belated phenomena of
reference, function like Derrida's writing and trace. Yet de Man
avoids ontology and metaphysics, restricting himself to close textual analysis, so that no messianic proclamations emerge that admit
to situating grammar and rhetoric at the site of the opening of
being and presence. Only the implication persists. Whether or not
de Man holds that grammar and rhetoric precede or accompany
the emergence into being, his theory of the sign operates, like
Derrida's *écriture*, as a disruptive and decentering force, an instrument of deconstruction, in the work of interpretation.

In his writings, Paul de Man articulates ideas *while* he reads texts;
consequently, his literary and critical theories are for the most part
embedded deeply in his works. He offers no programmatic statement about his deconstructive enterprise. Cagey and mysterious,
at times obscure and willfully unhelpful, de Man typically opens
canonical texts, with deliberation and extreme painstaking, to

ultimately breathless and original readings. One gets the impression, almost genuine, that Derrida need not have existed at all for de Man to carry out his work.

Crossing Over and Synthesizing the Sign

A critic must choose either the tradition of presence or the tradition of "difference," for their assumptions about language, about literature, about history, and about the mind cannot be made compatible.
—J. Hillis Miller

This choice was posed during 1971 in an essay on Georges Poulet's criticism.[5] Between the mid 1950s and late 1960s J. Hillis Miller worked as a devoted son of Poulet, the patriarch of the Geneva school of phenomenological critics. As a member of this continental front for the "tradition of presence," Miller published five widely read critical books. But sometime in the late 1960s his allegiance started to shift, and by 1970 he crossed over and emerged as a member of the Paris school of deconstructive critics—a group that, following the lead of Jacques Derrida, proclaims the "tradition of 'difference.'" In the early 1970s this new movement blossoms in America as the "Yale critics," and Miller quickly becomes the leading spokesman for the group. Since his shift Miller has written several dozen influential essays, most of which come from five books in progress.

The rift between Poulet and Miller dramatizes the either/or choice presented in the 1971 essay. Toward the end of his meticulously fair description of Poulet's criticism and his scrupulously impersonal exposition of the deconstruction of this phenomenology, Miller poses the clear choice. It is a primal scene: the son turns irrevocably from the father. Yet these same pages show Miller trying to align Poulet with Derrida—an attempt that succeeds only in part. Parallel to the break with Poulet is, in the next year, the split with modern humanistic scholarship, which occurs dramatically when Miller publishes a devastating review of M. H. Abrams' *Natural Supernaturalism* (1971). Precisely because "*Natural Supernaturalism* is in the grand tradition of modern humanistic scholarship, the tradition of Curtius, Auerbach, Lovejoy, C. S. Lewis," Miller criticizes the book or, more accurately, the tradition for having inadequate concepts of language, literature, history, and interpretation.[6] Here the profound division between traditional (logocentric) criticism and deconstruction emerges in public for the first time in America.

As early as 1970 Miller sketches out a rough theory of *difference* with the aid of Derrida's seminal essay "La Différance" (1968).[7] In fact, most of Miller's later deconstructive works are implicitly grounded on the operations in texts of difference. Here is Miller's most succinct formulation:

Each leaf, wave, stone, flower, or bird is different from all others. Their similarity to one another arises against the ground of this basic dissimilarity. In a similar way, language is related to what it names across the gap of its incorrigible difference from its referent.[8]

All similarities are produced out of differences. Thus difference is constitutive of resemblances, repetitions, and similarities. To say, for instance, that two birds resemble each other is to affirm subtly their initial difference. What is here true for birds is true of words also. A bird is not a b–i–r–d; that is, the body and feathers are not the four black ink marks on white paper. The word and referent are incorrigibly different.

What these observations emphasize is that the relations between entities are not based on unity and continuity; rather they are composed as differential and decentered formations. Applying this finding to words in general, Miller points out "all words are metaphors—that is, all are differentiated, differed, and deferred. Each leads to something of which it is the displacement in a movement without origin or end."[9] The force of difference undermines the traditional concepts of origin and unity. (The idea of a discontinuous and differential unity or origin is unthinkable.) To perform an easy test case on words, one need only trace the etymology of a word back to its roots, as Miller likes to do, to discover a labyrinth of semantic bifurcations and displacements ending in an impasse—the absence of authentic undifferentiated origin. "In the beginning was the *diakrisis*."[10]

Although he nowhere explicitly or fully proclaims his theory of the *sign*, Miller clearly situates the sign amid the disruptive forces of difference. Difference produces or constitutes the sign. Inevitably, the status of being and presence as points of origin comes into question. And, not surprisingly, difference—here as *diakrisis*—occupies the "beginning." One *must* choose either the tradition of presence or the tradition of difference; they cannot be made compatible. Without question, Miller's theory of the sign derives from Derrida.

For Miller all signs are rhetorical figures, that is, "all words are metaphors." In the Abrams critique Miller puts it this way: "Rather than figures of speech being derived or 'translated' from proper uses of language, all language is figurative at the beginning. The notion of a literal or referential use of language is only an illusion born of the forgetting of the metaphorical 'roots' of language" ("TD," 11). Employing the "rhetoric/reference" polarity, Miller here places the sign amidst the discontinuous and divisive forces of *rhetoricity*. This move undermines referentiality, setting the sign free to generate dizzying effects of semantic aberration. Clearly, Miller's theory of the sign derives from Paul de Man.

Signs, in Miller's view, are differentiated, differed, deferred. They displace the thing named, postpone its appearance, and substitute ink as reality. In the work of critical reading, this theory creates a continuous subversion of the stability of the sign. And the resultant flights of meaning appear beyond control or remedy. Truth always slips away. In addition, Miller conceives of the sign as figurative by nature. "Language is from the start fictive, illusory . . ." ("TD," 11). Hence truth doesn't, in fact, slip away; it isn't present at the outset. The referential function of language is here thoroughly undermined. Synthesizing elements of Derrida's and de Man's theories of the sign, merging difference and rhetoricity, Miller forges an instrument for the work of deconstruction. With this theory of the sign, derived from two different modes of deconstruction, Miller proceeds with notable success to deracinate the heretofore stable texts of the great tradition.

In the American grain, Miller thinks of himself and acts like a "practical critic." He devotes himself to careful readings of individual texts and authors. Nevertheless, he is regarded as a leading philosophical critic, mainly because he regularly attends to and employs continental philosophy. Since his turn to deconstruction, he allows himself occasionally to "theorize" without benefit of particular literary texts before him. Very rarely, though, does Miller write directly or at length about semiology, psychoanalysis or other extraliterary matters. The word "sign," for example, almost never shows up in his writings. In other words, Miller's theorizing, when it occurs, appears secularized and cleansed. No tortuous extended tangles with, say, Saussure or Heidegger or Derrida take place. Postioned as a major American literary critic, Miller manages to produce the expected and required practical criticism while staying more or less silently enmeshed in philosophical domains.

Given his position as practical critic in America, Miller does not and need not publicly wrestle with the theory of the sign. For this and other reasons we don't know why he adopts the theory of difference but not the attendant notion of *trace*. Nor do we know why he takes up the concept of rhetoricity, yet not the related theory of grammar. (If there are telling reasons for these omissions, we must extrapolate or guess them.) What you see is what you get. We can only say for sure that, using his own synthetic theory of the sign, Miller carries out an extensive deconstructive enterprise. At the same time he remains open to the charges of reductionism, unoriginality, derivativeness, and narrow practical criticism.

The development from Derrida to de Man to Miller manifests itself as continuous narrowing and reduction. The object of deconstruction changes from the entire system of Western philosophy to key literary and philosophical texts in the post-Renaissance continental tradition to major English and American literary works of the nineteenth and twentieth centuries. Loss in grandeur of sweep and boldness of approach seem to mar this history. Yet growing lucidity and succinctness mark the progression, as does economy of application. An accurate and reliable assessment of Miller ultimately depends upon the publication of all five of his books, which offer wide-ranging readings of post-neoclassical poetry and fiction as well as a theory of narrative. Throughout the first decade of deconstruction in America, the evaluation of Miller's project rested on assessments of his piecemeal publications and narrowly focused essays. He appeared last and least of three.

Unlike the early Derrida, Miller practices *deconstructive rhetoric*, tracing the aberrations of figures and the destabilizing flights of reference in texts. Derrida focuses upon concepts, reversing their terms and substituting new notions in place of the old truths. Generalizing his approach, Miller offers this program for the future of literary criticism:

The study of literature should certainly cease to take the mimetic referentiality of literature for granted. Such a properly literary discipline would cease to be exclusively a repertoire of ideas, of themes, and of the varieties of human psychology. It would become once more philology, rhetoric, an investigation of the epistemology of tropes. ("NLM," 451)

Next to historical, thematic, and psychological criticism, Miller would have rhetorical criticism. Such a move to deconstructive rhetoric is conceived, not as a happy escape from the simplicities of traditional criticism, but as a painful confrontation with the baffling epistemology of literary texts. Basically, rhetoric provides a way to move beyond the closure of referentiality—a way to break through the logocentric tradition of presence.[11] Yet the project of deconstructive rhetoric proceeds on hollow grounds. There are, after all, no literal designations; language is originarily figural. With this collapse of the "literal/figural" polarity, the work of rhetorical analysis is put in jeopardy. Rather than a referential/rhetorical structure, language is constituted as an infinite chain of figurative words, which have no extralinguistic origin or end. Deconstructive rhetoric, then, is not a science of truth: "the study of rhetoric leads to the abyss by destroying, through its own theoretical procedures, its own basic axiom."[12] Miller accepts this impasse and celebrates the abyss.

In the end we return to the enigmas of interpreting signs. Wide spaces open during the activity of interpretation, forcing the interpreter to play at prophet and rhetor. Occupying the edge or standing before the abyss, the visionary reader ultimately covers over the spaces and restricts the flight of the sign to understanding, to meaning, to truth. This process of stabilization and closure, shamanistic cure, gets done at the behest of one transcendent name or another, ranging from God to Author, from psychoanalytical Phallus to the present Being, from the spoken Word to the determined Center. As functions, God, Author, Phallus, Being, Voice, and Center all play a similar role: they reduce the flight of the sign and close the spaces of interpretation in a determination of stable meaning or truth.

II

VERSIONS OF TEXTUALITY AND INTERTEXTUALITY: CONTEMPORARY THEORIES OF LITERATURE AND TRADITION

Prologue: Notes and Aphorisms toward a Belated Manifesto

You confide
In images in things that can be
Represented which is their dimension you
Require them you say This
Is real . . .

—W. S. Merwin, "The Widow," *The Lice*

I

First Observation. The word "tree," an assembly of four letters, is not the wooden object. This sign marks the absence of the object. What to get out of this observation: you cannot get out of it. This Is real. . . .

(For an era of black astral holes and antimatter and strange quarks and traces we require a philosophy of *absence*.)

2

Other Dimensions. The relations between and among all entities are always constituted as discontinuous and differential. Such formations beget everywhere absences.

3

Toward Strategy. All repetitions or retracings are subversive since they summon up difference. To repeat—to retrace is to make a difference. To produce detour and absence. Nothing. Space.

4

The Insistence of the Figure. Signs displace and substitute; we inhabit a world of tropes and devices. Literal language does not exist, except for the illusion of it.

No language can have a literal ground. Consequence. No exit from the aberrations of reference. The ground always collapses.

A "literal interpretation" is an effect derived by single-minded reduction of grammatical, figural, and semantic oscillations in a writing.

Neither author nor critic can ultimately control the free play of signifiers in disseminating reference. No one escapes the chains of figurality, the flights of signifiers, and the network of differences in a writing. We confide always in images.

5

Note on Textuality. The world is text. Nothing stands behind. There is no escape. Here in the prisonhouse of language.

6

Model of the Critical Act. To construct a narrative of experience is to produce fissures in that experience. Criticism is such a perpetual displacement from immediacy.

7

On History. History is substitution, signifier, figure, difference, text, fiction.

8

Note on Interpretation. All facts, data, structures, and laws are assembled descriptions, formulations, constructions—interpretations. There are no facts as such, only assemblages.

There is always only interpretation.

All interpretive orderings, whether logical, psychological, historical, dialectical, thematic, rhetorical, or structural, are acts of willed mastery. Interpretation drives to control, insists on order, demonstrates authority.

9

Status of "Self," etc. The concepts "being," "consciousness," "identity," "presence," and "self" are creations, fabrications, patchworks—interpretations. Functions not facts. Effects of language, not causes. The same goes for "meaning."

10

On Meaning. Most texts can be made to generate an almost infinite set of refined statements about meaning. Why confide so exclusively in meaning? Meaning is belated production. Prohibition of play.

11

Criticism. (a) The idolatry of alluring language is criticism. Acting out this fetish, the lover violates the text, then bows in proud remorse and abject adoration.

(b) Critical readings are extravagant acts of fantasy abetted by seductive displacements, substitutions, and differences. None of this is a matter of choice, but of pleasure.

12

What is Reading? To reproduce, recuperate, or recreate intentional or objective meaning of (author's) text is goal and source of glory. Such effaced doubling of text enthrones critic as purveyor of truth.

When he repeats an element in text, critic changes it. As such, reading is transmutation, not transportation, of truth.

The creation of a reading, prophetic and rhetorical act, is the production of error. The condition of the edge.

> All reading is necessarily misreading.
> Texts are unreadable.

Criticism insists on performing what cannot be performed— reading texts. There can never be "correct" or "objective" readings, only less or more energetic, interesting, careful, or pleasurable misreadings.

13

On Intertextuality. The text is not an autonomous or unified object, but a set of relations with other texts. Its system of language, its grammar, its lexicon, drag along numerous bits and pieces— traces—of history so that the text resembles a Cultural Salvation Army Outlet with unaccountable collections of incompatible ideas, beliefs, and sources. The "genealogy" of the text is necessarily an incomplete network of conscious and unconscious borrowed fragments. Manifested, tradition is a mess. Every text is intertext.

14

The Strategy of the Weakest Link. Destruction is at least as important and necessary as creation.

15

Endnote on Dissemination. No one can control completely the play of floating signifiers and other differential forces across a writing: no final authority over dissemination. Always truth statements miss a part. Vice or versa.

4

The Truth of Literature

Of Being, Poetry, Truth, and Tradition

Language is the house of Being. In its home man dwells. Those who think and those who create with words are the guardians of this home. Their guardianship accomplishes the manifestation of Being. . . .[1]

poetry never takes language as a raw material ready to hand, rather it is poetry which first makes language possible. Poetry is the primitive language of a historical people. Therefore, in just the reverse manner, the essence of language must be understood through the essence of poetry.[2]

—Martin Heidegger

Human being resides in language and language results from poetry. To enter poetry is to encounter Being. Being dwells in poetic language. The circularity here, characteristic of Martin Heidegger, a dominant figure in modern phenomenological theory, requires some straightening out. We undertake this line of inquiry because Heidegger's monumental project inspires certain directions in deconstruction and inaugurates a particular movement of American "deconstruction." Ultimately, our primary thematics in the first section of this chapter will emerge as Heidegger's theories of poetry and tradition. We must go by way of eccentric paths and in the manner of quick cuts. In the second section, we take up the work of William V. Spanos, the leading American exponent of Heideggerian *destruction*. Here we encounter the reshaping of Heidegger for a contemporary "destructive" criticism. In the third and final section, we shall distinguish the project of *destruction* from *deconstruction*, maintaining our dual focus on questions of poetics and tradition.

The center of Heidegger's concern, early and late, is the meaning of Being. Yet ever more insistently this quest leads him to language and poetry—to sites where Being manifests itself. In this later situation, the quintessential question for *deconstruction* will be: "Which comes first—Being or language?" Put more peculiarly still, "Are we born into Being or into language?" Is *écriture* before existence or vice versa? Such a question is pre-logical; it concerns issues of governance, not chronology. On this question *destruction* and *deconstruction* are divided. But we are getting ahead of ourselves.

I

What is the relation of language to Being? In the traditional view, language serves as an instrument for the presentation and extension of man's will; it ex-presses and re-presents the mind or soul of man through bodily utterance; uniting sound and sense, language conveys man's opinion and knowledge, moods and resolutions, both real and unreal: it is clearly a useful tool in man's possession. Heidegger, knowing all this, works incessantly at and beyond the edges of such truth. Language for Heidegger is that locus where Being comes to place. As original condition of being-in-the-world, language, taking form in speaking, asserting, hearing, listening, heeding, and (even) remaining silent, lets Being first appear as such: it is the lighting and advent of Being itself.[3]

Nevertheless, Being, however pervasive, always appears mysterious and concealed. Language too, though very near, seems similarly mysterious:

> The one thing thinking would like to attain and for the first time tries to articulate in *Being and Time* is something simple. As such, Being remains mysterious, the simple nearness of an unobtrusive governance. The nearness occurs essentially as language itself. ("LH," 212)

Ever near, Being and language, simple and unobtrusive, while governing, stay in mystery. *Being and Time* wants to reveal that language speaks Being (*Sein*) to man as thinking (*Denken*). *Language speaks Being as thinking*. Language speaks Being. As thinking. To grasp Heidegger's obscure illumination is to conceive language and thinking as seemingly pure activities—without tangible substance or determined content. In their mere unfolding, language and thinking produce and reveal Being—which itself appears in and through them as something thoroughly abstract and ungraspable, yet ultimately and mysteriously present. (The obscurity seems forbidding.) "Everything depends upon this alone, that the truth of Being come to language and that thinking attain to this language. Perhaps, then, language requires much less precipitous expression than proper silence" ("LH," 223). The truth of Being, as it emerges in language and thinking, perhaps requires proper silence. Why silence? What constitutes such Being? Nothing. What? Nothing! Indeed, "because it thinks Being, thinking thinks the nothing" ("LH," 238). As activities without specific contents or as pure ontological processes, language and thinking, in their most rigorous moment, disclose the nothingness of Being. What, then, is Being? "Neither is Being any existing quality which allows itself to be fixed among beings. And yet Being is more in being than any being. Because nihilation occurs essentially in Being itself we can never discern it as a being among beings" ("LH," 237). Can we think or even conceive such an omnipresent, yet ever imperceptible nonentity, concept, trace, or possibility? Only in, through, and with language. Yet *this* language cannot be merely a tool or instrument—as tradition would have it. "Man acts as though *he* were the shaper and master of language, while in fact *language* remains the master of man."[4] Even nothing (no-thing) comes forth for man in language. The obscurity lingers—admittedly.

Typical of Heidegger, "thinking," like language, undergoes hypostatization. It is a highly abstract, fundamental ontological activity. On some occasions the giant in the land of Heidegger's philosophy appears as pure thinking. To be understood initially, thinking is perhaps best and most clearly thought beyond or before or separate from any particular thinker. Thinking in Heidegger, especially in the later works, reveals that language speaks Being. Being, as such, dwells in language. Thus the giant stalks Being—in, through, and with language.

Language itself must be understood through the essence of poetry. Poetry is the primordial source of language. Thinking, as a consequence, manifests itself fundamentally as poetic activity:

The poetic character of thinking is
    still veiled over.

Where it shows itself, it is for a
    long time like the utopism of
    a half-poetic intellect.

But poetry that thinks is in truth
    the topology of Being.

This topology tells Being the
    whereabouts of its actual
    presence. ("The Thinker as Poet," *PLT*, 12)

Here, in a section from a poem written in 1947 (published 1954), Heidegger links thinking and poetizing to Being: *thinking as poetry maps Being as presence.* Poetry, seeming a utopian form of thinking, allows Being to shine forth as present and locatable. The presence of Being manifests itself in poetic thinking. Making language possible, poetry gives Being a local habitation and a name.

Despite continuing obscurities, we can wonder for a moment whether or not Being is conceivable or possible outside poetry or separate from language. Does language allow and produce being, as Derrida's notion of *écriture* suggests? This question is crucial. In deconstruction, *writing* (or language) serves as ground of being while in Husserlian phenomenology and other forms of logocentric philosophy being grounds and precedes language. About the proper determination of language and being contemporary theorists expend much print and thought and emotion. In a sense, this problematic separates out the true deconstructors from the benighted others. A struggle over the body of Heidegger's writings on this issue animates current critical polemics (as we shall see in the next two sections and in chapter 5).

What is poetry? In "Hölderlin and the Essence of Poetry" (1936), Heidegger depicts poetry as an original act of establishing—an activity of inaugural naming. What is established and named is not the already known or existent, but these come to be in the very nomination and founding: "poetry is the inaugural naming of being and of the essence of all things . . ." (*EB*, 283). Disclosing

Being and founding existence, the poet stands between the divinities of the sky and the mortals of the earth. "The poet himself
stands between the former—the gods, and the latter—the people.
He is one who has been cast out—out into that *Between*, between
gods and men. But only and for the first time in this Between is
it decided, who man is and where he is settling his existence"
(*EB*, 288–89). Occupying the Between, the Open (*Lichtung*), the
poet confers names, but not like Adam, who named the already
known and existing. From out of the Between, poetry is originary
establishment, inauguration, founding.

Poetry is the source itself of language and art. "*All art*, as the
letting happen of the advent of the truth of what is, is, as such,
essentially poetry. The nature of art, on which both the art work
and the artist depend, is the setting-itself-into-work of truth."[5]
Heidegger stresses the *work-being* of the art work, deemphasizing
the role of the artist and the traditional decorative status of the
art object. The setting-itself-to-work, the primordial founding,
the inaugural naming—these appear as quintessential functions
and forces of poetry. (Poetry, of course, is now conceived broadly
as the source of all art as well as language.[6]) The work-being of
poetry is the advent of truth.

What then is truth? In a striking meditation on a Van Gogh
painting of peasant shoes, Heidegger observes:

Van Gogh's painting is the disclosure of what the equipment, the pair
of peasant shoes, *is* in truth. The entity emerges into the unconcealedness
of its being. The Greeks called the unconcealedness of beings *aletheia*.
We say "truth" and think little enough in using this word. If there occurs
in the work a disclosure of a particular being, disclosing what and how
it is, then there is here an occurring, a happening of truth at work.
("OWA," 36)

The work-being of the work is the advent of truth. Truth, *aletheia*,
is the activity or happening of unconcealing and disclosing the
being of an entity. When poetry, as inaugural naming and primordial establishing, operates, it discloses Being and it produces
truth. In poetry, the truth of Being comes to language as entities
stand to shine forth their being in presence. Poetry "tells Being
the whereabouts of its actual presence" (*PLT*, 12).[7]

In our discussions of Being and language, of thinking and poet-izing, of poetry and truth, whereabouts do we locate man? In the fourfold (*Geviert*). Existing on *earth* and under the *sky*, before the *divinities* and amidst *mortals*, man dwells among things in a simple and primal "oneness of the four" ("BDT," 149). "The unitary fourfold of sky and earth, mortals and divinities, which is stayed in the thinging of things, we call—the world."[8] Heidegger es-tablishes—arbitrarily yet simply—four sectors to the *world*. When it calls forth and names Being, when it discloses the truth of Being, poetry makes happen an opening, a clearing, a lighting, a Between amidst the fourfold of the world, and lets man realize for the first time where he is settling and who he is. For Heidegger *world* comes to presence for man amidst the Open of the fourfold ("LH," 229). This primordial occurrence happens *in time* as both event and historical founding. Through poetry man is located in the *world* and situated historically.

2

What is the relation of human being and time? Occupied with everyday issues, lost in current matters, forgetting all the rest, man lives in the present. This moment of being-in-the-world appears in Heidegger's thinking as "lapse" or perhaps "entrap-ment" (*Verfallen*). Yet man does exist with potentiality for future possibilities; ahead of himself, man plans tomorrow's projects. Heidegger calls this moment of being "existentiality." From affairs that lie behind him and past matters now out of his control, man is "thrown" from his personal history toward present and future paths. For Heidegger this moment of being-in-the-world is "fac-ticity." Taken together, these structures of time, rooting human existence in world, constitute Being as extended temporal activity. The historicality of Being—its entrapment, existentiality, and fac-ticity—situates man in world and community, involving him in his own fate and his society's destiny. Being dwells in, with, and through time.

"In order that history may be possible," observes Heidegger, "language has been given to man" ("HEP," 275). Extending this observation, he states: "Poetry is the foundation which supports history . . ." ("HEP," 283). Still more forcefully, he proclaims: "Art is historical, and as historical it is the creative preserving of

truth in the work. Art happens as poetry. Poetry is founding in
the triple sense of bestowing, grounding, and beginning. Art, as
founding, is essentially historical. . . . *Art is history in the essential
sense that it grounds history*" ("OWA," 77; my italics). As poetry
lets Being come into presence and allows truth to originate, it
opens time and grounds history. The work-being of poetry sets
history going. (In addition, the poetic works of the past, in a
creative preserving, make ancient primordial truth available to
us.) In its most radical sense, poetry is historical: it establishes
history.

But history weighs us down. Its concepts and categories,
boundaries and methods deaden our vitality. The answers of past
centuries pile up and bulge out of our libraries. The original questions, once vital, presently forgotten, now rarely even haunt us.
We have forgotten. We gather "truths" from shelves of death.
Burning the Library is the grand solution figured for our time by
William Carlos Williams in *Paterson*. History and tradition carry
death; destruction is necessary; the color of hope is black. Heidegger himself, in the Introduction to *Being and Time*, gives us
a plan for "The task of Destroying the history of ontology" (sec.
6). Here Heidegger calls for *de-struction* (*Destruktion*) not destruction (*Zerstörung*). Ultimately, Heidegger's task of destroying is an
effort at a creative preserving of history, as is the overall endeavor
of W. C. Williams in *Paterson*.

Heidegger calls for the destruction of the history of ontology
in *Being and Time*. Until such a process begins, the question of
Being fails to attain its proper dimension, its particularity, its
vitality.

If the question of Being is to have its own history made transparent,
then this hardened tradition must be loosened up, and the concealments
which it has brought about must be dissolved. We understand this task
as one in which by taking *the question of Being as our clue*, we are to *destroy*
the traditional content of ancient ontology until we arrive at those primordial experiences in which we achieved our first ways of determining
the nature of Being. . . . (*BT*, 44)

But this destruction is just as far from having the *negative* sense of shaking
off the ontological tradition. We must, on the contrary, stake out the

positive possibilities of that tradition. . . . On its negative side, this de-struction does not relate itself towards the past; its criticism is aimed at 'today'. . . . (*BT*, 44)

Tradition, while transmitting more and more knowledge, conceals truth; repository of self-evident, disembodied "truths," tradition, in the role of authority and master, blocks access to the genuine sources and primordial experiences in which truth originated. Since the well-springs are well hidden and forgotten, the work of return must seem at first unnecessary and incomprehensible. Once the return does appear essential, the work of de-struction begins in earnest to reclaim those elements of tradition which remain useful for today. *Destruction*, therefore, emerges as both negative and positive activity. Negatively, it rummages resolutely through tradition in a disruptive search for authentic materials of use to *contemporary* projects; it burns and blows away in a black wind of impatient criticism much that is conventionally regarded as sacred; it leaves in disrepute vast amounts of treasure, abjuring the antiquarian efforts at and pious respect for preservation and archeology. Positively, destruction renews tradition by conserving selected materials of value; it revivifies present thinking through concernful and genuine, yet critical, care of the past; and it pays homage to history by repeating the selfsame founding operations of tradition. The strategy of *destruction* assumes that tradition itself is two-faced. In one aspect tradition conceals truth by preserving only deadened "truths" (which appear insidiously as self-evident to us), thereby blocking off in forgetfulness all primordial and authentic origins. Yet, in another respect, tradition offers a way back to the founding and inaugurating moments of Being and truth. However it is viewed, man cannot escape history. His mode of being-in-the-world keeps him within time and his heritage.

When he returns to early Greek thinking and poetry—to Parmenides, Heraclitus, and Anaximander—when he laboriously traces the etymologies of words, and when he reconsiders the works of Kant, Hegel, and Nietzsche, Heidegger seeks to uncover inaugurating disclosures of Being missed or forgotten. This de-structive activity, so frequently practiced by Heidegger, keeps him continuously within the texts of the tradition so that his project

seems a grand final revision of Western metaphysics. But the
critical step back, the destruction, encounters a profound difficulty:

> That difficulty lies in language. Our Western languages are languages
> of metaphysical thinking, each in its own way. It must remain an open
> question whether the nature of Western languages is in itself marked
> with the exclusive brand of metaphysics, and thus marked permanently
> by onto-theo-logic, or whether these languages offer other possibilities
> of utterance—and that means at the same time of a telling silence.
>
> (*ID*, 73)

Heidegger's tone suggests that we are locked into a prisonhouse
of language, that we may actually be enchained in metaphysical
discourse, that we cannot effect escape from traditional thinking,
that destruction as a strategy inevitably courts impasse, that language as silence is perhaps the proper path for critical inquiry.
While this end of *destruction* as a possible mode of criticism remains
an open question, the irresistible impulse and necessity to return
ultimately to history persists to the end. "For every attempt to
gain insight into the supposed task of thinking finds itself moved
to review the whole history of philosophy" ("EPTT," 378). To
think is to confront history. To enter the domain of philosophical
language and tradition. Every new text then emerges as intertext,
caught up in a dependence on prior texts, codes, and languages.
The question of Being leads Heidegger back to the poetry of
Parmenides, Heraclitus, Anaximander. The contemporary destructive text proceeds to and from other earlier texts. The Heideggerian text contains cultural debris. With hammer and bucket,
Heidegger chips away at the ancient monuments for present purposes. The *traces* of the past infiltrate his work not only through
his destructive acts of deliberate preserving, but also, more insidiously, through the quiet and unwanted structuration of metaphysical thought itself inherent in Western languages. This *intertextuality*, implicit in all language and thinking, intuited by
Heidegger, shows itself as threatening barrier and ultimate limitation. Strategic silence admits the power of this prisonhouse of
language and tradition.

3

The publication in the postwar era of Heidegger's late works and
the spread of his early works through popular postwar existen-

tialism give Heideggerian philosophy tremendous prominence from the mid-1940s till the mid-1960s. In strictly literary circles, particularly in America, Heidegger comes to special prominence only during the 1960s and 1970s. In the next section we shall trace this transmission as it informs the project of an American *"destructive* criticism." Let us for now content ourselves with a provisional summary of Heidegger's conceptions of tradition and literature. We shall then close with some observations on Heidegger's influential style.

From his earliest to his latest works Heidegger carries out his project, resolutely and self-consciously, within a broad historical context, ranging from pre-Socratic to contemporary times. Tradition always looms large. Yet tradition must be destroyed so that it can be preserved in its vitality. Heidegger himself neither avoids nor escapes tradition. Given the temporality of existence, the indissolubility of Being and time, man is constituted and determined as a historical being, meaning, as a consequence, that no one can ever escape outside tradition. There is no outside. And, significantly, since language, as vehicle of tradition and house of Being, grounds history and existence, flight out of time or history or tradition is, strictly speaking, inconceivable as well as impossible. That a sense of enclosure and of closure here seems overpowering is obvious—if we forget the liberation of destruction. Destruction creates opening and renewal. And yet, in an almost unthinkable and an apparently invidious way, destruction itself appears doomed because language through its very structural constitution limits thinking to traditional metaphysical paths and modes of operation. Silence seems a way out of tradition. But even silence is a form of language. While not an overt theorist of *intertextuality*, Heidegger experiences and admits its sway and web at strategic moments of unwanted insight.

Poetry is the source and foundation of language and art and history and Being and time and truth. It is primordial founding, establishing, situating, naming. It brings forth existence. It produces thinking. There is nothing outside poetry. Strictly conceived, there is no "outside poetry." Not even "nothing" itself is outside poetry. This prisonhouse of language, coming to us from Heidegger's theory of poetry (and tradition), appears inescapable.

Existence is textualized through and through—from beginning to end. Language precedes Being. Yet such *textuality* in Heidegger is perhaps overstated—not to say problematic. For Being, significantly, may and does emerge in particular texts as prior to or, more often, concomitant with poetry. Disclosing Being as presence, poetry sometimes comes after or embodies—rather than produces—Being. Being precedes language. To hold Heidegger up as a thoroughgoing theorist of *textuality* is less purposeful or defensible here than to present him as a precursor on the way to the postmodern venture of triumphant textuality.

In some ways Heidegger's style is as provocative and distinctive as are his theories of poetry and tradition. The nearest thing in English to the unique surface of Heidegger's writing is D. H. Lawrence's similarly pulsating and repetitive, almost hypnotic, prose. Yet Heidegger is more lean and "unrhetorical," less given to pomp and purple. Certain words take on talismanic value, undergoing circular repetition and assuming ever-growing mantric value till finally the mere mention of such holy words brings on a knowing and fanatic nod or grin common to the true believer. Outside this circle of mesmeric charm, the uninitiated may be driven to worry beads. But inside, the powers of *Lichtung* and *Denken*, for instance, overwhelm towards elucidation and illumination—never mere explanation.[9] When, as usual, that which is elucidated is impalpable, Heidegger's lean and repetitive style belies the resultant nothing.

Reading texts and poems or tracing etymologies, Heidegger seeks to harness and rekindle the numinous energy of the source. He wants to disclose and unconceal. He aims to act out and produce truth before our eyes. In such moments, Heidegger takes analysis beyond explanation toward vision: he performs truth. The rapture and astonishment and primal wonder which result sweep Heidegger as well as his readers along. The impression that language speaks, not the author, is strong—very strong. As critical practice, Heidegger's writings eschew paraphrase and logic and textual fidelity to evoke and call into presence in celebration and in awe the dawning defamiliarization and unconcealment of truth. Forging a new poetics for critical writing, Heidegger pioneers a dramatistic mode of analysis; at its best his destructive enterprise emerges as a powerful performative project. Like poetry and truth, critical writing is an invaluable happening in- and of-itself—not a secondary phenomenon or mere instrument for communicating the already determined and validated Values.

The Destruction of Tradition
and the Being of Literature

When *Martin Heidegger and the Question of Literature: Toward a Postmodern Literary Hermeneutics*, edited by William V. Spanos, was published in 1979, the genuine importance of Heidegger for the contemporary movement toward *destruction* and *deconstruction* received convincing and definitive confirmation in America. Maybe such affirmation wasn't needed by 1979. This collection of fourteen essays plus photographs, poems, and a translated Heidegger text gathered together young and old critics writing on issues of compelling significance for the project of a new criticism. Published earlier as a special issue of *Boundary 2: A Journal of Postmodern Literature*, vol. 4 (Winter 1976), the Heidegger collection, when reissued for a larger audience in 1979, coincided with the important publication of a two-volume special issue of *Boundary 2*, vol. 7 (Winter and Spring 1979), edited by Paul A. Bové, devoted to "Revisions of the Anglo-American Tradition." Here twenty-one essays, covering significant authors from Chaucer to T. S. Eliot, aimed to "destroy" traditional Anglo-American literary history and critical practice. Spanos, founder of *Boundary 2* in 1972 and coeditor since then, emerged during the late 1970s as the leading American Heideggerian theorist of literary criticism; and Bové, a staff member of *Boundary 2* since 1975 and former student of Spanos, also emerged as theorist and practitioner of Heideggerian *destruction*. From the mid-1970s on, *Boundary 2* championed *destructive* poetics and hermeneutics, attracting to its venture other followers of Heidegger's critical phenomenology.

I

Paul Bové apparently wrote the first "deconstructive" dissertation accepted by an American university. In "A 'New Literary History' of Modern Poetry: History and Deconstruction in the Works of Whitman, Stevens, and Olson" (Ph.D. diss., State University of New York at Binghamton, 1975), Bové tries *destructive* readings of three major poets and of four major critics, including Cleanth Brooks, Harold Bloom, Walter Jackson Bate, and Paul de Man. His immediate aim is to *destroy* formalist and aesthetic criticism and to liberate the works of Whitman, Stevens, and Olson from stultifying misreadings.

At the same time Bové sketches a destructive hermeneutics based on Heidegger's *Being and Time*. This theory of interpretation calls forth and relies on distinct notions of textuality and intertextuality:

> Two crucial ideas for literary interpretation and literary history emerge from this discussion to support my original proposition that *literary texts are themselves interpretations*. All language is capable of authenticity and inauthenticity, i.e., it both discloses and covers up, often in the same movement. Therefore, for language to maintain what has been disclosed in a state of openness, it must itself be kept from solidifying into idle talk or "tradition" by the process of destruction. All authentic language reflects this destructive process. Criticism of literary language, insofar as it is authentic, must be aware of this interpretive process within the language being studied. . . . Moreover, literary history itself, . . . if it intends to be authentic, must be cognizant that *there is ongoing hermeneutical interaction within and among literary texts* to maintain what has been disclosed. . . . (106–7; my italics)

To Bové's mind, language itself is interpretation. In reading poetry, therefore, the critical job of keeping open the interpretive insights embodied in poetic language requires constant destruction—demands that reification into tradition or idle chatter be continually resisted and, when necessary, exposed. In effect, interpretation of poetry becomes a destructive hermeneutics of primordial hermeneutics. We approach here an abyss of interpretation: there is always only interpretation with no safe ground in sight. Moreover, Bové envisions the history of literature as a series of texts which destructively interpret other texts. In literary history we encounter poems (interpretations) that are interpretations of other poems (interpretations). Such intertextuality precedes literary historiography. In other words, the original series of historical intertexts or poems becomes the subject of later critical histories, and critical history, Bové urges, must attend to such constitutive intertextuality so as to hold open the valuable cumulative insights of poetic tradition. Through all of this, the text emerges as an interpretive discourse caught up in a network of other interpretive discourses.

Ultimately, however, Bové focuses less on the problematics of textuality and intertextuality and more on the operations in literature of being, nothingness, and truth. "All language has a dual potential because it emerges from the Nothing and Being of the source of all interpretations" (117). Tracing the disclosures of being in poetic texts, the critic, as he attempts to get to the bottom of things, comes upon the nothing—the point at which being itself springs out of nothingness or, to turn it around, the point at which being withdraws into the nothing. In the end, Bové's destructive criticism seeks primarily to disclose being itself. To uncover truth. Thus the endpoint of destructive analysis is the preservation of being in the texts of tradition through critical retrievals of truth. Texts, when finally disclosed, produce sightings of primordial being and truth. Since texts almost always exist surrounded by and encrusted with critical heritages, destructive criticism, in Bové's practice, works its way through prior mystified (mis)readings to the truth of the text. Reading texts destructively, therefore, necessarily involves destroying and revising literary history and tradition.

2

When Bové's revised dissertation entitled *Destructive Poetics* came into print in 1980, the work of Spanos remained available only in journal articles.[10] These lengthy essays focus on two main topics: hermeneutic theory and T. S. Eliot's major poetry. (They form the core of two books in progress.) Overall, Spanos develops a sophisticated Heideggerian *destructive hermeneutics*, and he enacts exemplary *destructive* readings of Eliot's major poems, especially *The Waste Land* and *Four Quartets*.[11] In taking up Spanos' Heideggerian project here, we shall draw out the main features of his destructive criticism so as to unfold its theories of tradition and literature. To conclude this chapter we shall distinguish the project of *destruction* from that of *deconstruction*. Let us begin with Spanos on tradition.

Following Heidegger, Spanos regards the ontotheological tradition, which spans from Plato to Husserl, from Greek tragedy to High Modernism, as pernicious in its covering over and forgetting of being and time. He devotes much energy to "destroying" this tradition, particularly its systematic mishandling of temporality. In Spanos' view, the tradition transforms, in two parallel ways, the temporality of being-in-the-world into an overall insidious "world picture":

(1) a flattened out, static, and homogeneous Euclidean space—a totalized and ontologically depthless system of referents (a map)—if the objectifying consciousness is positivistic or realistic; or (2) a self-bounded or sealed off and in-clusive image (icon or myth), if the objectifying consciousness is idealistic or symbolistic. In either case, this transformation allows *Dasein* [human being] to *see* existence from the beginning, i.e., all at once. In so doing it dis-stances him, i.e., disengages his Care, makes him an objective, a disinterested or care-less, *observer* of the ultimately familiar or autonomous picture in which temporality—its threat and its possibilities—has been annulled. ("BC," 427)

The "map" and "icon" paradigms of existence, which spring, respectively, from the world views of the scientific-pragmatic and the idealistic-symbolist mind-sets, situate human consciousness above the tumult of life, affording man a measure of objectivity and distance from things as they are. As observer, man is enabled to look over the whole of life and to grasp its order, to make sense of its origins and ends. In constructing a view of the world and of existence, ontotheological man can assume a stance of disinterest and impersonality; he can distinguish through observation the permanent from the changing; he can withhold his care and interest. Thus man is able to place before or to present to himself in presence and in certainty objects for analysis, manipulation, and calculation; he can exercise will and power over the world. In all of this, metaphysical man expresses a profoundly *spatial* view of existence.

Spanos aims to "destroy" the traditional spatial model or world view in favor of a temporal systematics. What does such *destruction* entail? "By 'destruction' I do not, of course, mean 'annihilation'; I mean, rather, a hermeneutic project grounded in an understanding of truth . . . as *a-letheia*—bringing into the open from hiddenness or oblivion (*BT*, 57)—and assuming the form of a destruction—a dis-assembling of a spatial figure—such as that which Heidegger undertakes in his dialogue with . . . the systematic philosophy of what he has called the Western 'onto-theo-logical' tradition" ("R," 229). In a Heideggerian manner, Spanos conceives *destruction* as an interpretive enterprise oriented toward overturning the systematic philosophy of tradition, especially its spatial paradigm, in order to reveal hidden and forgotten possibilities through careful de-structuring of the now dominant metaphysical formations of truth.

Destructive inquiry, as it opens a text and progresses through time, disarticulates the spatial point of view, bringing into the open the indefinite or vague insights into being that lie hidden in tradition. It discovers being as *be-ing* in the actual temporal process itself, and discloses that interpretation is a ceaseless experience of concealing and unconcealing the truth of being. As an historical being-in-the-world, the destructive interpreter proceeds with interest and care to move independently yet intimately into the being of the text to re-enact for himself and his time the truth of being in an activity of retrieval or repetition (*Wiederholen*). As *repetition*, interpretation repeats and recaptures primordial historical existence, transforming it into a new beginning. Here the beginning is not reduced to the past (or to a form of detemporalized *recollection*), but is begun again with all the dangers and insecurities of authentic beginning. This process of destructive interpretation "makes time man's element and ceaseless exploration in the openness of time his (saving) activity" ("HM," 563). Man is thrown into an endless interpretive existence. There is never closure.

In summing up and explaining the fundamentals of the destructive project, Spanos reveals how closely he follows Heidegger's phenomenology. This constitutes a crucial passage for contemporary destructive criticism, deserving extended quotation:

It will suffice for my purposes to draw the obvious conclusions from Heidegger's destruction of the tradition: that the literary hermeneutics suggested by Heidegger's "Existential Analytic" in *Being and Time* is an anti-metaphysical, phenomenological hermeneutics of dis-closure in which temporality is ontologically prior to [metaphysical] Being (or Spatial Form). It thus demands a phenomenological reduction (*epoché*) of the metaphysical perspective, a "return to the things themselves," not, as in Husserl, in the sense of a recovery of a logocentric origin, an *arché* as source, but of recovering one's original status as being-in-the-world (*in-der-Welt-Sein*). Here, we recall, [1] the actuality, the primordial Situation, into which the interpreter as *Dasein* finds himself thrown (*Befindlichkeit*); [2] the Understanding (*Verstehen*), that which reveals *Dasein*'s possibilities as Being-in-the-World; and [3], most important for my purposes, the Saying, the making explicit, of this Understanding (*Rede*, the *logos* as *legein* [talk])—all are equiprimordial and *radically temporal*: un-grounded or, rather, grounded in Nothing, i.e., open. Here also—and because of his temporality—*Dasein* . . . is characterized, not by disinterestedness, but by *Anxiety*, which . . . discloses its being, that is, as *Care*. . . . ("BC," 443–44)

Rather than unpack this telling quotation line-by-line, let us foreground the understructure of thought that directs this and previous passages. A set of oppositions continually patterns Spanos' thinking. In this network the first term invariably receives phenomenological privilege:

temporal/spatial	activity/stasis
careful/careless	anxiety/disinterest
original/derived	beginning/end
opened/closed	nothing/ground
vocal/visual	saying/observing
projective/retrospective	repetition/recollection
disclosed/concealed	remembering/forgetting
subjective/objective	truth/error
diachronic/synchronic	process/object
dialogic/monologic	history/eternity
contingent/reified	difference/identity
changing/permanent	absence/presence
explorative/coercive	letting-be/will-to-power
authentic/inauthentic	be-ing/Being
phenomenology/metaphysics . . .	

This detailed pattern of thinking, suggesting a fully elaborated philosophy of world and existence, can be further simplified and framed into a reductive narrative. Thrown into the world, man finds through his understanding and language that time is constantly unremitting and that existence is groundless; the encounter with nothingness produces anxiety and concern (care); in his original or beginning situation, man experiences his personal existence as a chaotic and risky venture. Now when we contrast even this oversimplified formation with the familiar and hardened onto-theological account, we set Spanos' phenomenological thinking in relief. Inheriting the spatial world view, man observes and reflects upon reality and existence as they present themselves to him objectively; he determines or derives the nature of being and world dispassionately through logical or experimental calculation and manipulation; using discourse to communicate his conclusions, which assume form in formulas, graphs, and systems based on refined principles of order, coherence, conciseness, and completeness, man re-presents and extends through time his valid findings—his truth—for the practical use of future generations. Setting the metaphysical against the phenomenological account, we uncover and foreground the general directions of Spanos' thinking: he values a recovery of man's original status or situation of primordial being-in-the-world; he seeks to situate temporality prior to all spatial formations; he desires a return to things themselves and their basis in nothingness; and he intends to hold being, understanding, and discourse on an equal footing as ontologically equiprimordial. Stated negatively and simply, Spanos aims to overturn thoroughly ontotheological thinking and tradition.

Not surprisingly, Spanos, as literary critic and theorist, takes out after formalism, structuralism, semiotics, myth criticism, Geneva criticism, and other forms of metaphysical thinking. For each of these modes of criticism initiates inquiry with a predetermined sense of the "whole picture" or with an opening commitment to "overall form." The end is in sight before the reading begins. Sure expectations of one sort or another coerce the temporal medium of literature into an inclusive message or immobile object—a closed circle, a detemporalized presence. That meaning, like form, is infinitely open eludes these metaphysical interpretive systems. In their demands for and expectations of totality, in their will-to-power over texts, in their repressed anxiety in the face of continuous uncertainty, these spatial methods turn disorder into

Order, differences into Identities and words into the Word. Unable to let texts be in openness, traditional criticisms seal off the unfolding disclosures of truth. Spatializing the temporal processes of be-ing, all metaphysical criticism practices a particularly invidious strategy: "*It is, in other words, a strategy that is subject to a vicious circularity that closes off the phenomenological/existential understanding of the temporal being of existence, and, analogously, of the temporal being—the sequence of words—of the literary text*" ("HK," 116).[12]

But before we move further into the circularity of understanding and the temporal being of the literary text, let us pause for a moment to recapitulate Spanos' thinking thus far about tradition. Philosophy and literary criticism, in their traditional forms, suppress the temporality of existence and of discourse in favor of spatial representations and coercive ways of thinking. This strategy begets a massive and powerful systematics that overlooks the temporality of being and the disclosures of truth, producing instead numerous and ubiquitous spatial models and modes of understanding. Two mega-models, in particular, dominate this history—the *map* and the *icon*. To counteract and undo ontotheological history and tradition, destruction is necessary. Destruction, in essence, emerges as the painstaking effort to overturn and disassemble the many and various spatial forms taken by the metaphysical tradition. It seeks to retrieve authentic being and time in a ceaseless activity of exploration and analysis. Like Bové, Spanos conceives the destructive enterprise as essentially endless. Yet, unlike Bové, Spanos hardly ever mentions intertextuality. Apparently, ontotheological history and tradition, in his view, invade and direct philosophical understanding and literary interpretation; but they do not seem prone, in his practice, to infiltrate and determine the actual constitution of literary texts. Everything rests in reading and in interpretation—not in *writing*.

3

As a way into Spanos' theory of literature, we pick up again the discussions of the circularity of interpretive understanding and of the nature of the reading activity.

Following Heidegger's famous analysis of the hermeneutic circle,[13] Spanos affirms that all inquiry is grounded beforehand by

what it seeks, and he confirms that the meaning of being is available to us, though only vaguely, as an existential fore-structure
of all temporal interpretation. Although we cannot avoid circularity, we "may" ground reading in temporality and thereby allow
interpretation to become discovery and disclosure. In this way,
"It *opens up* the infinite possibilities of the meaning of be-ing that
reside in the reader/text (time/form) relationship, those possibilities which are *closed off*, covered over and forgotten, by the spatial/
metaphysical imagination" ("BC," 450). Adapting ideas from
Kierkegaard and Gadamer as well as Heidegger, Spanos conceptualizes temporal interpretation as a process of *repetition* as opposed
to the *recollection* of spatial hermeneutics. With the end in mind
from the start, recollective interpretation repeats backwards the
verbal experience of the text in a job of verification, whereas
projective hermeneutics retrieves the text by repeating forwards
the sequence of words in an activity of exploration (*aletheia*). As
exploration, interpretation manifests itself ideally in a dialogic
relationship of an interested and care-ful reader with the being of
a text and ultimately with being itself.

As he elaborates the destructive project, Spanos criticizes the
spatial formations of tradition and celebrates the temporality of
literary texts. In so doing, he stresses the *processes* and *performances*
of reading and interpretation.[14] Where traditional literary criticisms emphasize the craft of the author or the structure of the
text, destruction attends rather to the activities and discoveries of
reading. For a destructive reader the experience of the text is
fraught with both positive possibilities and potential dangers because any encounter with a text may destroy reified formations
and present beliefs. They may also result in outright misunder-
standings. Significantly, reading texts is always risky adventure.

What is crucial here for the theory of literature is Spanos' opening of the text to the individual creative activities and discoveries—
the being—of the reader. In effect, Spanos breaks both the critic's
and the author's authority over and spatial perspective on the text.
No longer does the critic or poet hover above the text in Olympian
contemplation and complete understanding. To come to life, the
poem must be unfolded care-fully and intimately in a continuous
dialogue between reader and text. The "form" of the text is a

belated and recollective construction; it does not exist. Readers do not encounter form. The flow of words, the temporal being of the text, requires from the reader active involvement and interested exploration. Thus *the text is an event*—an event occurring within the reader's temporal horizon, an event experienced necessarily as interpretation, an event dis-covering the temporality of being in and for the present ("BC," 445). As action and event, the poem produces Form through process, Meaning through interpretation, Being through be-ing; these are not entities or substances inserted into or extractable from texts. They are retrospective constructions. Engaging the reader in open-ended actualizing, the literary work defers closure, demanding an ongoing interrogative mood and projective stance while refusing totalizing interpretation. The text sets going an activity of continuous participation and revision. When it is stopped, reduction and reification ensue as pernicious recollection.

If we stop and think back for a moment, we may be surprised to have come this far with Spanos without hearing a word about language, about the sign, about the referent. Working out of the phenomenological tradition, Spanos steers clear of most specialized linguistic and semiological terminology. Yet he holds a definite theory of language, which ultimately determines his theory of literature. He assigns parallel and equiprimordial status to Existence, Understanding, *and Discourse*. (In this he adheres closely to Heidegger's teaching in *Being and Time*.) Like being and thinking, language emerges primordially in (as) the founding moment of existence ("HK," 138). Nevertheless, words too often appear to us as images, that is, signs become static pictures for us to oversee and to contemplate, not to hear. Such spatializing requires destruction. To Spanos' mind, "the essential existential structure of human life is language as human speech . . ." ("HK," 138). Given this view of language as primordial *speech*, Spanos works against the drift of much contemporary literary criticism and theory. He knows it:

the reification of language, the transformation of words into image, by the mystified logocentric hermeneutics of Modernist criticisms—the New Criticism, the myth criticism of Northrop Frye, the "phenomenological" criticism of consciousness of Georges Poulet, and the struc-

turalism of Todorov and Barthes—closes off the possibility of *hearing the temporality of words, in which the real "being" of a literary text inheres.*
("BC," 443; my italics)

And what was [wrongly] conceived as an artifact [spatialized text] to be read from a printed page, an image to be looked at from a distance, an It to be mastered, becomes *"oral speech" to be heard immediately in time.* . . .
("HK," 139; my italics)

The theory of language determines the theory of the text. The real being of literature occurs in the temporal hearing of words. The literary text is *oral speech* heard in time. As image, as print, as object for mastery, the word appears in an invidious spatial guise. But as evanescent sound activated in and through body and mind, the literary word comes into its proper temporal being. *Language is Saying and literature is Oral Speech.*[15] When manifested only as print and image, language and literature obliterate and spatialize time; they need human speech and hearing to get underway toward being.

Spanos' theory of literature relies heavily on the *intentionality* of the reader. Rather than theorize about what the "original" or "probable" *intention* of the author was, Spanos continually emphasizes what the *reader*, as care-ful and interested historical being-in-the-world, discovers—hears. In other words, the notions of *care* and *interest* confer upon the reader intentionality. Since the experience of the text is open-ended, Spanos doesn't talk about *intention*. The reader has no particular intent; the experience of the text may and can lead anywhere. For Spanos the authentic being of literature lies in interested and careful hearing.

What is literature? According to Spanos, a literary text consists of a sequence of words that enter into human existence as primordial speech. To be activated or experienced, the temporal being of a text, its voice or saying, requires interested and careful hearing. When heard, the text has the capacity to alter present understanding and being. Yet the unfolding adventure of the text-reader dialogue must proceed, not through coercive spatialization or recollective interpretation, but through circular participation in and exploration of the actual temporality of be-ing. In this way, the literary text opens up infinite possibilities for the meaning and truth of being. Most importantly, this risky open-ended event of the literary text resists all closure. Any reduction of such "textuality" calls for destruction.

Destruction versus Deconstruction

There are two Heideggers: the *destructive* and the *deconstructive* Heidegger. The latter is the creation of Jacques Derrida, Paul de Man, J. Hillis Miller, Joseph N. Riddel, and others. Occasionally William Spanos complains. He does so in the Preface to *Martin Heidegger and the Question of Literature* (p. x) and in his essay for the volume: "Derrida's and de Man's Heidegger is not the Heidegger of *Being and Time* but a Heidegger interpreted (or deconstructed) through post-Structuralist eyes" ("HK," 148). The body of Heidegger's writings is the site of a struggle. The house of "de(con)struction" is divided. Phenomenology versus poststructuralism.

In a way, the dispute seems simple enough. Spanos relies almost exclusively on *Being and Time* (1927), Heidegger's acknowledged masterpiece, while the poststructuralists purportedly investigate the master's later works, those on poetry and language and on Hölderlin and Trakl, which were written between the mid-1930s and the late 1950s. Spanos relates this story:

> As Derrida has suggested in his deconstruction of Heidegger's thought, Heidegger's late quest for originary language—"the one word"—tends to reappropriate the metaphysics he intended to overcome. His "hermeneutic" project in the essays on poetry, language, and thought, therefore, does not suggest an interpretive method radical enough. . . . It is, rather, his existential analytic in *Being and Time*, by which (through its hermeneutical violence) he intends to gain access into being, that points to a hermeneutics of literature commensurate with the crisis of contemporary criticism. ("BC," 422–23)

The literary application of the Derridian version of Heidegger's destruction, i.e., deconstruction, has indeed yielded provocative and fruitful initial results concerning the question of literary history. However—and here my comments apply equally, if in a different way, to the hermeneutic methodology underlying the later, the post-*Being and Time*, Heidegger's exegetical dialogues with Hölderlin, Trakl, and George—it is subject to significant error—or blindness—in interpretation and even lends itself to willful misreading *because it continues to begin the hermeneutic process from the end . . . to read particular historical texts or oeuvres spatially.* ("BC," 447)

These details are revealing. Spanos and the deconstructors agree that the later Heidegger is metaphysical—that he isn't radical enough. But when the deconstructors present Heidegger as the last metaphysician of the logocentric tradition, they presumably overlook his radical work in *Being and Time*, focusing mainly on the later works. Spanos himself, to be sure, depends almost completely on *Being and Time*, aiming to extend only the postmetaphysical, the radical, Heidegger. Specifically, Spanos wants to preserve the violent existential hermeneutic that seeks access to being; he abjures the quest for originary language. And he disdains Heidegger's later literary interpretations, which, in blindness and error, allegedly produce misreadings through a backsliding spatial hermeneutics.

When Heidegger sets out to uncover the essence of language, he goes amiss. His earlier disclosures of being, however, deserve preservation and extension. In particular, his early interpretive strategies—the destructions—can be extended and refashioned into a contemporary literary hermeneutics fully adequate to the crisis of our time. Spanos' project, then, is to produce out of *Being and Time* such a literary hermeneutics. This systematics requires "extensions" of Heidegger for our time.

Yet the full scope of Spanos' project goes beyond simply fashioning a new temporal hermeneutics for reading literary texts. Ultimately, he seeks a new literary history. "*This temporal, as opposed to spatial, orientation is the key not only to reading a literary text but to the discovery of a new literary history*" ("HK," 116). In Spanos' view, destruction "opens up the possibility of a perpetually new—a postModern or an authentically modern—literary history, a history that, in focusing on dis-closure, both validates the inexhaustibility of literary texts (i.e., literary history as misreading) and commits literature to the difficult larger task of 'overcoming metaphysics'—a history, in other words, that puts literature at the service of being rather than being at the service of literature" ("BC," 446). Using temporal hermeneutics, the destructive critic discovers that texts are inexhaustible. To read a text is necessarily to misread it. All readings are misreadings. Texts are perpetual. Therefore, literary history is by definition permanently open and continuously new. Temporal hermeneutics is destructive precisely in that it reveals, accepts, and extends the inexhaustibility of texts and of literary history. In his project for a new literary history, Spanos extends Heidegger's distinctive performative mode of phenomenology toward a theory of history and tradition as ceaseless happenings and inexhaustible performances.[16]

Calling for a new literary history, Spanos aims to put "literature at the service of *being* rather than being at the service of literature." When he takes up Heidegger, he praises his quest for *being* and criticizes his search for originary language. Arguing with Derrida, Spanos attacks the poststructuralist celebration of *écriture* at the expense of *parole* (*saying*); and he accuses Derrida and other deconstructors of a spatial hermeneutics, which forces them to miss "the text's temporality, blinding themselves, that is, to its version of being, of how it stands with be-ing in that text" ("BC," 447). Through all of this argumentation runs a dominant opposition: being versus literature, being versus language, *saying* versus *écriture*, being (temporality) versus text (spatiality). Spanos everywhere and always seeks access to being. The agencies of being are literature, language, *écriture*, the text. While in theory he casts these modes of writing as equiprimordial with being, in practice he stages them in a struggle with being. The ground of literature is being. The purpose of literary criticism is to uncover being. The job of literary history is to reexperience and restore the disclosures of being in previous texts. Being, being, being. Spanos, of course, is a phenomenologist. As such, he is heir to Derrida's definitive critique of Husserl as well as his scattered skirmishes with Heidegger.

Deconstruction, in practice, sets writing or language as ground. The random flights of signifiers or the vertiginous freeplay of grammatical, rhetorical, and referential linguistic strata preclude any final commitment or even credible search for the disclosures of primordial being or truth. Such a phenomenological quest is inconceivable as well as impossible. It appears monomaniacal and blind. It is patently logocentric. No more proof of such logocentrism (and phonocentrism) is needed than the destructive theory of literature that hypostatizes *speech*, or the conceptualization of reading that celebrates authentic *hearing*, or the notion of tradition that absolutely insists on recovering primordial *truth*. The most telling point of contention between destruction and deconstruction, however, is not the theory of literature or of interpretation or of tradition—these are each crucial, of course; it is the theory of language. Insofar as the constitution of primordial language as *either* speech *or* writing (*écriture*) directs and determines all other theorizing about poetics, hermeneutics, and historiography, the entire destructive/deconstructive house stands to rise or fall on this ground.

Spanos is a vigilant theorist. In his mind, "writing" in Western literary tradition insidiously preserves presence, stabilizes being, and spatializes time. Thus he calls for a literature grounded in free speech, that is, a speech which is the act of an instant of being-in-the-world. Unlike the oracular speech of the tribal seer—an Olympian spatialized orality—Spanos' speech is kinetic, explorative language with "its source not in presence (a substantial self), but, as Heidegger insists in *Being and Time*, in Nothingness, a groundless ground" ("HK," 147). Spanos' speech is not the "oracular" *parole* of Derrida; it is *Rede* or *legein*, "which, in being temporal, precludes a definitive revelation of any being" ("BC," 445). In other words, language (as speech) rules out presence through its radical temporality and, as such, eliminates definitive appearances of being; it is grounded in nothingness. With this special view of language (*legein*), Spanos is able to keep the literary text open: the text is inexhaustible; its meaning cannot be fixed, only played through time in ceaseless dialogue with readers. Textuality. In addition, Spanos can maintain a destructive stance toward tradition because, historically, "writing" has suppressed *legein* in order to privilege spatial form, stabilize being, and reify tradition. What results, then, is a view of language that allows Spanos to operate his own special "deconstructive" project.

And yet, despite all the *destructive* theories, the suspicion persists that the single-minded phenomenological quest for being and truth is a logocentric enterprise. What, after all, is the "authentic" reader truly *interested* in? What does she actually *care* about? The truth of being out of literature—always. Just what Heidegger sought in his later works. The intentionality of such a reader supersedes the nothingness of the ground. Uncovering truth, the reader stays the nothing and comes away a changed person. However risky the adventure, the didactic gift of change, no matter how evanescent or insignificant, exhausts the perpetual text in a moment of satisfying and acceptable learning. Approving the reduction, though infrequently and perhaps guiltily, *destruction* fails to keep the text open. In the end the reader attains security and self-possession. The death of dissemination in the birth of truth. This seems a small matter. Such little threads of humanism, however, hold down and tie up the project of destruction. Finally, the destructive enterprise, in Spanos' hands, largely ignores the disruptive forces of inter*textuality* because it insists on a theory of literature as instantaneous and original, free speech, sealing the poet's text off—in practice—from the disruptive invasions of tradition. The *trace* is systematically undervalued: the denial of differance. The resulting primordial privacy of the text silently restores the base of the spatial monument. In "La parole soufflée" (1965), Derrida foresaw this outcome when he noted the "necessary dependency of all destructive discourses: they must inhabit the structures they demolish, and within them they must shelter an indestructible desire for full presence, for nondifference . . ." (*WD*, 194).

5

The Dissemination of the Text

Beyond Being and Truth toward Textuality as Intertextuality

The earliest large-scale work of deconstructive criticism written by an American is Joseph N. Riddel's *The Inverted Bell: Modernism and the Counterpoetics of William Carlos Williams*, published in 1974.[1] When it was reviewed by J. Hillis Miller the next year in *Diacritics*, the first major split within American deconstruction surfaced publicly.[2] The rift was further opened and dramatized in the subtle and telling reply of Riddel to Miller in the fall of 1975.[3] This season of attack and counterattack reveals a great deal about deconstruction, as we shall see momentarily. Almost predictably it opens and closes on the question of Martin Heidegger's influence.

Examining three moments in the deconstructive career of Joseph Riddel, we move beyond the interpretive quest for being and truth to the critical celebration of textuality as intertextuality. Like other American literary critics, Riddel goes past formalism to phenomenology during the late 1960s and very early 1970s and then in the early and mid-1970s he takes up deconstruction.[4] In the deconstructive phase, which is our concern, Riddel associates closely with the *Boundary 2* enterprise, publishing during the 1970s five important articles there, contributing a crucial essay to William Spanos' *Martin Heidegger and the Question of Literature*, publishing a piece in Paul Bové's special issue on "Revisions of the Anglo-American Tradition," and recruiting both Spanos and Bové to write works for a special number of the journal *Genre* on "The Long Poem in the Twentieth Century" (1978), edited by Riddel.[5] Finally, in 1979 Riddel joins the editorial board of *Boundary 2*.

Tinged by this association with a hint of Heideggerianism, Riddel, nevertheless, carries out ever more singularly a deconstructive, as opposed to destructive, enterprise. Like both Miller and Spanos, Joseph Riddel produces a spate of admirable essays during the 1970s, most of which constitute major work in progress—in Riddel's case a book on American poetics from Poe to Olson—yet of necessity definitive assessments can occur only in the 1980s when these essays come together in final form. In other words, the period of the 1970s for American deconstruction is mainly a time of ground-breaking and sowing. The 1980s promise harvest. *The Inverted Bell*, however, provides an exception, as does Paul de Man's later *Allegories of Reading* (1979)—a gathering of twelve deconstructive essays written between 1972 and 1978. During this decade of beginnings one of the more interesting and telling events is the Miller-Riddel controversy.

In the first section of this chapter we shall attend to the Miller-Riddel debate so as to open to view a serious critique of the Yale school of deconstruction and to present Joseph Riddel's deconstructive theory of textuality as intertextuality. In the second section we shall investigate the popular poststructuralist theories of the text and intertext promulgated by Roland Barthes initially in connection with the *Tel Quel* group and then in the context of an erotics of reading. In the concluding section we will consider an important comment on textuality by Jacques Derrida, published in the Yale-school manifesto of 1979, situating this consideration within a summary reflection upon the contemporary deconstructive theory of the disseminating *text*. Overall, then, we stage here amidst some hubbub a hearing of the *Yale* and *Tel Quel* theories of literature and tradition while foregrounding the individual, distinctive projects of Joseph Riddel and Roland Barthes. Throughout chapter 5 we focus on deconstruction, letting phenomenology and structuralism fall more and more into the background.

I

Reviewing Joseph Riddel's text on William Carlos Williams, J. Hillis Miller notes at once the work's strategic "constant trian-

gulation from Heidegger and Derrida" ("DD," 24). Further, he
observes that Riddel relies on the later Heidegger and that he
employs a highly selective early Derrida. This configuration raises
questions. Does Riddel, for example, grasp Heidegger? Derrida?
Williams? Can three very different discourses, in any event, be
made compatible? "Riddel tends to assume that Heidegger, Derrida, Williams, and he himself are each more or less self-consistent,
and that all four are saying roughly 'the same thing.' This means
that one can follow Heidegger and Derrida at once" (25). Of
course, Derrida carries out here and there across his oeuvre a
critique of Heidegger. Their two discourses are discontinuous.
And Heidegger's corpus is itself divided. Not surprisingly, "Riddel's criticism," concludes Miller, is "heterogeneous, dialogical
rather that monological. His commentary wavers or oscillates. . . .
At one moment Riddel sounds something like Derrida. . . . The
next moment, on the same page, he falls back into Heidegger"
(27). In a manner of speaking, Miller offers valuable insight: Riddel's text is situated between Heidegger and Derrida. But precisely
this condition "distinguishes" Riddel's early deconstructive work.
Unlike Miller, who follows Derrida and de Man, and unlike Spanos, who adopts Heidegger, Riddel diligently works both sides
into his enterprise. To Miller this venture appears regressive: Riddel "*falls back* into Heidegger." Apparently, however, Spanos regards the effort more positively: he regularly publishes Riddel's
work; in the Preface to the Heidegger collection he singles out
Riddel's *deconstructive* appropriation of Heidegger and judges it
"indeed viable" (*QL*, x). For Miller the damning conclusion about
Riddel's heterogeneous deconstruction is, ultimately, that "Heidegger, on the whole, wins the day" (28). He extracts as evidence
a dozen or so samples from Riddel's text of Heidegger's distinctive
diction and style. Finally, Miller gently instructs Riddel in ways
of improving his project: "He perhaps accepts a bit too much at
face value the Heideggerian formulas about '*aletheia*. . . .' His
book would have been clarified if he had remained more faithful
to his intermittent insight into the difference between Heidegger
and Derrida" (29). And yet, despite all these complaints, Miller
detects virtue, however unintended: "Riddel's book may in fact
have its greatest value in its apparently unintentional demonstra-

tion of the irreducible heterogeneity of the languages of poetry, of philosophy, and of criticism" (30).

What sets Riddel's deconstructive text apart from those of Miller and of de Man is most obviously a heterogeneous style. (There are, to be sure, other important differences, which we shall explore.) Characteristically, Riddel in his stronger moments deploys within small spaces numerous quotations from various poets and philosophers to marshal his "points." Actually, Riddel never single-mindedly aims for points; he orchestrates directions for thinking by arranging a score of diverse, yet provocative, variations. Unnerved, the reader may long for the scrubbed surfaces and singular purposes of Miller or de Man. Where Miller effects overall stylistic clarity and certainty and where de Man exhibits relentless interpretive concentration on the tiniest particulars, Riddel practices a deliberately nebulous yet highly suggestive stereophonic prose. Three or four tracks are the norm. These differences seem oddly comparable to the distinctive atmospheres usually associated with the hospital X-ray den, the brain-surgery suite, and the emergency room: the carnivalesque mode of the latter differs strikingly from the quiet efficiency and the rigorous attention characteristic of the former two. While there appears something of the confident radiologist-technician in Miller, the hermetic, sometimes arrogant, head surgeon in de Man, and the distracted general practitioner in Riddel, we recognize in this scene the recurring figure of the contemporary medicine man. The heterogeneous discourse of Riddel, his *bricolage*, is not, as Miller surmises, simply unintentional. Ironically, Riddel most nearly resembles Derrida in his stereographic mode of discourse, more so than most other American deconstructors, especially Miller and de Man. Only Harold Bloom and Jeffrey Mehlman vie with Riddel in constructing the multitrack text.

More damning evidently than either the stigma of his Heideggerianism or the displeasures of his stereographic text is Riddel's employment of a theory of literary history and tradition that presupposes "progress." As we move from one period of literature to another—in Riddel's view—changes occur, development happens, new world views emerge. In particular, as we go from Modernism to Postmodernism, which is one of Riddel's main topics in *The Inverted Bell*, a paradigm shift and historical improvement take place. Miller marks this operation:

> Basic to Riddel's argument is a more or less strict equivalence between "Modernism" and what Derrida, in "Structure, Sign, and Play" calls the "nostalgia for origin" of Rousseau or of Lévi-Strauss. On the other hand, Riddel makes an equivalence between "Post-Modernism" and what Derrida describes as "the Nietzschean *affirmation*—the joyous affirmation of the freeplay of the world. . . ." (26–27)

Miller uncovers an evolutionary theory of periodization at work in Riddel's text. Although Riddel's historical casting of recent tradition relies heavily on Derrida, Miller, himself a Derridean, expresses very serious doubts. "What validity, in any case, does periodization any longer have in the study of literature?" (25). Miller aims toward deconstructing the concept of "periodization." Apparently, Riddel holds an undeconstructed or a traditional notion of *periodization*. Yet his specific portrait of the postmodern world view appears ingenious. (It is worth noting that Spanos, Bové, and Riddel share a common commitment to writing literary history and hold similar notions of the differences between the modern and postmodern world views.) On this issue of literary history Miller seems earnest and unforgiving: "The idea of homogeneous literary periods must be discarded. Each period is itself equivocal" (31). He goes on to recommend the revisionist histories of Harold Bloom and Geoffrey Hartman—two members of the Yale school—neither of whom is otherwise as radical a deconstructor as Riddel.[6] In Miller's assessment, Riddel's deconstructive reading in *The Inverted Bell* founders upon an unexamined logocentric theory of history and tradition.

More telling than his critique of Riddel's theory of tradition is Miller's attack on Riddel's theory of literature. Here the special blending of Derrida and de Man, which characterizes Miller's philosophy of language, clashes with Riddel's purported Heideggerian *literal* view of language and literature:

> Riddel's theory of language, like that of Heidegger, with his belief in "ein einziges, das einzige Wort," is in fact literal or mimetic. He tends to take the Heideggerian figures literally, as referring to extra-linguistic reality. . . . For Derrida, on the other hand, language is "originally"

figurative, or rather, since in the absence of literal or "unique" naming the distinction between literal and figurative breaks down, each word is seen as a link in an endless chain of substitutions and displacements, with nowhere a fixed extralinguistic beginning or ending. . . . (29–30)

According to Miller, Riddel holds to a mimetic theory of language and literature: the language of poetic texts mirrors objects and events of the outside world; language is an instrument that conveys knowledge and information about extralinguistic reality; each literary sign has an external referent. Riddel follows Heidegger. Yet Miller obviously goes off here. Heidegger's notions of language and literature, early or late, are hardly literal or mimetic. Moreover, Miller's characterization of "Derrida's" theory of language is more accurately de Man's conceptualization of *rhetoricity*. What is most revealing in this critique is the raw confrontation, however unmotivated, between a traditional theory of literature as *mimesis* and a deconstructive theory of literature as *textuality*. The "endless chain of figures with no extralinguistic beginning or ending" versus the "limited sequence of words with determinate referential values." In all of this Riddel gets lost, but he later responds point-blank to Miller's critique—as we shall observe in a moment.

At the end of his review Miller propounds a *special* deconstructive theory of literature, derived from de Man. This conclusion has little to do directly with Riddel, Derrida, or Heidegger. But it will stir up negative responses from Riddel and later from Spanos—both of whom correctly attribute it to de Man's masterful deconstruction of Derrida's *Grammatology* in *Blindness and Insight*. Following de Man, Miller proclaims that every literary "text performs on itself the act of deconstruction without any help from the critic" (31). In his closing paragraph, Miller sums up: "Another way to put this is to say that great works of literature are likely to be ahead of their critics. They are there already. They have anticipated explicitly any deconstruction the critic can achieve" (31). This theory of literature, which Miller offers in place of Riddel's supposed Heideggerian notions, joins together two concepts—that of rhetoricity and that of the "self-deconstructing text." Such a version of textuality, distinct from Heidegger's, Derrida's, Spanos', and Riddel's, continuously surfaces in the deconstructive works of Miller and de Man, causing various complaints and critiques. Riddel's will be the first attack forcefully mounted and widely read.

2

Reading Miller's review essay, we get the impression that Riddel practices a Heideggerian destructive phenomenology, that he misconstrues and defuses Derrida, that his concepts of language, literature, and tradition remain caught up in logocentric thinking, and that his critical discourse displays incoherence. Specifically, Riddel too readily accepts Heidegger's notion of *aletheia* and believes in the literal or extralinguistic truth of literature. And he thinks of literary tradition as a regulated evolutionary progress. While he produces an exemplary multitrack method of inquiry, Riddel essentially stumbles onto this method, assuming naively that his points of reference and his sources agree harmoniously rather than clash in a productive heterogeneity. In a corrective discourse, Miller offers, succinctly and lucidly, the proper deconstructive theories of language, literature and tradition. We glimpse rhetoricity and textuality, and we come to understand the self-deconstructing text. Derrida is restored; Heidegger put in his place. And Riddel, well, Riddel remains just on the fringe of the authentic deconstructive project. He must relinquish Heidegger, take up Derrida more fully and carefully, and learn the right versions of textuality and intertextuality.

Reading the response essay, however, we receive the impression that Riddel operates a Derridean deconstructive venture, which in certain ways is more radical than Miller's and de Man's and more faithful to Derrida; that he goes about his work less naively and far more self-consciously than Miller allows; and that he understands quite clearly the important implications of the differing versions of textuality and intertextuality.in question. The question of Riddel's Heideggerianism seems laid to rest by the response. Most importantly, a struggle over the body of Derrida's doctrine begins in earnest between these leading American deconstructors. (This initial struggle will be carried on later by ever-growing numbers of theorists within the American deconstructive movement.) Joseph Riddel opens this Pandora's box publicly for the first time.

Significantly, Riddel constructs his response to Miller less as a defense of his enterprise and more as a broad critique of Yale-school deconstruction. While he aims mainly to deconstruct the project of the Yale critics, Riddel does offer, here and there, defenses of his own deconstructive endeavor. In particular, he immediately dismisses Miller's charge that he champions a mimetic theory of language and literature. He complains "to say that I really believe in some originary, pre-linguistic event is ridiculous, since the metaphors are not mine. . . . I present them as figures, and note that they are fictions" ("MT," 59). Furthermore, "I (literally) indicate that the 'origin' is already a reconstruction (a re-membering) of traces (already double signs) . . ." (59). From these impatient comments we infer that, for Riddel, literary language does not mirror originary prelinguistic events, that linguistic figures are fictions, and that signs are redoubled traces. Riddel puts it succinctly at the opening of *The Inverted Bell*: "In the beginning was writing, language and not pure song" (7). Like Derrida, Riddel sets *écriture* as ground. Obviously he holds to a theory of textuality.

Yet Riddel's book, unlike the response, plays out a Heideggerian track. For example, "In saying, words and things, ideas and things (or in Heidegger's restoration of the original pre-Socratic terms, *logos* and *physis*) arise into being, into a field of difference. They come to light; they *are* because they have place, are gathered" (9–10). Here *saying*, not writing, serves as ground for the emergence into *being* of words, ideas, and things. How to splice together or harmonize Riddel's Heideggerian and Derridean tracks? May we suppose that *saying*, for Riddel, is a form of writing or language (*écriture*)? Perhaps. But accepting the mode of his discourse as is, we acknowledge Riddel's generic heterogeneity in *The Inverted Bell*, and simply point out that in his later works Heideggerian "being" and "truth" give way more and more to freeplay and dissemination under pressure of Derridean textuality and intertextuality. At the same time we understand now Miller's difficulties as reviewer.

Riddel exhibits little genuine sympathy with Miller. Even though he believes "all texts . . . are not only open to, but perhaps command, their own misreading" (56), he nevertheless castigates Miller for miscasting his project and, in particular, he fulminates against the Yale critics' taming of Derrida. In Riddel's judgment, Miller and de Man attempt to restore the status of the author (if only as a function) and to valorize *literary* language. This conservative preservation of the institution of literature, in a move typical of the "humanistic tradition," stages literature as a superior and sacred form of human wisdom and creativity. Miller, we recall, does believe that great works of literature are often ahead of their critics. As Riddel portrays this view, the Yale critics' self-proclaimed "Derridean" project ultimately elevates literature and deflates criticism. When all is said and done, Miller, following de Man, hypostatizes *literature* as the highest form of deconstruction. Criticism merely imitates or belatedly repeats the exemplary (self-deconstructed) works of the tradition.

Miller's enterprise, then, is a footnote to de Man's most heroic attempt to contain Derrida, and thus to maintain the possibility of an "exemplary text". . . . This puts a hedge around Derrida's "Nietzschean joy" of open, endless interpretation. . . . It ironizes Derrida, . . . it "thematizes" his questioning. It turns him into a philosopher, and thus reduces him. . . .

This containment of Derrida is certainly evident in the exemplars of the new literary history. . . . Both Geoffrey Hartman and Harold Bloom acknowledge the severity of the Derridean question. . . . But unlike Miller, neither presumes to embrace him as an exemplary critic, for neither will accept his reduction of the text to a play of differences, to the play of language (without reference) itself. (63)

The net effect of Riddel's critique is to contain and diminish the Yale critics. In particular, Hartman and Bloom refuse both the freeplay of differences and the end of referential language, that is, they deny textuality. Miller's work is merely a "footnote" to de Man's. De Man refuses the endless interpretive activity celebrated by Derrida, shifting such disruptive power away from the interpretive activity itself and assigning it to the powers of literary language. As a result, literary texts emerge as the most awesome and wonderful creations. Reading and interpretation become puny belated attempts at harnessing the inherent deconstructive energies of great texts. The openness and play of interpretation wither so that the sacred text and the divine author may both endure and prevail. Miller does proclaim that:

great works of literature are likely to be ahead of their critics. They are there already. They have anticipated explicitly any deconstruction the critic can achieve. A critic may hope with great effort, and with the indispensable help of the writers themselves, to raise himself to the level of linguistic sophistication where Chaucer, Spenser, Shakespeare, Milton, Wordsworth, George Eliot, Stevens, or even Williams are already. They are there already. . . . ("DD," 31)

Just here Riddel appears to have the goods on Miller and de Man. Yale deconstruction preserves and recanonizes the great writers, works, and tradition. We know the roll call: Chaucer, Spenser, Shakespeare, Milton, Wordsworth, etc. Yale deconstruction humbles the critic before these great prophetic geniuses, who are always already ahead of any and all critics. Critics, poor inferior beings, need the help of the authentic poets. So omniscient are these great vatic fathers that they already deconstruct their own works. At one point Riddel wonders sardonically whether or not Yale criticism is much different from American New Criticism with its belief in the sacredness and independence of the Great Poem and its Maker.

As far as Riddel is concerned, the Yale deconstructors either deny, as do Hartman and Bloom, or tame, as do de Man and Miller, *écriture*. They privilege *literary* language and texts. They keep the author as genius alive. They preserve the great tradition undisturbed. They delimit interpretation. Curiously, they imply that literature is complete and that we do not need more texts. This latter notion seems oddly structuralist in its synchronic or spatial reduction of literary history. No room remains for contemporary literature.

About *The Inverted Bell* Riddel ultimately rebuts "I will simply reassert that I was writing the 'story' of a kind of literature which is attempting a double deconstruction, of itself and also of its immediate predecessors, in an attempt, not unlike de Man's, to make 'literature' an irreducible but empty 'bottom'" (63). Disentangling this assertion, we learn that Riddel, in conceiving literature as irreducibly empty, accepts textuality, and that, in regarding literature as cannibalistic toward earlier literature, he implicitly confirms intertextuality. Without missing sight of the irony, Riddel affirms that literature itself is deconstructive not only by virtue of its inherent intertextuality, but by dint of its self-deconstructing nature. Significantly, however, Riddel limits this peculiar self-deconstructing feature to W. C. Williams' work and by implication to other *postmodern* texts. In his view, the autodestruction of contemporary poetic texts distinguishes them from their modernist predecessors. In short, Riddel takes a strictly historical view of the self-deconstructing text, unlike Miller and de Man, who regard this feature as constitutive of all great works.

3

About a year after the controversy Joseph Riddel published an essay entitled "From Heidegger to Derrida to Chance: Doubling and (Poetic) Language," which appeared in *Boundary 2* and later in Spanos' *Martin Heidegger and the Question of Literature*. Once again, Riddel displays a deep sympathy with the Heideggerian venture, believing that this severe questioning of the ontotheological tradition remains crucial and unavoidable, though still misunderstood in America. At the same time he recognizes Heidegger's limits and accedes to (while extending) Derrida's "definitive" deconstruction of the phenomenological project. (He tells us frankly that his own text is "not Heideggerean"—*QL*, 234.) And, unexpectedly, Riddel demonstrates that Paul de Man derives his theory of the self-deconstructing text from Heidegger. Overall, this essay shows Riddel championing a fullblown deconstruction inspired by Derrida, maintaining respect for but further relinquishing Heidegger and, surprisingly, turning Paul de Man into a Heideggerian. Most important for our purposes, the essay foregrounds explicitly Riddel's post-phenomenological, deconstructive theories of literature and tradition.

   In illustrating Riddel's concepts of literature and tradition, we aim here to highlight, through commentary on a pastiche of five telling citations, his particular version of textuality as intertextuality. Like some Yale critics, Riddel derives his theories from Derrida:

Derrida deprives us of literature in its relation to truth, only to give us back "literature" already in quotation marks, a text whose meaningfullness resides in its play of differences, including the insertion within it always of disruptive re-marks, other texts, signs that are not filled with meaning but are always already doubled. . . . (*QL*, 247)

a text is never self-sufficient or self-present, never in itself a totalization
of meaning or a concealment/unconcealment of a unitary sense. (248)

readings of the thematic or semantic richness of work only reveal that
the depth of the text is a semantic mirage generated by the play of
heterogeneous signifiers which refuse to be commanded by any single
element within (meaning) or without (author) the text. (248)

[differance (or its various surrogates)] functions to upset the illusion that
in literature there can be truth, or the "appearance" of an unrepresented
in the represented, the concealed which is unconcealed yet hidden, a
unity of consciousness or the "reality" of an imaginary "world." (248)

The literary text is a play of textuality, not simply in the obvious sense
that a "work" of art always originates in the historical field of predecessors. Its own play of differences mirrors its displacement and reap-
propriation of other texts, and anticipates the necessary critical text which
must "supplement" it. . . . (249)

Riddel merges intertextuality with textuality; that is, he presents
the literary text as irreducibly infiltrated by previous texts. (He
does not start with the sign.) The resident earlier texts open out
the present text to an uncontrollable play of historical predecessors. The predecessor-texts themselves operate intertextually,
meaning that no first, pure, or original text ever can or did rule
over or delimit the historical oscillations at play in texts. Thus all
texts appear doubled: they are uncontrollably permeated with
previous texts. The disorienting effect of the invading predecessors
resembles the disruptive functions at work in the sign: a play of
differences operates, bringing about, not fullness of meaning, but
generic disturbances and discontinuities—random flights of signifiers. In place of pure signifiers, though, we have here contam-
inating pieces of various intertexts. The sign, as such, is constituted as originarily intertextual. Because prior texts reside in
present texts—that is, in their signifiers—no text itself is ever
fully self-present, self-contained, or self-sufficient: no text is
closed, total, or unified. The forces of intertextuality, in Riddel's
view, fundamentally infiltrate the operations of the sign, disal-
lowing any notion of pure or nonintertextual textuality.
    Just as a barrier separates the signifier from the signified, so the

intertext divides the text from itself. The gaps between signifiers and signifieds and those between texts and intertexts open numberless spaces where a constituting play of differences prevails. To be accurate, Riddel installs the signifier and intertext as an equiprimordial, indivisible entity. The signifier is intertextual from the outset. Since a work of literature consists of many signifiers, the amount and variety of differences at play are incalculable. The text is infinite. What traditional thematic and semantic critical readings, taken all together, reveal is precisely the infinite possibilities of "meaning combinations." The play of heterogeneous or doubled signifiers refuses definitive ordering or successful totalization. There will always be some surplus or remainder. Texts do not hide or conceal unity or meaning, which can be discovered or reconstructed through careful interpretation. (Nevertheless, the mirages of unifying "deep structures," or of controlling "authorial intentions," or of solidifying "references" and "representations" still underwrite strong conventional belief and faith in the truth of literature.) The lesson of textuality as intertextuality is that truth in (of) literature is an illusion: there is only always the deracinating play of myriad differences. Infinite meanings are broadcast across textual surfaces. In deconstructive theory, such *dissemination* takes the place of truth.

Because both literary and critical history are by constitution a series of texts (as intertexts), we can foresee that all future texts will emerge out of present and past ones. In a manner of speaking, all texts anticipate their future appropriation. And texts, as they await future interpretation, can anticipate misreading and critical supplementation. For, in Riddel's account, reading is constituted as misreading. Stopping the infinite play of the text at a particular point—that is, halting dissemination—the reader willfully or wearily confers meaning in an activity of (mis)reading. "Misreading is not an incorrect reading, but the errancy or deviation of every reading."[7] While interpretation seeks totalized readings, closure of play and unity of meaning, deconstructive "hermeneutics" undermines such traditional values with its theory of reading as misreading and its theory of textuality and (as) intertextuality.

The concept of textuality as intertextuality—which begets the attendant notion of misreading—suggests that every reader is

caught in the historical logocentric webs of discourse and that all
are condemned to use traditional language and concepts, even in
the most radical moments of criticism and deconstruction. There
is no outside and no escape from the logocentric enclosure. (Heidegger, we recall, intuited this.) Tradition is inescapable. Derrida
insists on this point.

Finally, textuality must be construed as thorough—total. "For
Derrida does *textualize the world*, or sees it reduced everywhere
to a text (in the sense that language is the inescapable reduction
and that the concept 'world,' like 'life,' 'experience,' 'perception,'
etc., is originarily metaphorical, or metaphysical, and hence textual)" ("RC," 242; my italics). Textuality applies to all (poetic)
language. These parentheses, as in Riddel's title for the 1976 essay,
hint at an important issue. Does textuality extend to the whole
world, as Derrida implies, or only to *literary* language, as de Man
and Miller believe? Riddel sides with Derrida. The immediate
result is that literature becomes "literature" (already in quotation
marks); that is, literature is no longer a miraculously omniscient
and highly privileged form of self-deconstructing textuality; it is,
like all language, *écriture*. Overturning the old hierarchy, in which
literature is the highest form of language, Riddel immediately sets
criticism on an equal footing with literature; he situates performative and cognitive language equally amidst the webs of textuality; he denies the ontological separation of types of discourse.
Literature is only one among many forms of *writing*. The Yale
hierophants should cower before such radical textuality.

4

Historically speaking, deconstruction emerges in our time as a
severe critique of and an "alternative" to both phenomenology
and structuralism. At the outset Derrida undermines both Husserl
and Saussure. American deconstructors, however—many of
whom are former phenomenologists—tend to critique only phenomenology and sometimes formalism (New Criticism). Such deconstructive attacks constitute one part of the complete works of
de Man, Miller, Spanos, Riddel, and others. In other words,
American deconstructors largely bypass examinations of structuralism (and of its "sign") since it never really established a sig-

nificant foothold in America. Thus we find a poststructuralist criticism taking root without benefit of a native structuralism. The movement beyond *structuralism* occurred primarily on French soil. For Americans, the deconstructive critique is more a general assault on all logocentrism or traditional thinking and less a focused attack on phenomenology, structuralism, or formalism. Thus many American deconstructors tend to start with Derrida and go forward from there, taking his critiques of contending philosophies and literary theories as complete and definitive. Like other postwar criticisms, therefore, American deconstruction tends more and more to show up as a narrow method of practical literary analysis. That this instrumentalizing of deconstruction occurs is no surprise to Americans. It does, however, spur cries of heresy and charges of reductionism. (I will not list the ever-expanding bibliography on this point.) What distinguishes Joseph Riddel as well as William Spanos is an atypical, deep and continuing immersion in Heideggerian phenomenology. In the case of Spanos we witness a serious effort to recast Heidegger to meet the challenge of deconstruction; with Riddel we see an attempt to keep Heidegger vital and effective for a Derridean deconstructive project. (With de Man we observe a return to Nietzsche for theoretical guidance and inspiration.)

In France the deconstructive enterprise, like other contemporary intellectual endeavors, comes into an environment deeply respectful of, or at least extremely attentive to, psychoanalytic and Marxist theories. Neither of these discourses holds sway in America. Indeed, American deconstructors proceed pretty much as though Marxism were not an issue. Since Derrida himself has never fully confronted Marxist theory, limiting himself at first to rare footnotes and later to occasional comments, the avoidance of Marxism in America has been facilitated. Still, the works of some critics, like Fredric Jameson and John Brenkman, attend carefully to Marxism, though neither of these avant-garde theorists is, strictly speaking, a deconstructor. Psychoanalysis is another matter. Derrida works meticulously and frequently with such texts. American deconstructors, inspired, no doubt, by Derrida, sometimes take up psychoanalysis. We find this effort on occasion in Miller and

Riddel, but rarely in de Man. Bloom, Hartman, Johnson, Mehlman, and others are more fully steeped in and committed to psychoanalytic theorizing.

When we consider Roland Barthes as deconstructor, we shall come upon an urban and lucid former structuralist, who practices an agile "Marxism" and psychoanalysis, both of which condition his theories of textuality and intertextuality. The project of Barthes, therefore, presents a rich and productive contrast to the work of most American deconstructors.

From a Poetics to an Erotics of the Text

to pursue the reading of the text—its dissemination, not its truth.[8]

there are very few writers who combat *both* ideological repression and libidinal repression. . . .[9]

—Roland Barthes

From the late 1950s till the late 1960s Roland Barthes played out the role of influential dean of literary semiological structuralism. To be sure, his work focused on sociological and cultural matters as much as on literary topics. During this time he castigated the bourgeois life-style and its reified thinking, employing a persuasive structuralism and a supple Marxism. But sometime during the late 1960s he turned toward deconstruction, as did other leading French intellectuals, particularly those associated with the journal *Tel Quel.*[10] From 1968 until the early 1970s Barthes carried out an impressive, seemingly collective, post-structuralist project. The masterpiece of this era is *S/Z* (1970), which we shall consider in Part III. When he published *The Pleasure of the Text* in 1973, followed by *Roland Barthes* (1975) and *A Lover's Discourse: Fragments* (1977), it became clear that Barthes had begun a highly personal and provocative, erotic variety of deconstruction. In this later phase the discourse of psychoanalysis more fully permeates the texture of Barthes' writing. At the same time his Marxism appears ever more individualistic and diffusive. Always more a man of letters than a scholar and generally more a gifted essayist than a writer of tedious tomes, Barthes displays his considerable erudition much more lightly and gracefully than most other cultural theorists. This apparent lack of rigor and philosophical painstaking relegates him within the academy to the outer sanctum of the Great Scholars' Pantheon—a marginal site he instinctively occupied and appeared to relish, as he suggests more than once in his autobiography.

As we look into the poststructuralist writings of Roland Barthes, we shall proceed outward in a rippling movement from the theorizing of the *Tel Quel* period to that of the later erotic phase. Again, we focus on formations of the text and intertext without forgetting the wider issues and general directions of the expanding deconstructive project.

I

In "The Death of the Author" (1968), Roland Barthes sketches out poststructuralist notions of the text and intertext. In particular, he reconsiders and recasts the concepts "author" and "reader," asserting that "writing is the destruction of every voice, of every point of origin" (*IMT*, 142). Disconnecting the originating voice from its text, Barthes nudges the author towards "death" so that *writing* (textuality) may commence. Language speaks, not the author. No longer is the author *the* voice behind the work, *the* owner of the language, *the* origin of the production. The "text's unity lies not in its origin but in its destination" (148). We enter the age of the reader. Unsurprisingly, "the birth of the reader must be at the cost of the death of the Author" (148).

Subverting the authoritarian status and powers of the "author," Barthes substitutes those of the new "scriptor," who practices a different kind of writing:

The Author is thought to *nourish* the book, which is to say that he exists before it, thinks, suffers, lives for it, is in the same relation of antecedence to his work as a father to his child. In complete contrast, the modern scriptor is born simultaneously with the text, is in no way equipped with a being preceding or exceeding the writing. . . . (145)

Barthes directly assaults the expressive theory of literature, which conceives the work as a portrait of the inner soul of the author. Rather than conveying the past experience of the poet, the text unfolds now in a performative manner, forbidding access to the life or consciousness of the scriptor. With the death of the author, biographical, historical, and psychological inquires into the lives of writers become defunct in favor of a receptionist theory of criticism, in which the reader, like the scriptor, activates the text in the present moment. As a result, "*writing* can no longer designate an operation of recording, notation, representation, 'depiction'. . ." (145). It is performative. In effect, Barthes also assaults the mimetic theory of literature, which regards the work as a mirrorlike reflection of preexisting life and reality. The scriptor inscribes language out of the ready-formed and immense dictionary that he bears within him. This storehouse of signs and citations, drawn from numerous areas of culture, can only be mixed and blended. "Thus is revealed the total existence of writing: a text is made of multiple writings, drawn from many cultures and entering into mutual relations of dialogue, parody, contestation . . ." (148). In place of both the "inner soul" of *expression* and the "world or reality" of *mimesis*, Barthes establishes the "heterogeneous dictionary" of *intertextuality*. The text of the scriptor is a sequence of signifiers taken from the intertextual repository of language. And "there is one place where this multiplicity is focused and that place is the reader . . ." (148).

When a work has an "author," it offers a limit—a final signified. Accordingly, to read a work is to restore the author or, the same thing, to recover a preexisting reality. Criticism then seeks to resurrect body beneath the work; it aims to determine or fix an ultimate signified. The poem becomes pretext for meaning.

[However,] writing ceaselessly posits meaning ceaselessly to evaporate it, carrying out a systematic exemption of meaning. In precisely this way literature (it would be better from now on to say *writing*), by refusing to assign a 'secret,' an ultimate meaning, to the text (and to the world as text), liberates what may be called an anti-theological activity, an activity that is truly revolutionary since to refuse to fix meaning is, in the end, to refuse God and his hypostases—reason, science, law. (147)

Let us give up "literature" for *writing*. In doing so, we forego "meaning," the "final signified," the "author," "law," "science," "reason," and ultimately "God." We accept the freeplay of the world and of signs without truth and without origin. We go

beyond humanistic man. We celebrate endless active interpretation. As our diction suggests, Barthes' early deconstructive thinking parallels that of Derrida. Deconstruction in the late 1960s
presents a revolutionary face as it disarticulates traditional conceptions of the author and the work and undermines conventional
notions of reading and history. Instead of mimetic, expressive,
and didactic theories of "literature," it offers textuality (*écriture*).
It kills the author. Turns history and tradition into intertextuality.
And celebrates the reader. The "work," now called *text*, explodes
beyond stable meaning and truth toward the radical and ceaseless
play of infinite meanings spread across textual surfaces—*dissemination*. In these circumstances, traditional criticisms, whether biographical, formalist, historical, structuralist, or receptionist, appear inadequate, if not defunct. The tone of raw radicalism,
evident in Barthes' project, distinguishes *Tel Quel* deconstruction
from the Yale version.

The Yale critics keep the author alive—however diminished she
may now be. And the Yale critics, to some extent, preserve "literature" with the idea of the great self-deconstructing text. Nevertheless, their *text* does give way to dissemination. Foregoing the
ancient worship of truth, the Yale critics (i.e., de Man and Miller)
relinquish almost completely mimetic, expressive, and didactic
theories of literature for *textuality* (*rhetoricity*). (Bloom and Hartman, however, straightforwardly resist the end of expressive poetics.) We say "almost completely" because the notion of *rhetoricity*
maintains, when all is said and done, a "referential" dimension
and potentiality for language. Admittedly, this last dimension
erodes under the vertiginous forces of grammatical and rhetorical
linguistic operations and through the necessities of misreading,
yet referentiality holds a place in the theory.

From an American point of view a distinctive feature of *Tel
Quel* deconstruction, which separates it clearly from the Yale variety, is its political thrust. Barthes, in subverting the traditional
notion of "author," provides an instance:

The author is a modern figure, a product of our society insofar as,
emerging from the Middle Ages with English empiricism, French rationalism and the personal faith of the Reformation, it discovered the
prestige of the individual, of, as it is more nobly put, the 'human person.'

It is thus logical that in literature it should be this positivism, the epitome and culmination of capitalist ideology, which has attached the greatest importance to the 'person' of the author. The *author* still reigns in histories of literature, biographies of writers, interviews, magazines, as in the very consciousness of men of letters anxious to unite their person and their work through diaries and memoirs. The image of literature to be found in ordinary culture is tyrannically centred on the author. . . . (142–43)

The job of deconstructing the authority of the *author* involves desedimentizing a historical formation, which long ago installed itself as a purposeful ideology. So long has this notion reigned that it seems "natural" to us now. Yet this "social natural" serves demonstrable political and economic purposes. Propounding the death of the author, Barthes uncovers the pernicious combined forces of empiricism, rationalism, individualism, positivism, and capitalism—as they influence and direct a theory of literature and criticism. Deconstruction, of the telquel variety produced during the late 1960s and early 1970s, springs forth with an ideological agenda and a political mission. The absence of this thrust in most American deconstruction, particularly the Yale versions, marks an important difference. Occasionally, charges of American reductionism and political naïveté accompany discussions of this profound difference.

When he writes "From Work to Text" (1971), Barthes organizes the theory of the *text* into seven "propositions." In summarizing them, we paraphrase these familiar points as helpful clarifications. (We defer quotation marks here, admitting complete theft. Let us follow Barthes' own order.)

1. Unlike the traditional "work," the *text* is experienced exclusively in an *activity* of language production.
2. Exceeding all genres and conventional hierarchies, the text confronts the limits and rules of rationality and readability.
3. The text practices the infinite deferment of the signified through a radically disruptive freeplay of signifiers, which cannot be centered or closed.
4. Constructed of intertextual citations, references, echoes, and cultural languages—which are anonymous and un*trace*able—the text accomplishes the irreducible plural of meaning, answering not to truth but to dissemination.

5. The inscription of the "author" is no longer paternal or privileged but ludic; neither origin nor end of the text, the author may visit the text only as a guest.
6. The text is opened out and set going—produced—by the reader in an act of collaboration, not consumption.
7. The text is bound to utopia and to (sexual) pleasure.

Everything on the list has been discussed earlier, except the last point where Barthes merely hints at an erotics of textuality. (We shall consider this point a bit later.) What is telling in this essay is not just the package of propositions, which outlines a compact systematics, but the closing remarks. Barthes fully acknowledges that he has "done no more than pick up what is being developed round about him" (*IMT*, 164). We repeat his gesture.

In hasty conclusion, Barthes touches on the problematic of "metalanguage." It is only just a touch, but let us make the most of it. When discussing the theory of the text, we ourselves have assumed a position of "judge, master, analyst, confessor, decoder" (164), employing a safe and external language. Yet the theory of the text denies metalinguistic expression; the discourse about the *text* should itself be nothing other than textual activity. Since there may be no safe distance from *writing*, the theory of the text calls all metalanguage into doubt. How, then, can we discuss the text and yet remain safely beyond or before it? This enigma continues to trouble deconstruction. Barthes responds "it may be necessary provisionally to resort to meta-language . . ." (164). But more and more we see deconstructors practicing textuality; the lines separating literature from criticism give way and "criticism" becomes "literary." Metalanguage crumbles. The reign of *writing* crosses all borders. Critical texts become interesting and energetic "literary" works. We shall have more to say about metalanguage later.

Significantly, the most radical versions of textuality and intertextuality are checked in "Writers, Intellectuals, Teachers," published by Barthes in *Tel Quel* in 1971. Distinguishing two types of deconstructive criticism, Barthes calls for a halt on ideological grounds to the most extreme type. The historical moment requires a different, more moderate strategy. What are the two types of criticism? The first pushes the signifier as far as it will go beyond polysemy to asemy—dissemination. It wonders: why stop? why practice restraint? It presumes a utopian state of freedom and operates outside of historical forces and cultural dialectics, believing that the old laws are completely lifted. Yet situated in a particular alienated intellectual milieu, this criticism manifests itself as triumphant petit-bourgeois subjectivity. *My* reading turns into manic *personal* liberation. "At best," concludes Barthes, "one can simply say that this radical criticism, defined by a foreclosure of the signified (and not by its slide), *anticipates* History, anticipates a new, unprecedented state . . ." (*IMT*, 208). Perhaps the future holds for us the possibility of this new criticism, but the time is not right now. Strategic considerations demand that the *signified* slide, not disappear totally under floating signifiers.

What is the second type of deconstructive criticism? This criticism applies itself to the flights of meaning and the problematics of interpretation without exceeding the grounds of semantic possibility. "In a society locked in the war of meanings and thereby under the compulsion of rules of communication which determine its effectiveness, the liquidation of the old criticism can only be carried forward *in* meaning (in the volume of meanings) and not outside it" (208). To be effective as an ideological instrument, deconstruction must carry out its project, self-consciously and deliberately, within the bounds of meaning. To abjure this work in favor of the infinite signifier is to celebrate bourgeois subjectivity—to turn away from society and political praxis and to court impotence and accede to alienation. The limit on the freeplay of the text is self-imposed for strategic ideological (historical) purposes. Still, the ultimate goal remains precisely to erase the signified: "the signified, exemption of which is the materialist task par excellence, is more easily 'lifted' in the *illusion* of meaning than in its destruction" (208). While the aim is clear, timing and tactics are subject to historical considerations of praxis. At this point in history the illusion of meaning requires preservation. Destruction is out. And yet, as we shall see, these imperatives of Marxism conflict with those of psychoanalysis. The pleasures of dissemination seemingly lure Barthes away from tactical control toward blissful free play and more immediate gratification.

2

utopia begins: meaning and sex become the object of a free play, at the heart of which the (polysemant) forms and the (sensual) practices, liberated from the binary prison, will achieve a state of infinite expansion. Thus may be born a Gongorian text and a happy sexuality. (*RB*, 133)

If we were charting influences, we would observe that Barthes moves from Marx-Sartre-Brecht to Saussure, then to Kristeva-Derrida-Sollers and finally to Lacan and perhaps Nietzsche. His analytical practice progresses from Marxist cultural criticism to semiological structuralism to *Tel Quel* deconstruction to erotic deconstruction. And the idols of his contemplation change from History and Truth to Validity and Truth to Partial Textuality and Dissemination to Infinite Textuality and Pleasure. A quarter of a century pointing towards final utopian thinking: the sumptuous Gongorian text and polymorphous sexuality. Yet there remains a mysterious longing and curious call beyond even this desire and this extreme textuality: "the texture of desire, the claims of the body: this, then, is the Text, the theory of the Text. But again the Text risks paralysis: it repeats itself, counterfeits itself in lusterless texts, testimonies to a demand for readers, not for a desire to please: the Text tends to degenerate into prattle (*Babil*). Where to go next? This is where I am now" (*RB*, 71). What lies beyond the infinite expansion, the utopia, of erotic textuality? What new ravishment awaits the insatiable seeker?

We defer an answer. For now we attend to Barthes' immediate post-*Tel Quel* ideas of literature and tradition or, more properly, theories of textuality and intertextuality.

What form does intertextuality take in Barthes' theorizing? According to Barthes, it is impossible to live outside the infinite text—to escape, for example, newspapers, books, TV shows, and billboards. This larger cultural "book" confers meaning on life not only through overt influence but also by subtle infiltration. Figures, metaphors and thought-words create a kind of "muzak" that permeates the environment so that every text relays this lulling hum (*PT*, 32, 36). And yet the theory of intertextuality works less as a positive notion about social-historical determinations in (of) language and more as a tactical instrument to arrest the extensions and continued expansions of ideological repressions. That is to say, intertextuality, as a critical instrument, combats the "law of context," which always attempts to set borders on dissemination. Somewhat like the limited concept "ambiguity," intertextuality is a machine for battling the tyranny of correct or controlled meaning (*RB*, 172). For Barthes, then, intertextuality presents two faces: it appears as historical crypt, that is, as formation of cultural ideology; and it shows up as a tactical device for critical deconstruction. In the first role, it seems a prison; in the second, an escape key.

The perception of confinement and closure calls for strategies of release. *S/Z* offers some ways, which we shall explore in Part III. *The Pleasure of the Text* recommends escape from binarism toward Derridean deconstruction: the production of third terms or *undecidables* (*PT*, 54–55). And the autobiography *Roland Barthes* promotes *decomposition:*

> Suppose that the intellectual's (or the writer's) historical function, today, is to maintain and to emphasize the *decomposition* of bourgeois consciousness. Then the image must retain all its precision; this means that we deliberately pretend to remain within this consciousness and that we will proceed to dismantle it, to weaken it, to break it down on the spot, as we would do with a lump of sugar by steeping it in water. Hence *decomposition* is here contrary to *destruction*: in order to *destroy* bourgeois consciousness we should have to absent ourselves from it, and such exteriority is possible only in a revolutionary situation. . . . (63)

In theory, escape outside the intertextual network is possible—in a revolutionary situation. But here and now we remain locked in. Decomposition, not destruction, offers a way beyond closure toward utopia. Precision and patient scorching are called for. Dissembling too. Another possibility is an antistructuralist criticism that turns up a work's disorder, that foregrounds its heterogeneity and that produces its irrational polygraphy (*RB*, 148). Part of the decomposition involves the decomposer himself: "by decomposing, I agree to accompany such decomposition, to decompose myself as well, in the process: I scrape, catch, and drag" (63). The disintegration of the self—a tactic—becomes part of the project. Using the stable self, we can dismantle the self; employing the intertext, we can dissolve rigidifying intertextuality; and examining the work, we can decompose it and produce the *text*. Such amoral oscillation possesses strategic value.

One of the more curious and extreme aspects of poststructuralist theory is the deconstruction of the self. In place of a unified and stable being or consciousness, we get a multifaceted and disintegrating play of selves. (When we look at *Anti-Oedipus* in Part III, we shall encounter a dramatic version of this morcellation.) This idea of the deconstructed subject attaches to the notions "author," "reader," and "critic." In a sense, the forces of differance, freeplay, and dissemination ultimately affect and textualize the *self*. Barthes' versions of this visitation deserve notice since they help distinguish his project from others.

As he develops the implications of intertextuality in *S/Z*, Barthes extends them to the self of the reader. "I is not an innocent subject, anterior to the text, one which will subsequently deal with the text as it would an object to dismantle or a site to occupy. This 'I' which approaches the text is already itself a plurality of other texts, of codes which are infinite. . . ."[11] Within the reader-subject resides a multiplicity of texts and codes, and this "resource" effectively rules out any conception of the reader-text transaction as a simple relation of subjectivity to objectivity. The invasions of intertextuality into the self of the reader disintegrate that enclosed self. The borders collapse, producing a disorienting complicity. The *reader*, like the text, is unstable. Focusing on the "proper name," Barthes also undermines the stable self of the (literary) character, just as he does with the self of the reader: "What is obsolescent . . . is the character; what can no longer be written is the Proper Name" (95; see 191). Most extreme are Barthes' deconstructions of the self in his autobiography.

Essentially, deconstruction regards the subject as an effect of language. The "ego," a rational formulation, emerges out of a play of signifiers. "I am not contradictory, I am dispersed" (*RB*, 143). In fact, *Roland Barthes* meticulously and luxuriously unfolds this dispersion. We can read the text as an extended deconstruction of the self. Tracing a pattern in his life's work, Barthes empties his existence of content:

he systematically goes where there is a solidification of language, a consistency, a stereotypy. Like a watchful cook, he makes sure that language does not thicken, that it doesn't *stick*. This movement, one of pure form, accounts for the progressions and regressions of the work: it is a pure language tactic, which is deployed *in the air*, without any strategic horizon. The risk is that since the stereotype shifts historically, politically, it must be followed wherever it goes: what is to be done if the sterotype *goes left*? (162)

As a super gadfly and arch antinomian, Barthes attacks whatever stereotype currently holds sway. If that stereotype happens sometime to be leftist ideology, he will be compelled to criticize it. He is "a *political misfit*" (170). There exists no substance to his enterprise. No specific content. Only a movement of denial. What is the self of Roland Barthes? An operation of cancellation. Even this form or structure, described as a language tactic, comes to us as a language tactic. When Barthes assigns the epigraph to his text, he sets up the entire scene of *auto*biography in an abyss: "It must all be considered as if spoken by a character in a novel." The self is fiction: of the reader, character, writer, and critic.

In a section of *The Pleasure of the Text* entitled "Subject," Barthes, who rarely quotes anyone in this text, cites Nietzsche: "We have no right to ask *who* it is who interprets. It is interpretation itself, a form of the will to power, which exists (not as 'being' but as process, a becoming) as passion" (62). The activity of reading exists as passion; this process (of becoming) exceeds the subject (being). To this quotation Barthes immediately replies: "Then perhaps the subject returns, not as illusion, but as *fiction*" (62). He goes on to characterize identity as an invention—a "rarest fiction." And, provocatively, he suggests a revealing typology for readers:

We can imagine a typology of the pleasures of reading—or of the readers of pleasure; it would not be sociological, for pleasure is not an attribute of either product or production; it could only be psychoanalytic, linking the reading neurosis to the hallucinated form of the text. [1] The fetishist would be matched with the divided-up text, the singling out of quotations, formulae, turns of phrase, with the pleasure of the word. [2] The obsessive would experience the voluptuous release of the letter, of secondary, disconnected languages, of metalanguages (this class would include all the logophiles, linguists, semioticians, philologists: all those for whom language *returns*). [3] A paranoiac would consume or produce complicated texts, stories developed like arguments, constructions posited like games, like secret constraints. [4] As for the hysteric (so contrary to the obsessive), he would be the one who takes the text *for ready money*, who joins in the bottomless, truthless comedy of language, who is no longer the subject of any critical scrutiny and *throws himself* across the text (which is quite different from projecting himself into it). (63)

Reading is a form of pleasure. Pleasure seekers, of course, take their pleasures in different ways and with different styles. The reading of an obsessive person differs from that of a hysteric. They produce different texts. Using psychoanalysis, we can differentiate classes of readers: the fetishist, the obsessive, the paranoiac, the hysteric.[12] Traditional criticism is obsessive; contemporary deconstruction is hysteric. Unlike fetishistic, obsessive, and paranoiac readers, who are enchained to their egos, the hysteric manifests undiluted id. Only the hysteric reaches authentic bliss (*jouissance*)—an orgasmic experience beyond mere pleasure (*plaisir*). The hysteric, an extreme visionary and lunatic rhetorician, is continuously celebrated by Barthes. His *A Lover's Discourse: Fragments* seeks to monumentalize hysterical discourse. (Notice the move beyond *Tel Quel* philosophy.) Despite the appearance in the typology of fixed types or stable personalities, Barthes labors to undo rigidifying determinations of the subject. Commenting indirectly in his later autobiography on the typology of readers in *The Pleasure of the Text*, Barthes suggests that solidified formations or models of self ultimately break up: "you unite in yourself supposedly distinctive features which henceforth no longer distinguish anything; you discover that you are at one and the same time (or alternately) obsessive, hysterical, paranoiac, and perverse to the last degree (not to mention certain erotic psychoses) . . ." (144). The self disintegrates; it is multiple. The apparent distinctive features of the subject give way to a panoply of different selves.[13]

For the reader of pleasure the text offers a freeplay of meaning and sex, opening out toward complete freedom. The polymorphous reader comes to the polymorphous text. The reader and the meaning disseminate sumptuously toward infinity. The disintegrations of the reader's self as well as the writer's unfold as the text is set going: "the text is made, is worked out in a perpetual interweaving; lost in this tissue—this texture—the subject un-makes himself . . ." (*PT*, 64). This loss of the self is an orgasmic happening. Ideally, the reader and the writer should come to-gether. A poet's utopian "vision then appears: that of infinitely spread-out languages, of parentheses never to be closed: a utopian vision in that it supposes a mobile, plural reader, who nimbly inserts and removes the quotation marks: who begins to write *with me*" (*RB*, 161).

There are two kinds of texts: the *readerly* and the *writerly*. The *writerly* text is that which the reader can "write" along with the scriptor; its signifiers can be set going toward infinity; and its pleasure can be worked up and experienced in an orgasmic activity. The *readerly* text, however, can only be consumed, not pro-duced—read, not written; it manifests itself in a structure of sig-nifieds or in fixed patterns of meaning; it calls for a serious, in-transitive, and impotent reader (*S/Z*, 4–6; cf. *RB*, 118).

Barthes delivers a playful allegory of the reading activity. It deals with soothsayers and bird signs. So we return to the Homeric scene where we began. It is different now:

> The text, in its mass, is comparable to a sky, at once flat and smooth, deep, without edges and without landmarks; like the soothsayer drawing on it with the tip of his staff an imaginary rectangle wherein to consult, according to certain principles, the flight of birds, the commentator traces through the text certain zones of reading, in order to observe therein the migration of meanings, the outcropping of codes, the passage of citations.
>
> (*S/Z*, 14)

The borderless expanse of the text gets cut and divided for con-venience into neat shapes and zones, and these patches produce the flight of signifiers and the variegated plumage of citations: text and intertext. The exact cut and the commentator's criteria—these are unimportant, imaginary. The interpreter is a soothsayer. A mad man.

> it must have been a fine thing to see, in those days: that staff marking out the sky, the one thing that cannot be marked; then, too, any such gesture is mad: solemnly to trace a limit of which immediately *nothing*

is left, except for the intellectual remanence of a cutting out, to devote oneself to the totally ritual and totally arbitrary preparation of a meaning.

(*RB*, 47)

Five years after *S/Z* Barthes sees his deconstructive project differently. During his telquel days he was a soothsayer, a mad man, cutting up the sky in an attempt to prepare the ground of "a" meaning. And so solemnly. The interpreter's limit, ritual and arbitrary, now encloses nothing—inscribes evanescent marks on an always transformed sky. No longer simply a single-minded and detached soothsayer who reads airy nothingness, the deconstructive reader is an amorous desiring body, seeking pleasure and bliss in an excess of polymorphous love play. At once he is an erotic lunatic not only like the obsessive soothsayer, who repeatedly disconnects and divides the text so as to return it after careful and correct interpretation; but like the fetishist whose piece of the text stays and extends the satisfactions of forepleasure; and the paranoiac who saturates the text in delirious and deluded, complete readings; and the hysteric who naively and boisterously exalts the text and the disintegrating self in excesses of truth and bliss. No longer a soothsayer, but a Satan-figure, Barthes intimates "I am legion."

The Borders of Reference Overrun

I

Let us appear flip for a moment. Make up an utterly ridiculous tale. Put everybody in a fix. Suppose we were language police working the graveyard shift. Orders come down to round up all the nearby wandering crazies. Someone stole the *referent*, and we are overrun with sliding signifieds and floating signifiers. Who stole the referent? Out of the paddy wagon and into the interrogation room come Barthes, de Man, Derrida, Heidegger, Husserl, Lacan, Lévi-Strauss, Miller, Riddel, Saussure, and Spanos. And a blind man—Hector. Or is it Homer? Anyway, we have a dozen. Who stole the referent?

In the morning there are twelve reports to read. At first glance it seems that this wretched dozen did the job. Saussure, in particular, appears to be the instigator. A bad influence on most of the others. Yet evidence of lingering reverence for the referent shows up in the reports from de Man, Heidegger, Husserl, Lacan, Lévi-Strauss, Miller, Spanos, and the other Greek. Under interrogation Heidegger, Husserl, and Spanos separately admit respect, even admiration, for the referent, though their speech is difficult to decipher. Only Barthes, Derrida, Riddel, and Saussure stay hostile. The others quibble and hem and haw. De Man and Miller seem to say "Yes, but. . . ." Lévi-Strauss appears indifferent. And Lacan obfuscates, perhaps unintentionally. The silent Greek doesn't talk and his eyes won't give him away. He looks innocent.

Everybody keeps staring at Derrida. Some seem miffed while others appear attracted to him. He must be the ringleader. A quick examination of him turns up enough circumstantial evidence for conviction. He's our man. The evidence on Saussure and Riddel is convincing but skimpy and that on Barthes is massive but a bit contradictory. (We continue to stack the deck here.) The people who know Derrida, both friends and enemies, reinforce our suspicion. That's it. He stole the referent. No doubt, Saussure taught him. And Heidegger, Husserl, and Lévi-Strauss unwittingly pointed out potential traps. And Barthes and Riddel went along. And de Man and Miller, though demurring, offered encouragement and a hide-out. And the two Greeks—well, Spanos is innocent and the other fellow seems harmless. And Lacan—who knows? Maybe he tried to steal the referent but grabbed the wrong thing. Evidently, Derrida beat him to it. Quick hands. Everybody is more or less agreed: Derrida is our man.

Anyhow, what happened to the referent? Rumor says it got dissolved in a bath of atheistic acid. (Some believe it's indestructible.) Others suggest that it is buried here or there or somewhere. "Maybe it's in the eye of the beholder," offers another group. These people are very tolerant and engaging. Where is the referent? Without it we've got signifiers cluttering the atmosphere. We're choking. The air of truth runs out. Everything gets unhinged and the world goes mad. Dissemination.

2

Several weeks before the decade of the 1970s came to a close the Yale critics published their manifesto—*Deconstruction and Criti-*

cism—which contains essays by Bloom, de Man, Derrida, Hartman, and Miller. In the Preface, Hartman, the group scribe, tells us that Derrida, de Man, and Miller are "boa-deconstructors" and that Bloom and Hartman are "barely deconstructionists." While the reluctant two "even write against it on occasion," the three stranglers appear "merciless and consequent," as "each enjoys his own style of disclosing again and again the 'abysm' of words."[14] A cold, winter book, a gift of advent, *Deconstruction and Criticism* announces the growing pertinence of two issues: (1) the progression of criticism beyond pedagogical and academic functions toward a separate literary-philosophical realm of its own; and (2) the movement of literary language toward a position of priority by virtue of the signifier's strength over the signified (vii). And then Hartman outlines intertextuality and textuality:

Each text is shown to imbed other texts by a most cunning assimilation whose form is the subject both of psychoanalytic and of purely rhetorical criticism. Everything we thought of as spirit, or meaning separable from the letter of the text, remains within an "intertextual sphere". . . . [Criticism] has always shown that a received text means more than it says (it is "allegorical"), or that it subverts all possible meanings by its "irony"—a rhetorical or structural limit that prevents the dissolution of art into positive or exploitative truth. (viii)

Assuming a nondeconstructivist point of view and tone, Hartman depicts intertextuality as a tricky and seductive force of inclusion that produces states of closure and compromises meaning. And he characterizes textuality in two ways: (1) as polysemous and, therefore, allegorical, and (2) as asemous or unreadable and, consequently, ironic. In either case, textuality, the excess and subversion of meaning, has always been shown by criticism. Thus textuality is tamed. It has *always* been demonstrated. It is allegory. It is irony. This rhetorical containment, reminiscent of de Man and Miller, comes forth, nevertheless, as a barrier that resists the reduction of (privileged) art to truth. Even this most moderate and uncertain of deconstructors gives up the truth of literature at the behest of (one version or another of) textuality; and, though a conservative deconstructor, he admits the contamination and closure of (one version or another of) intertextuality. Finally, deconstructors, whether moderate or extremist, whether Hartman or Derrida, characteristically and continuously emphasize the signifier over the signified, and rarely, if ever, mention the lost and forgotten referent. Only the opponent of deconstruction thinks to name the referent. Put bluntly, if someone wants to discuss the referent, you may presume she is hostile to deconstruction.

Who stole the referent? Derrida. And consequently the world becomes an infinite, borderless text. A cosmic library. Riddel says it forcefully: "Derrida does *textualize the world*. . . ." In the Yale manifesto Derrida, seemingly bemused, observes:

The question of the text, as it has been elaborated and transformed in the last dozen or so years, has not merely "touched" "shore," *le bord* (scandalously tampering, changing, as in Mallarmé's declaration, "*On a touché au vers*"), all those boundaries that form the running border of what used to be called a text, of what we once thought this word could identify, i.e., the supposed end and beginning of a work, the unity of a corpus, the title, the margins, the signatures, the referential realm outside the frame, and so forth. What has happened, if it has happened, is a sort of overrun [*débordement*] that spoils all these boundaries and divisions and forces us to extend the accredited concept, the dominant notion of a "text," of what I still call a "text," for strategic reasons, in part—a "text" that is henceforth no longer a finished corpus of writing, some content enclosed in a book or its margins, but a differential network, a fabric of traces referring endlessly to something other than itself, to other differential traces. Thus the text overruns all the limits assigned to it so far (not submerging or drowning them in an undifferentiated homogeneity, but rather making them more complex, dividing and multiplying strokes and lines)—all the limits, everything that was to be set up in opposition to writing (speech, life, the world, the real, history, and what not, every field of reference—to body or mind, conscious or unconscious, politics, economics, and so forth). ("LO," 83–84)

There are two texts: the old and the new. The old "text" possesses a title, margins, signature (author), a beginning, an end, overall unity, and limited content. Outside its frame lies a "referential realm." This piece of writing is distinguishable from reality, the world, history, life, and speech; and it is distinctive from the realms of the body, mind, consciousness, the Unconscious, politics, and economics. All these boundaries, frames, divisions, limits—*borders*—mark out and enclose the old "text," making it a very special and highly differentiated entity and object. Since the late 1960s, however, a new *text* has come to our attention. It touches and tampers with—it changes and spoils—all the old boundaries, frames, divisions, and limits. The identity of "text" alters. The overrun of all the old borders forces us to rethink the "text." (Partly for strategic purposes we keep the word "text," but we extend its conceptualization.) The new *text* consists of a string of differential traces that refer to other differential traces; it is a differential network. Its excesses complicate all borders, multiplying and dividing them in a process of luxurious enrichment; significantly, the *text* does not level or bury or otherwise erase the old boundaries. This new *text* has happened, "if it has happened," since 1967.

But this description of the overrun of the borders serves mainly as preface to what follows. Here we pick up Derrida where he left off:

Whatever the (demonstrated) necessity of such an overrun, such a *débordement*, it still will have come as a shock, producing endless efforts to dam up, resist, rebuild the old partitions, to blame what could no longer be thought without confusion, to blame difference *as* wrongful confusion! All this has taken place in nonreading, with no work on what was thus being demonstrated, with no realization that it was never our wish to extend the reassuring notion of the text to a whole extra-textual realm and to transform the world into a library by doing away with all boundaries, all framework, all sharp edges (all *arêtes* [ridges]: this is the word that I am speaking of tonight), but that we sought rather to work out the theoretical and practical system of these margins, these borders, once more, from the ground up. I shall not go into detail. Documentation of all this is readily available to anyone committed to breaking down the various structures of resistance, his own resistance as such or as primarily the ramparts that bolster a system (be it theoretical, cultural, institutional, political, or whatever). What are the borderlines of a text? How do they come about? ("LO," 84–85)

The overrun of the borders produced shock, followed by vigorous efforts to reconstruct and preserve the crumbling limits. In particular, charges of error and confusion were lodged against the theory of *difference*. But those shocked and angry people did not read Derrida. Neither the necessity of the overrun, nor the demonstration—ample and available—of such necessity were attended to in careful work. In the main, Derrida asked rigorously and continuously: What are borders? How do they happen? He sought to examine thoroughly the system of theory and practice underlying the establishment of borders. He inquired into titles, beginnings, endings, signatures, margins, unities, contents, speech, and so forth. In doing so, he encountered resistances of all kinds. He never wished to stretch the old notion of the "text" to the whole world; nor did he wish to transform the extratextual realm into *writing* by erasing all borders. He mainly problematized borders by multiplying, not leveling, them.

This curious passage, which we divided for convenience, summarizes *textuality* (in opposition to the old logocentric notion of the "text"), enumerating the many new excesses as well as the destroyed older boundaries. And yet it evidently takes back for a moment the entire enterprise. Retrospeculation. Like Hartman or Bloom, Derrida acts reluctant. Surely this is coyness. The whole regressive argument ultimately relies on Derrida's self-proclaimed "original intention" and his audience's inept "reading": "it was never our wish . . . to transform the world into a library. . . ." That Derrida has formerly rendered suspicious simple authorial intention and scrupulous reading goes without saying, much less demonstration. What then is the effect of this passage? It calls us back to the borders—to the most basic of questions.

The question of the borderline precedes, as it were, the determination of all the dividing lines that I have just mentioned: between a fantasy and a "reality," an event and a non-event, a fiction and a reality, one corpus and another, and so forth. ("BL," 82–83)

What is a version? What is a title? What borderline questions are posed here? I am here seeking merely to establish the necessity of this whole problematic of judicial framing and of the jurisdiction of frames.

("LO," 88)

Hence no context is saturable any more. No one inflection enjoys any absolute privilege, no meaning can be fixed or decided upon. No border is guaranteed, inside or out. ("LO," 78)

It is always an *external* constraint that arrests a text in general. . . .

("BL," 171)

Derrida resurrects and revitalizes the "founding" question: the enigma of borders. It is almost as though he were now seeking and promoting rededication to his "original" inspiration. (At the same time he silently unifies his oeuvre around a single question.) Actually, the *question of the* BORDER is the question of difference—but in a new guise. Every boundary, limit, division, frame, or margin installs a line separating one entity or concept from another. That is to say, every border marks a difference. The question of the border is the question of difference. Examining borders, Derrida finds "No border is guaranteed, inside or out." Applied to texts, this finding becomes "no meaning can be fixed or decided upon." When directed to the intertext, the result is "no context is saturable any more," which is to say no genealogy of a text can ever be complete. The only way to arrest the disseminating play of the text is to impose an external constraint (border). About the attempt to constrain a text by surrounding it with a stablizing intertextual context, Derrida observes: "An apocalyptic super-imprinting of texts: there is no paradigmatic text. Only relationships of cryptic haunting from mark to mark. No palimpsest (definitive unfinishedness). No piece, no metonymy, no integral corpus" ("BL," 136–37). There can be no limit to intertextuality. Not even the liberal model of the *palimpsest* can delineate intertextuality because it smacks too much of the bounded and definitive.

The excesses of textuality and intertextuality overrun the referential realm. In place of the referent we observe the differential trace referring endlessly to other differential traces. Rather than anchor lines of "influence" or "source," which refer a present text to earlier texts, we encounter disruptive and apocalyptic, cryptic overlays where one signifier haunts another, producing the exact opposition of integration. The disintegration of the borders, which includes the deconstruction of the referential function of language, comes about under the force of difference. In place of the referent stands the trace.[15] The question of the border opens for inquiry the law of all limits. Ultimately, deconstruction overruns the old jurisdictions and limits, as it elaborates their sway and complexity.

3

Reducing deconstruction to a coherent and succinct, single paragraph, we can produce an abstract: deconstruction takes the semiological theory of the sign (signifier + signified) beyond the sliding signified to the floating signifier. (Notice that it eschews the referent.) Since language serves as ground of existence, the world emerges as infinite Text. Everything gets textualized. All contexts, whether political, economic, social, psychological, historical, or theological, become intertexts; that is, outside influences and forces undergo textualization. Instead of literature we have textuality; in place of tradition, intertextuality. Authors die so that readers may come into prominence. In any case, all selves, whether of critics, poets, or readers, appear as language constructions—texts. What are texts? Strings of differential traces. Sequences of floating signifiers. Sets of infiltrated signs dragging along ultimately indecipherable intertextual elements. Sites for the freeplay of grammar, rhetoric, and (illusory) reference. What about the truth of the text? The random flights of signifiers across the textual surface, the disseminations of meaning, offer truth under one condition: that the chaotic processes of textuality be willfully regulated, controlled, or stopped. Truth comes forth in the reifications, the personal pleasures, of reading. Truth is not an entity or property of the text. No text utters its truth; the truth lies elsewhere—in a reading.[16] Constitutionally, reading is misreading. Deconstruction works to deregulate controlled dissemination and celebrate misreading.

6

The (Inter) Texualization of Context

When it finds its way into a current text, a chip or piece of an older monument appears as source, influence, allusion, imitation, archetype, or parody. When, for example, we read a contemporary sonnet, we recognize a stanza pattern, rhyme scheme, conventional thematics, and we recall perhaps Petrarch, Wyatt, Ronsard, Spenser, or Milton. As craftsmen and free creative spirits, our poets employ such sources and historical forms for literary effect. The educated reader or critic recognizes and attends to these effects of literary history and tradition. Knowing the grammar, rhetoric, syntax, and lexicon of the language and the forms and conventions of the literature, the critic reexamines Petrarch, Wyatt, Ronsard, or the others in order ultimately to situate, decipher, and assess the new text. All this critical work, diligent and self-effacing, is scholarship and, when extended to cover many sources, forms, and texts, becomes literary history. To widen the circle to include the politics of patronage or publication, the economics of printing, the theology of poetics, and the aesthetics of the other fine arts is to write on a grander scale—to produce cultural history. The rings of context surrounding the text appear ever expandable. Through all this activity the isolation of demonstrable data and the use of established techniques of empirical evidence guide the limiting production of history and tradition. But (inter)textuality undermines such contextualization.

In an uncanny glimpse Heidegger guessed that the structure of language may control our thinking. In this vision, we are not aware of such limitation. Unknown forces pattern thought and history. And Joseph Riddel noted that the signifier consists of a history: not just a sequence of tabulated denotations but a set of unexamined cultural and personal connotations divide the signifier in its constitution. Here the sign shows up as unpurifiable cultural debris dragging along an unchartable history. Such history can never be fully exhumed and narrated. As he decomposes the authority of the author and the stability of the reader, Roland Barthes singles out the founding role of heterogeneous language, pictured as an immense unabridged dictionary, in the historical construction of the enclosed "self." He disperses the determining subject and denies the centering consciousness, voiding the grounds of contextual history. In effect, the theorists of the (inter)text undermine, directly or indirectly, the various older notions and practices of writing (about) tradition and history.

Reexamining "author," "reader," "text," "language," and "history," deconstructors turn up a barely realized realm, a cultural Unconscious perhaps, a reservoir of *traces*, which manifests itself as an infinite universal discourse that (un)grounds all conceptual formations. To turn it around, the careful and conscious constructions of scholarship and history rest upon a wild profusion whipped into order. Below the smooth surfaces lie numerous unrestored and unrecoverable jagged remains and surpluses. Just as an individual may avoid his Unconscious, so may a culture, but this disruptive underside will not ignore the individual or the culture. If the ultimate horizon and context of every literary work is cultural history, this history is understood to include unconscious as well as conscious materials and constraints. To reconstruct or otherwise restore *all* such materials and patterns is patently impossible. When established, they serve to limit, protect, and explain. Such severe reduction amounts to facile deception. Historical research necessarily sets borders around textual dissemination and simplifies critical reading.

During the last two decades our understanding of history has undergone extensive reconsideration and revision. Within the structuralist movement the work of Hayden White particularly stands out as a celebrated example of a new and influential form of theorizing about history. Within the poststructuralist movement no theorist has examined more prodigiously and relentlessly the discourse of history, the buried cultural archive, than Michel Foucault. And no deconstructor has entered an analogous realm more strenuously and obsessively with an extended sense of its importance for *literary* history than Harold Bloom. We shall survey the distinctive projects of these three theorists in this chapter.

In the first section, we shall review the fourfold model of history, a rhetoric of historiography, proposed by Hayden White. Our purpose is to examine a carefully articulated theory of history as writing. In the second section, we shall look at the tetralogy on poetic misprision of Harold Bloom, considering his theory of tradition, his notorious Map of Misprision, his conceptualization of (inter)textuality, and his role in American deconstruction. Our goal is to review Bloom's general project in detail so as to understand his particular practice of deconstructive literary history. In the third section, we shall attend to the influential work of Michel Foucault, examining his notions of discourse and archive, his theories of textuality, intertextuality, and archaeology, and his formulations on knowledge and power. Our aim is to explore this wide-ranging contemporary theory of history, which offers the richest poststructuralist model yet to account for modes of "context." To conclude our discussion, we shall sample some contemporary subversions of the traditional conceptualization of *context*, focusing on Foucault's program for *genealogy*, Derrida's notion of *iterability*, and the general deconstructive strategies for *intertextuality*.

History as Written

Throughout the 1970s Hayden White develops and refines a poetics and hermeneutics of historiography—a meta-analytics of historical interpretation and writing. Focusing on the major historians and philosophers of history in nineteenth-century Europe (including Michelet, Ranke, Tocqueville, Burckhardt and Hegel, Marx, Nietzsche, Croce), White in *Metahistory* (1973) creates a machine for a project of metahistory ultimately as fully articulated and agile as Harold Bloom's eccentric machine for a literary poetics and hermeneutics, which we shall examine in the next section.

According to White, history, as verbal discourse, usually favors a particular mode of emplotment. A historical text may emerge as romance, tragedy, comedy, or satire. Other genres get subsumed under these dominant ones. Each such controlling form exhibits an affinity for a particular mode of ideological implication. Correlated with the types of plot are, respectively, anarchist, radical, conservative, and liberal points of view. Variations, within limits, occur. Homologous with the kinds of plot and ideology are specific forms of argument. Such broad explanations, hypotheses, or laws of history display certain preferred modes of deduction, including formist, mechanistic, organicist, and contextualist methods. Taken together, these structural sets or modes of emplotment, argument, and ideological implication describe the manifest aesthetic, epistemological, and ethical aspects of a work. They characterize historiographical *style*.

Between an unexamined historical record, a primitive chronicle, say, and a finished text of history, a written book in your lap— between such basic stages—the historian performs certain processes of selection and arrangement, producing forms of plot, explanation, and ideology. These productions, in White's account, are inherently hermeneutic:

> Interpretation thus enters into historiography in at least three ways: aesthetically (in the choice of a narrative strategy), epistemologically (in the choice of an explanatory paradigm), and ethically (in the choice of a strategy by which the ideological implications of a given representation can be drawn for the comprehension of current social problems). And I have suggested that it is all but impossible, except for the most doctrinaire forms of history-writing, to assign priority to one or another of the three moments thus distinguished.[1]

Three levels of interpretation constitute the historical text. When it comes to a reader, a history is already triply interpretive. It is usually impossible to ascertain which level of interpretation, if any, controls the others. Still, despite what history-writers believe, such metahistorical hermeneutic operations determine the text.

"And although professional historians claim to be able to distinguish between proper history on the one side and metahistory on the other, in fact the distinction has no adequate theoretical justification. Every proper history presupposes a metahistory which is nothing but the web of commitments which the historian makes in the course of his interpretation on the aesthetic, cognitive, and ethical levels differentiated above" (*TD*, 71). Every history is metahistorical: the narrative of the past always exhibits three hermeneutic moments or levels.

White grounds his history of history in a theory of language. Before a historian can ever represent, explain or value the data of a historical field, he must prefigure or constitute the field as an object of thought. This generative act is linguistic in nature. "This preconceptual linguistic protocol will in turn be—by virtue of its essentially *prefigurative* nature—characterizable in terms of the dominant tropological mode in which it is cast."[2] Preceding his formal analysis of the field, the historian creates his object and thereby predetermines his style of interpretation. The four tropological modes or master tropes, correlated to the modalities of emplotment, argument, and ideological implication, are metaphor, metonymy, synecdoche, and irony. As human thought makes contact with the world of experience, relationships within and among phenomena occur. The tropes describe these relationships or, to put it more accurately, "thought remains the captive of the linguistic mode in which it seeks to grasp the outline of objects inhabiting its field of perception" (*Metahistory*, xi). Thus tropological modes underlie and inform all preconceptual materials in the historical field. Tropes constitute the latent level or deep structure of every historical text.

In history, I have argued, the historical field is constituted as a possible domain of analysis in a linguistic act which is tropological in nature. The dominant trope in which this constitutive act is carried out will determine both the kinds of objects which are permitted to appear in that field as data and the possible relationships that are conceived to obtain among them. . . . These precritical commitments to different modes of discourse and their constitutive tropological strategies account for the generation of the different interpretations of history which I have identified. . . . (*Metahistory*, 430)

As the historian prefigures the historical field linguistically, he commits himself implicitly to particular modes of explanation, emplotment, and ideological implication. Within this structural *set*, as defined by White, few permutations appear possible.

With this establishment of a linguistic base for historiography, our understanding of historical interpretation alters. The cognitive, aesthetic, and moral levels now emerge as projections of various founding tropes. Historical interpretation becomes the formalization of life's phenomena and experiences in line with tropological determinations. History-writing is the working out of possible plots, arguments, and ethical implications contained in tropological formations. As a discipline, White's metahistory, the interpretation of historical interpretation, seeks to uncover and explicate the hermeneutic effects of precritical tropological constitutions.

White specifies how historical discourse is produced and how all such productions are inherently intrepretive. In short, he demonstrates how every poetics of history is always already a hermeneutics. Then he shows how such hermeneutics depend upon tropology.

Ultimately, White construes all history as *writing*. History is writing in two senses: it derives from a troplogical constitution and it deploys a generic mode. In the first case, history is textuality; in the second, it is literature.

White severely limits the play of the historical *text*. Though he never celebrates truth, he ignores dissemination. The sign stays intact. His interests are in regulated forms of consciousness, modes of tropology, and types of discourse, that is, in the rules that govern their formations. His is a structuralist enterprise. While he demystifies history, he inaugurates no project for destruction, decomposition, or deconstruction. To the extent that White conceives history as regulated by a small set of preconscious tropes, he fosters a limited notion of intertextuality. Tropological modes determine the paths of thinking and the patterns of discursive history. Authors are not free to alter such linguistic controls.

White believes strongly in the efficacy of human reason, will, and morality. As humanist and moralist, he closes his Introduction to *Tropics of Discourse* (1978), saying "Kant's distinctions among the emotions, the will, and the reason are not very popular in this, an age which has lost its belief in the will and represses its sense of the moral implications of the mode of rationality that it favors. But the moral implications of the human sciences will never be perceived until the faculty of the will is reinstated in theory" (23). Like Bloom, White holds onto the self, as heroic agency of the will, despite the massive assault of deconstruction on the possibility of any self. Embattled, White affirms, "I will not apologize for this Kantian element in my thought . . ." (*TD*, 22).

While White realizes and confirms that his own history from Hegel to Croce works within an ironic mode, he seems unhappy about this tropological situation, which is common to modern historiography. He wants to transcend irony. He believes he can do so through aesthetic and/or moral choice. Yet he is caught between his metacritical understanding that preconscious tropological constitutions determine historiographical modes and his stubborn desire to escape this truth. He cannot will a particular tropological investment of the historical field, but he obstinately longs to do so. There is no escape from (inter)textuality. Neither history as written nor the historian as writer can turn away the constituting forces of language.

Mapping Tradition

it is not possible to return wholly to a mode of interpretation that seeks to *restore* meanings to texts. Yet even the subtlest of contemporary Nietzschean "deconstructors" of texts must *reduce* those texts in a detour or flight from psychology and history. Nothing prevents a reader with my preferences from resolving all linguistic elements in a literary text into history, and similarly tracing all semantic elements in literary discourse to problems of psychology.[3]

—Harold Bloom

The most prolific of American "deconstructors," Harold Bloom during the 1970s published six critical books and numerous essays, all of which distinguish themselves deliberately *against* the seemingly monolithic background of the desconstructive enterprise headed by Jacques Derrida and Paul de Man. The centerpiece of

Bloom's antithetical criticism is his tetralogy on "poetic misprision," which includes *The Anxiety of Influence* (1973), *A Map of Misreading* (1975), *Kabbalah and Criticism* (1975) and *Poetry and Repression* (1976). In Bloom's view, deconstruction avoids and voids history and psychology through its reductive emphasis upon linguistic and narrowly defined rhetorical elements in literary texts. Continually expanding and revising his poetics and hermeneutics, Bloom ultimately creates an eccentric and inimitable countermonolith, recuperating for literary and critical theory the threatened contexts of psychology and tradition. In so doing, Bloom becomes a major explorer of *literary* intertextuality—a role parallel to that of Michel Foucault, premier poststructuralist analyst of the *cultural* intertext.

In taking up Bloom's project, we shall examine his theory of tradition, his Map of Misprision, his formulation of (inter)textuality and his position in American deconstruction. We aim to explore Bloom's overall enterprise in order to understand his special practice of literary history.

I

The focus of Bloom's historical concern is the post-Enlightenment poetry of major English and American poets. He names the period from 1740 up to the present "Romantic." Within this Romantic era he studies the (destructive) influence of strong poets on other strong poets. In this endeavor, the canons of Wordsworth and Whitman dominate down to present times. The true fountainheads of the deluge of poetic influx are Milton and Emerson. Before Milton, poets experienced influence as a healthy and generous force. But when poetry became subjective, influence began to create profound anxieties. Bloom examines the anxiety of influence in scrupulous detail and in occasional revulsion. Typically, his portrayals of literary history and tradition hold back none of the horrors nor any of the unromantic psychological realities of the post-Enlightenment era.

Opposing a "Scene of Instruction" to Derrida's Scene of *Writing*, Bloom elaborates a six-phase psychology of poetic origins and development. This staging is the ground of his intertextual theory of tradition. The young post-Enlightenment poet is seized by an older poet's power (*election*), whereupon ensues an agreement of poetic visions (*covenant*), followed by the choice of a counter inspiration or muse (*rivalry*), after which the apparently liberated ephebe offers himself as the true manifestation of the authentic poet (*incarnation*); eventually the latecomer comprehensively revalues the precursor (*interpretation*) and ultimately recreates him in a new way (*revision*).[4] Using Freudian notions as analogues, Bloom pictures this formation of the strong poetic *ego* as an unconscious and unavoidable process in which the precursor is lodged, not in the *superego*, but in the *id*. The relations between poets, similar to those in the Freudian Family Romance, commence, therefore, with a *primal fixation of influence* in the emergent poetic psyche. However idealized or composite the precursor, he presides over a scene of authority and priority as well as a scene of love and competition. The ephebe's consequent assimilations and accommodations, his self-withdrawals and self-representations, his devotions and aggressions reveal to us further the workings of a *primal repression*, which accompanies the initial fixation on the precursor. What is repressed is the new strong poet's ravenous demand (or desire or wish) for autonomy and for immortality. Without such an overpowering *will-to-divination* a newcomer cannot emerge and succeed as a strong poet. The repression, more a continuously modified force than a stable state of being, brings into play revisionary operations designed ultimately to insure the survival, independence, and triumph of the belated strong poet against the precursor and tradition.

The Scene of Instruction, which encompasses both the origin and the end of poetry, stages a theater, a virtual globe, of inescapable intertextuality. Every text is necessarily an intertext. The ground of any text is always another text. Poems do not exist— only interpoems do. When Bloom maps the precise revisionary relations (or ratios) between numerous latecomer and precursor texts, he sketches the larger historical picture of the post-Enlightenment poetic universe. At the same time he gives us the blueprint or deep structure of *the* Romantic poem. (We shall look at this map shortly.) The point is that Bloom is a literary historian of both the individual and the epochal intertext.

The site of the Scene of Instruction is the psyche. The self

precedes poetic language. Resolutely, Bloom refuses to "abandon
the self to language."[5] He denies the Scene of Writing (*écriture*).
"A poetic 'text,' as I interpret it, is not a gathering of signs on
a page, but is a psychic battlefield upon which authentic forces
struggle for the only victory worth winning, the divinating
triumph over oblivion . . ." (*PR*, 2). The indomitable will to
overcome death and time, to survive belatedness and gain immortality—to be canonized in the tradition—underlies the real
project of the strong poet. This will, repressed from the moment
of the primal fixation of influence, defends itself against extinction,
deadening influence, and loss of poetic power through revisionary
acts of figuration—through rhetorical troping. Rhetoric plays a
fundamental role in Bloom's literary theory, just as it does in
White's historiography. For Bloom rhetoric *serves* the poetic will.
Insistently, he denies the theories of language proffered by Lacan
and Derrida, and he specifically refuses the *rhetoricity* of de Man
and Miller. Like Spanos, he holds onto the "subject," though his
post-Freudian "subject" ultimately gazes upon us as embattled
rags on a stick, rivaling a Giacometti figure in severity of di-
minishment. Although Bloom is a master analyst of intertextuality,
he is a heroic refuser of textuality.

Actually, Bloom employs a limited theory of textuality. Like
Heidegger's *Being*, his *will* undergoes textualization, which becomes most evident in his account of rhetorical processes of
"psychic defense." We shall consider this legerdemain later. For
now "Poems are not psyches, nor things, nor are they renewable
archetypes in a verbal universe, nor are they architectonic units
of balanced stress. They are defensive processes in constant
change, which is to say that poems themselves are *acts of reading*"
(*PR*, 25–26). In our view, Bloom's poetics never completely escapes one or another paradigm or figure of textuality. His celebration of an iron-willed stickman, present behind every (inter)text,
is more stubborn than persuasive. The humanist dies hard. But
the (inter)text survives.

Bloom admits his logocentrism. His poet's "will to poetic
power," the dynamo that drives the psyche, functions as a "transcendental signifier" that *centers* the wandering significations of
the text. The context of this will is the inescapable historical in-

tertext. Like White, Bloom insists on a version of the creative will-to-power. To the extent that the newly formed poetic *id* serves as a repository of literary tradition, which undergoes creative destructions in a Heideggerian fashion, Bloom resembles Foucault: he explores surface disorders and distortions—discontinuities—smelted in the Unconscious, the vault of effective history. However, Bloom's successful strong poet possesses a degree of autonomy and freedom—Emersonian self-reliance—unmatched in other poststructuralist theories of tradition and the individual talent. The "deconstructed" self, however hollowed out by history and the Unconscious, finally retains a backbone and an aggressive posture. Without these rare virtues—reserved for the relentless and fit few, the strong—tradition would stifle and choke all creative life.

What is tradition? "Out of the strong comes forth strength, even if not sweetness, and when strength has imposed itself long enough, then we learn to call it tradition, whether we like it or not" (*MM*, 200). What value has tradition? "It is now valuable precisely because it partly blocks, because it stifles the weak, because it represses even the strong" (*MM*, 29).

2

To protect himself in relation to an anxiety-producing precursor, a latecomer poet has recourse, most often unconsciously, to a panoply of "psychic defenses." Recasting Anna Freud's ten into six, Bloom maps a pattern of such *defenses*, which regularly show up in post-Enlightenment poems in a specified manner, but this order "may" be juggled: reaction formation; turning against the self or masochistic reversal; undoing, isolation, and/or regression; repression; sublimation; and introjection and projection. These traditional modes of defense, which we defer defining, appear in poems as specific *tropes*. A trope embodies a defense. Bloom correlates six figural processes with his six defenses: irony; synecdoche; metonymy; hyperbole/litotes; metaphor; and metalepsis. If we read or write a poem, the defenses, incorporated in figural patterns, appear for us as *images*. Such images show particular configurations (and they correlate with the six defenses and tropes): images of presence and absence; part for whole or whole for part; fullness and emptiness; high and low; inside and outside; and early and late. Putting this information together, we find that the ephebe's first psychic defense of "reaction-formation" comes forth as a trope of irony in images of presence and absence. The five other stages also combine the specified defenses, tropes, and images into single processes of revision. Bloom assigns memorable names to each of his six revisionary ratios (relations): *clinamen, tessera, kenosis, daemonization, askesis,* and *apophrades.* Clinamen suggests a process of "swerving" from the precursor; tessera intimates a revisionary movement of "completion" of the precursor; kenosis indicates an "emptying" of the self in relation to the precursor; daemonization implies the extraction, countering, and celebration of an "alien," though present, element in the precursor; askesis denotes an effort of "self-purgation" aimed at attaining a sacred solitude against the precursor; and, finally, apophrades depicts an uncanny "return" of the precursor, reminiscent of the flooded apprenticeship, yet now the mature latecomer seems, strangely enough, the true author of the precursor's characteristic works.

What claims does Bloom make for this *Map of Misprision*?

To begin with, he asserts and demonstrates that many of the best strong poems written over the past two centuries follow the six phases of the Map. The Romantic *crisis-poem,* sometimes also labeled the "Wordsworthian poem," emerges as the dominant lyric form or poetic genre of the post-Enlightenment epoch. Moreover, the Map offers a full-blown theory of poetry—a psychopoetics—that accounts for the psychological origins as well as the ends of Romantic lyric poetry. In constructing the Map, Bloom practices an eccentric brand of literary history, predicated firmly on a theory of intertextuality. In addition to his poetics of the lyric and his literary history of the post-Enlightenment era, Bloom offers in his Map a hermeneutic method. Like J. Hillis Miller and many other Americans, he often insists that he is primarily a "practical critic." The first words of *A Map of Misreading* are: "This book offers instruction in the practical criticism of poetry, in how to read a poem, on the basis of the theory of poetry . . ." (p. 3). The opening paragraph of *The Anxiety of Influence* declares two aims: to de-idealize the relations between poets and "to provide a poetics that will foster a more adequate practical criticism."[6] The Map teaches one how to read a poem; it is meant as a useful hermeneutic. Although he never develops the notion, Bloom sometimes hints that the Map also characterizes the unacknowledged psychological operations at work in acts of critical reading. The implication is that critical interpretation itself is a psychical process involving fixations, repressions, and defenses as well as revisionary tropes and images of a chartable sort. A poetician and practical critic, Bloom exhibits little sustained interest in such metacriticism. Like Barthes' typology of readers, Bloom's implied Map of Critical Misreading is a tantalizing throwaway.

A complete Bloomian reading of a poem, of its images, figures, psychological processes and historical relations, employs the Map to get at the last phase of the Scene of Instruction—the stage of revision. Five other rungs on the ladder of interpretation remain. With his devotion to *strong* poems and poets only, Bloom has abjured developing further his hermeneutic machine. He focuses on the sixth stage. One can imagine intricate refinements, which would aid in analyzing, among other things, cases of arrested development. Presumably, one could take a weak poem and pinpoint its stage of failure. And one might be able to characterize schools and periods of literary history by their practice of a dominant ratio. Poets of mid-eighteenth-century sensibility, for example, favor hyperbole—*daemonization*. To practice such criticism would be to employ a diachronic rhetoric, which Bloom has lately started to do.

Not until his essay "Poetic Crossing" (1977), which appeared just after the tetralogy, did Bloom fully refine his *dialectic of revisionism*, which had always been part of the Map of Misprision.[7] Basically, Bloom reduces his Map to three dialectical movements or tiered processual planes: (1) clinamen ↔ tessera; (2) kenosis ↔ daemonization; and (3) askesis ↔ apophrades. (In theory, these processes can move either way.) Three times the strong latecomer contracts or withdraws himself, experiencing a "negative moment," followed by a "crossing" over into expansive acts of "positive" self-representation. Transgression of a taboo leads to transcendence. A whole set of structural homologies emerges in the Map. For example, irony, metonymy, and metaphor oppose synecdoche, hyperbole, and metalepsis. In other words, two dominant classes of tropes exist: (1) *tropes of action*, which exhibit a language of need and powerlessness; and (2) *tropes of desire*, which display a language of possession and power. The first group of figures produces and demonstrates a lack in language or in the self, revealing a dearth of meaning; the second class of figures strengthens language and the self, creating excess of meaning. Without belaboring all the refinements that accompany the dialectic of revisionism, we can see that the production of poetic meaning results, in Bloom's view, from a volatile substituting process, which is inherently liminal and transgressive. Moving through repressive limitations to representations or through sublimating representations to limitations, the belated poet's images create meaning in disruptive tropes of expansion and contraction and in assertive and stifled acts of defense. Meaning emerges out of an inconstant relation between language and psyche, or rhetoric and will, or writing and voice or the Other and the self. In opposition to deconstruction, Bloom aims to save the human psyche, will, voice, and self from extinction by language, rhetoric, writing, and the Other. His theory of meaning rests somewhere between Heidegger's *aletheia* and Derrida's *dissemination*. On the one hand, poetic meaning unfolds states of being through temporal and figural processes of realization; on the other hand, meaning is produced in an unstable play of figural substitutions or crossings. The dialectic of revisionism, a crucial element in the Map of Misprision, accounts for both the production and the sliding of fickle meaning across the poetic text.

Significantly, the dialectic of revisionism, the true dynamic of Bloom's Map, introduces discontinuity and difference into the poetic text and its hermeneutic deciphering. Each repetition of contraction and of expansion and each new substitution or crossing opens a space for difference. From the initial primal identification of ephebe and precursor in *election*-love up to the final analogous identification in the grand revision of *apophrades*, from start to finish, Bloom monumentalizes difference through his stratified paradigm of finely differentiated ratios. The effect of such difference is to enforce and perhaps authorize his most fundamental concept—*misprision*.

When he sketches his project at the outset of the tetralogy, Bloom celebrates deviation and discontinuity, deliberate error and distortion—all forms of difference that characterize the theory of misprision and its dialectic of revisionism:

> *Poetic Influence—when it involves two strong, authentic poets,—always proceeds by a misreading of the prior poet, an act of creative correction that is actually and necessarily a misinterpretation. The history of fruitful poetic influence, which is to say the main tradition of Western poetry since the Renaissance, is a history of anxiety and self-saving caricature, of distortion, of perverse, wilful revisionism without which modern poetry as such could not exist.* (AI, 30)

Misprision (meaning mistaking, misreading, and misinterpreting), both necessary and inescapable, occurs between one poet and another and between a critic and a text because, essentially, exact repetition or identification is impossible and because, quintessentially, identity is slavery and death; difference is freedom and vitality. The dialectic of revisionism, borrowed from late Kabbalistic theory, seeks to map the disruptive play of difference in intra- and inter-poetic relations. It's success is a measured failure, as Bloom realized early: "The six revisionary movements that I will trace in the strong poet's life-cycle could as well be more, and could take quite different names than those I have employed" (*AI*, 10–11). Once let loose, there is no secure limit to the play of difference, nor any comprehensive representation of such force, which Derrida's essay on *differance* so tortuously demonstrates.

Bloom acknowledges three levels of misprision. The latecomer misreads the precursor; the critic misinterprets the text; and the poet mistakes his own poem. On each level there are various forms of misprision. Bloom charts six varieties on the first level with his Map. The implication is that these six apply on the other levels as well. "Poets' misinterpretations or poems are more drastic than critics' misinterpretations or criticism, but this is only a difference in degree and not at all in kind. There are no interpretations but only misinterpretations . . ." (*AI*, 94–95). To understand the theory of misprision is to learn that there is only always misreading. This formulation derives initially from de Man, which we shall discuss in Part III. Bloom adopts this notion with some reluctance and with limitations. "I do not agree wholly with de Man that reading is impossible, but I acknowledge how very difficult it is to read a poem properly, which is what I have meant by my much-attacked critical trope of 'misreading' or 'misprision.' With three layers of troping perpetually confronting us, the task of restituting meaning or of healing a wounded rhetoricity is a daunting one. Yet it can and must be attempted" (*D&C*, 16). Published in 1979 in the Yale manifesto on deconstruction, this statement reveals Bloom's conservatism. As a hermeneutic, his Map of Misprision prescribes interpretive procedures designed to restore meaning. He denies the radical textuality of de Man's rhetoricity. Bloom's proclamation, "Yet it can and must be attempted," declaimed in heroic tones reminiscent of Milton's Satan, who is much beloved by Bloom, sounds more stubborn than assured. Like White, Bloom will not apologize.

On the safe side of the abyss of misreading, the theory of misprision deliberately and perhaps desperately sets limits to the dissemination of poetic meaning. Meaning, in Bloom's work, is ultimately restored in disruptive and tattered intertextual forms. Most admired by Bloom are prize passages of daemonization where rare moments of Romantic sublime and countersublime sometimes present instances of meaningful passion and beauty against the grim background of tradition. Bloom enjoys most a particular phase of meaning.

3

When Bloom talks about any (inter)text, he has five conceptual languages at his disposal: the languages of psychological defense, rhetorical figure, poetic imagery, revisionary ratio, and dialectic of movement (revisionism). In any given instance, he may read an (inter)poem or (inter)passage in one or more of these modes, though, to be sure, he intends to exhaust all possibilities. Occasionally, Bloom employs the language of the Scene of Instruction, which affords him a sixth option for critical reading. With Bloom most everything comes in sixes. With White it's fours.

Generally speaking, Bloom uses his typology, the Map of Misprision, to ponder the intricacies of poetics, to practice hermeneutic decoding, to propound elements for his history of genre (the post-Enlightenment crisis-lyric) and sometimes to produce broader literary history. As he develops his basic notions, he often mulls over aspects of the theories of intertextuality, misreading, and textuality, using insights from psychoanalysis, Kabbalistic and Gnostic hermeneutics, and classical rhetoric. Let us examine his conceptualization of (inter)textuality.

Since he regards every text as inherently an intertext and every poet as inescapably influenced by precursors (hence the "inter-poet"), Bloom is fundamentally a historical critic. But he is a *literary* historian. Rarely, if ever, does he mention economic, political, religious, cultural, or other nonliterary events or histories. For Bloom literary history is primarily a drama of clashing strong personalities. An (inter)poem is a psychic battleground but not an Armageddon of impersonal heterogeneous *traces*. Intertextuality is limited and psychologized.

Not surprisingly, Bloom aims to be a strong critic. He invents his own monolithic system; and he defines himself against strong contemporary critics, especially Jacques Derrida and Paul de Man. He admires Kenneth Burke and Geoffrey Hartman. One finds in Bloom as critic moments of anxiety, instances of repression, and cases of revision. This is particularly true on the crucial matter of *textuality—which in Bloom is an aspect of the mapped concept of intertextuality*.

Bloom's Scene of Instruction presents a primal moment of fixation and repression—the moment of the origin of intertextuality. This spot of time precedes the creation of any complete text. The ground of "textuality" is intertextuality. The Map of Misprision charts textual patterns and operations in adamant relation to precursor intertexts. All talk of defense, trope, image, ratio, dialectical movement, and misprision involves "texts" with intertexts. A "text" is a psychological production. An affair of two or more people. Not a simple play of tropes. On this site tropes and images, whose play is charted through specific ratios and movements of misprision, issue out of the fixated and repressed psyche as it defends itself against the influence of the Other. To succeed, the anxious latecomer must possess an inordinately strong will-to-divination; he must hunger after independence and immortality.

(Rhetoric is only one of his means.) His "text" is necessarily an intertext.

The poetic self as seen by Bloom is Promethean. Behind every belated (inter)text resides an embattled stronger-than-average subject. As he undergoes the anxieties of influence and as he operates his defenses—as he refuses or revises literary history—the hero begins to thin out and lose parts of himself. Typically, Bloom's poet-hero appears destined for costly defeat or, at best, questionable victory. Crack-up and mutilation are often the wages of success. Silence is the price of failure. The successful self of the Romantic poet, in Bloom's history, is Satanic in strength of will and in eventual fate: he fades and falls from youthful bright glory to darkening and inglorious vengeful maturity. Diminished thing, stick-man of indomitable will, the modern poet, in the end, seems another version of the deconstructed subject. Done in by psychic battle instead of lawless and unfaithful language. But done in. This ultimate portrayal is meant, no doubt, to comfort us. Stubborn, the poetic self, in Bloom's account, chooses destruction by fierce struggle with the invulnerable Other rather than deconstruction by the insistent forces of decentering rhetoric.

In discussions of defenses, tropes, images, ratios, dialectical movements, and misprisions, defenses usually come first. That is to say, psychic events precede linguistic and all other operations. The psyche or its will-to-power is the *center* of the text. Bloom offers an expressive, not a textual or mimetic, theory of poetry. (When "mimetic" elements appear, they result from revisions of precursor-texts.) With the idea that a defense may be structured like a trope, Bloom is quite comfortable, as his "correlations" of defenses and tropes show. He holds no commerce, however, with the notion that a defense is structured *by* a trope. To accept this formulation would be to accept a textual theory of poetry.

Yet Bloom hedges on the crucial question of priority. Which comes first—the trope or the psychic defense?

An antithetical practical criticism must begin with the analogical principle that tropes and defenses are interchangeable when they appear *in poems*, where after all both appear only as images. What I have called "revisionary ratios" are tropes and psychic defenses, both and either, and are manifested in poetic imagery. A rhetorical critic can regard a defense as a concealed trope. A psychoanalytic interpreter can regard a trope as a concealed defense. An antithetical critic will learn to use both in turn, relying upon the substitution of analogues as being one with the poetic process itself.

Arbitrarily, I will begin with defenses, and then pass on to tropes. . . .

(*MM*, 88–89)

Once again, it hardly matters whether one calls a defense a concealed trope or a trope a concealed defense, for this kind of concealment *is* poetry. (*MM*, 179)

But eventually Freud was to assert that "the theory of the drives is so to say our mythology. Drives are mythical entities, magnificent in their indefiniteness." To this audacity of the Founder I would add that defenses are no less mythological. Like tropes, defenses are turning-operations, and in language tropes and defenses crowd together in the entity rather obscurely called poetic images. Images are ratios between what is uttered and what, somehow, is intended. . . . (*D&C*, 20)

Engaged in practical criticism, Bloom confronts imagery. While this poetic material crowds together psychic defenses and rhetorical figures, it is essentially the imagery—the phenomena of the text—that a reading critic comes upon and cares about. It makes little practical difference whether a critic interprets images as defenses or as tropes. Either way is fine. A trope is a defense; a defense is a trope. It's all the same. (The "defense," in any case, is a myth.) Only in imagery can a defense or trope come forth. Bloom undermines his psychopoetics.

In the name of "practical criticism," Bloom subverts the priority of defense over trope. He promotes "phenomenological" notions that the trope and defense are coeval, that surface imagery is most important, and that the poet's intent directs the poetic and interpretive enterprises. Intentionality, however central, is yet mysterious. "Images are ratios between what is uttered and what, *somehow*, is intended. . . ." Behind the (inter)text lies the intentional voice of the poet. So it is that for Bloom the intending subject survives, even though his intentions, unconscious and defensive, Promethean and Satanic, are evasive exercises in vengeance and failure. (Inter)texts are intentional.

4

Like other leading contemporary American literary critics, Bloom seems a besieged phenomenologist. He perhaps shares this uncertain status with Hartman and Spanos. Former phenomenologists, de Man, Miller, and Riddel, no doubt, appear to have gone too far in championing deconstruction. What finally is at issue between these groups? What are the impasses? With the theories of the subject, intentionality and textuality. Where can *compromise* be effected? Partly with intertextuality, (mis)reading, and meaning. But what about history?

Bloom, Hartman, and Spanos practice literary history, whereas de Man, Miller, and Riddel, who have often seemed to avoid such practice, are only lately working in this direction. Still, all these critics, early or late, "deconstructors" or deconstructors, deal with *literary* history. The wider social and cultural contexts, taken up by Michel Foucault, Fredric Jameson, and Edward Said, for instance, remain mostly unexplored—which explains why Marxist theoreticians (cultural historians), in particular, regularly oppose deconstruction. They are not alone. Deconstruction creates the impression that the literary text lies outside, beyond or before historical culture. Or that it subsumes or textualizes culture in poetic language, which cannot be crossed over. As a hedonism of the disseminated text, as self-indulgent and licentious practical criticism deconstruction appears to be just another decadent version of always narrow formalism. (We shall not soon hear the end of all manner and variety of this most basic insight.) Ultimately, deconstruction must figure in history. With its cause and effect and narrative chronicle, history explains and limits, represents and restricts: it still lies before deconstruction.

Celebrated as the leading deconstructive historian of literature, Bloom offers little enough of history or hope to the remaining humanists among us:

Emerson denied that there was any history; there was only biography, he said. I adapt this to saying that *there is no literary history,* but that while *there is biography, and only biography,* a truly literary biography is largely a history of the defensive misreadings of one poet by another poet.[8]

Next to Foucault's poststructuralist theory of history, predicated on the "death of the subject," Bloom's odd version of the "great man theory," based on the Satanic strength and vitality of the subjected poet, remains within the ancient humanist tradition—but near its end.

The Discourse of History

In attempting to uncover the deepest strata of Western culture, I am restoring to our silent and apparently immobile soil its rifts, its instability, its flaws; and it is the same ground that is once more stirring under our feet.[9]

The traditional devices for constructing a comprehensive view of history and for retracing the past as a patient and continuous development must be systematically dismantled. . . . History becomes "effective" to the degree that it introduces discontinuity into our very being. . . .[10]

—Michel Foucault

Throughout the 1960s and 1970s Michel Foucault's extensive enterprise appears singularly dedicated to uncovering the deepest strata of post-Renaissance Western culture. Continuously, he reveals the rifts and instabilities that crisscross and carve up our historical discourse. This operation begins in earnest with *Madness and Civilization: A History of Insanity in the Age of Reason* (1961) and *The Birth of the Clinic: An Archaeology of Medical Perception* (1963), reaches a particularly intense manifestation in *The Order of Things: An Archaeology of the Human Sciences* (1966), and broadens out energetically in *I, Pierre Rivière . . .* (1973), *Discipline and Punish: The Birth of the Prison* (1975), and *The History of Sexuality*, vol. 1 (1976). Investigating the discourses of psychiatry, medicine, the human sciences, penology, and sexology, Foucault dismantles traditional historiography and single-mindedly introduces *discontinuity* and *difference* into History. He publishes systematic theoretical accounts of his "differential historiography" in *The Archaeology of Knowledge* (1969) and "The Discourse on Language" (1971). Labeled a structuralist in the early days, Foucault ever more stridently refuses structuralist ways, just as he regularly does with all manner of phenomenology and hermeneutics. Something of a poststructuralist, though by no means a card-carrying deconstructor, Foucault typically emphasizes accidents, not universal rules; surfaces, not depths; multiplicities, not unities; flaws, not foundations; and differences, not identities. Nevertheless, these distinctions become exceedingly hard to maintain when one is lost in the intricacies of a Foucault text. The impression prevails that he seeks depths, rules, and foundations. Ultimately, Foucault produces forms of order as disorder—not instances of disorder as order. But the considerable time spent in articulating "forms of order" creates an enduring impression of structuralism—even though all orders undergo final subversion. Foucault, as we shall see, appears a most structuralist poststructuralist in his constructions of history.

I

The heart of Foucault's historical concern is the transition from classical age to nineteenth-century culture. In all of his works a similar narrative framework emerges: the relatively open and free-wheeling world of the sixteenth century gives way, in turn, to the classical age and then the densely regulated nineteenth century. (In our own time another momentous mutation seems underway.) To dramatize epochal shifts, Foucault painstakingly details the configurations of each era. Significantly, the *epistémè* of each period, its epistemological field, is presentable only in terms of specific disciplines and their discursive practices. Thus Foucault undertakes individual studies of psychiatry, clinical medicine, the human sciences, penology, and sexology. Instead of broad and continuous (period) histories, Foucault offers fragments from an era. He denies the possibility of traditional forms of history: there can be no "progress of reason," "spirit of the age," "unity of assumptions," or "dominant world view." There are only discontinuous fields of discourse. Some follow the same pattern and others don't. For example, the histories of early nineteenth-century mathematics, biology, and psychopathology constitute three very different manifestations of historical formation. In Foucault's theory, the *epistémè* appears highly specified, being limited to certain historical phases of disciplines; yet in his practice, the *epistémè* often emerges as the overall epistemological understructure of an entire era. One imagines that the more discontinuous and fragmented the *epistémè*—the more differentiated it is—the closer it approaches Foucault's singular inspiration and enterprise.

Foucault situates most forms of cultural history within the concept of *discourse*. Everywhere he looks, he turns up discourse. When he examines the discourses of diciplines, he seeks to discover the *rules* that form their specific configurations. He is not interested in who speaks, nor in what linguistic laws determine speech. He wants to know which particular objects and concepts appear in discourse and what rules render them possible. In the discourse of an *epistémè* some things and theories take shape, subsist, change, and disappear—all according to definable rules. Relentlessly, Foucault collects and analyzes the rules of formation and transformation of such elements within specific discursive fields. History is the descriptive analysis of "regulated changes" in discourses.

In any era certain matters and topics are not tolerated in discursive practice. Both stipulated and secret, rules of exclusion systematically control and delimit discourse. Some words, for example, are forbidden. The writings of madmen and the language of falsity or error may be suppressed. Frequently, discourse is submitted to rigorous interpretation or commentary and associated closely with an individual author or stance. These practices set limitations, silent safeguards, to discourse. In the field of medicine or of biology or of law, for example, a speaker must be "qualified" to talk; he has to belong to a community of scholarship; and he is required to possess a prescribed body of knowledge (doctrine). Despite the benefits of this system, it operates to constrain discourse; it establishes limits and regularities. Nevertheless, Western culture conceptualizes discourse as an ideal repository of truth freely created through rigorous rationality in the interest of knowledge. The exchange of knowledge, proffered by such discourse, occurs in a seemingly transparent operation of reading that penetrates lucid writing to arrive at substantial thinking. The thinking subject collects the truths or facts that pre-exist in the world and packages them or uncovers them in discourse. Discourse itself, its materiality and free play, is nullified. When applied to discourse, the various rules and practices of exclusion, in fact, designate systematically who may speak, what may be spoken, and how it is to be said; in addition, they prescribe what is true and what false, what is reasonable and what foolish, and what is meant and what not. Finally, they work to deny the material existence of discourse itself.[11]

Writing history, Foucault delineates the particular configurations of such exclusionary rules as they emerge, stand, and shift
within a single discipline, discursive practice, or field of knowledge (*connaissance*). When he applies this procedure to groups of
disciplines—the human sciences, for instance—he discovers homologous as well as discontinuous formations and transformations
of such rules. As they surface and produce an outline of an overall
epistemic structure, the rules take on unexpected status: they seem
less at the disposal of the historical individuals who apparently
deployed them than a set of forces determining and perhaps dom-
inating the thinking, practice, and knowledge of an era (*savoir*).
Eluding the consciousness and formulation of any historical individual, the rules, widely operative across the discourses of disciplines, form a *positive Unconscious* of knowledge. Foucault aims
to get at this highly stratified site.

In the formation of individual discourses, rules emerge to define
objects proper to the field, to construct fundamental concepts,
and to build effective theories. This group of rules for discursive
practice constitutes the system of *formation*, which is subject to
various historical thresholds. Over a period of time a discipline
delimits a field of objects, defines legitimate perspectives, and fixes
norms for the production of conceptual elements. Accordingly,
discursive practices establish shifting historical prescriptions to
designate choices and exclusions. Foucault describes four *thresholds*
in the emergence of a discursive practice: the thresholds of posi-
tivity, epistemologization, scientificity, and formalization (*AK*,
186–87). Essentially, these phases mark out the passage of a discipline from dawning individualization and autonomy to mature
institutionalization. Constructing history, Foucault traces the
unique distributions in time of these thresholds. A discourse need
not move successfully through all phases, nor do contemporary
discourses necessarily follow the same chronologies. Across an era
a set of different discourses may exhibit discontinuous and fractured histories of formation. (As ideal models, therefore, the
"regular interval," the "evolutionary phase," or the "stage of
maturation" fail to account for the overall formation of historical
discourse.) Not merely ways of creating regulated discourse,
emergent disciplines produce patterns of behavior, technical proc-

esses, institutional procedures, pedagogical forms, and modes of transmission. As they manifest an expanding will-to-knowledge, which exceeds any single agent or author, each discursive practice follows a specific and ever more insistent process of formation.

Statements produced within a discourse adhere to specific regularities. The volume of utterances in the discourses of an era reflect such regularities. The rules of utterance for an era, which underlie its discourses, are subject to determinable historical formations and transformations. Between what can grammatically and logically be said and what is actually said lies an entire domain of epochal discourse, which can be accounted for neither by linguistics, nor by logic, nor by antiquarian history. Foucault always focuses on this domain, which he names the *archive*. In the various discourses of a period, statements are made in accordance with specific rules and practices. Other utterances are disallowed through regulation. Systems of discursivity produce regions of discourse, which in their multiple existences exhibit unique durations. The *archive* is not a uniform or nondifferentiated volume of discourses; rather it is the highly differentiated "*general system of the formation and transformation of statements*" (*AK*, 130).

To us the *archive* appears as "Other"—as difference. It is impossible to uncover our *own* archive "since it is from within these rules that we speak, since it is that which gives to what we can say—and to itself, the object of our discourse—its modes of appearance, its forms of existence and co-existence, its system of accumulation, historicity, and disappearance" (*AK*, 130). When we successfully examine the archive of another era, we indirectly testify to our own distance and difference and implicitly deny any uniform teleological progress of ascent or simple genetic line of descent in the realm of history. We confirm discontinuity and difference. As our epigraph suggests, "History becomes 'effective' to the degree that it introduces discontinuity into our very being. . . ." The theory of the *archive* voids notions of origin and destiny; it celebrates chance and discontinuity. In the end, it situates and names "the" positive Unconscious of cultural knowledge and history.

In employing the special concept *transformation*, Foucault deliberately suspends any commitment to traditional models of historicity. Whether history is circular, cumulative, progressive, or fluctuating depends ultimately on certain expectations of change and causality, that is, on notions of continuity or regularity. In place of cause and change, Foucault offers accounts of mutations and derivations, which occur within and across particular discursive practices, on different specified levels, through individual moments of succession and in various modes of connection. In short, Foucault substitutes analyses of different types of transformation for all abstract models of change and cause. He sets aside conventional forms of continuity and stresses the intensities of difference. In a telling essay, published in the late 1960s, Foucault outlines three classes of transformation.[12] (1) *Derivations* (*intradiscursive dependencies*): changes by deduction or implication, by generalization, by limitation, by passing to the complementary, by passing to the other term of an alternative, by permutation of elements, by exclusion or inclusion. (2) *Mutations* (*interdiscursive dependencies*): displacement of boundaries defining the field of objects, alteration of role and position of the speaking subject, modification of language's function with respect to objects, institution of new forms of social circulation, and localization of discourse. (3) *Redistributions* (*extradiscursive dependencies*): reversal in hierarchical order, change in directing role, displacement in function. Although in outline only, this typology of *transformation* indicates the number and types of "changes" Foucault assigns to different states of discourse, suggesting both his wide-ranging deployment of discontinuities and his use of polymorphous correlations in place of simple or complex causality. Amidst the objects, operations, and concepts of discursive formations and transformations there occurs a disruptive and multileveled play of dependencies. "History is the descriptive analysis and the theory of these transformations" ("HDD," 233). Thus the archive emerges as an ever-shifting, stratified, yet regulated configuration of cultural knowledge.

2

What is history? An immense panoply of heterogeneous discursive practices. What is a discursive practice? A set of rules and procedures for the formation and transformation of writing and thinking within a limited field of inquiry. How are such rules mani-

THE (INTER)TEXUALIZATION OF CONTEXT   149

fested? Through systems of exclusion and inclusion operative in the discourses of cultural disciplines. What are these disciplines? Individual epistemological fields, which, when taken together, constitute something like culture's positive Unconscious—its archive. Where do we discover the archive? In the overall or general system of rules for the formation and transformation of all discourse. In view of the dominance of such rules, how does change ever occur? Through chance, which appears to us as discontinuous transformation. Is the archive valid for all history? Always an unstable collection of heterogeneous and stratified regularities, the archive of an era, which can be reconstructed through descriptive analysis, is valid for a particular, limited, brief period of time; each era produces different durations for the archive.

This reductive rehearsal, this catechism, stages Foucault's idea of history in order to highlight its obvious textuality. In Foucault's account, evidently nothing precedes discourse and nothing escapes it. Yet, strictly speaking, some things are nondiscursive. For example, the nondiscursive aspects of clinical medicine would include institutions, social relations, and economic and political circumstances. If there exists any *pre*discursive domain, it is essential silence. Discourse is a practice we impose upon things. These things come to us in discourse. Only in some imaginary realm can they exist in a pure state free of discourse. One does not escape the textuality of discourse. Even the nondiscursive domain is an effect of discursive practices.

Significantly, the various theories of textuality usually associated with deconstructors and that propounded by Foucault diverge on the crucial matter of context. Imagine a writer producing a discourse: she necessarily operates within the confines of the archive. Certain definable historical regularities channel her text. In short, an entire system of cultural rules determine the production, distribution, and consumption of the discourse. Writing is not a private or free, creative exercise of the linguistic signifier; rather it activates a complex historical archive that effectively delimits the flight of the signifier. The archival limit to the free play of the sumptuous signifier works at the level of a culture's base, not the superstructure. In its writing and in its reading, the text encounters historical constraints. (To be sure, these barriers may show up as "natural," "indirect," "neutral," or "acceptable." Or they may remain "invisible.") To produce or to analyze a text is necessarily to situate it within a historical or archival network. While the deconstructor's signifier, separated from any transcendental signification or position, floats free and thereby decenters the logocentric enclosure, Foucault's signifier functions within the regulated exchanges of the *epistémè*. In other words, Foucault exercises a limiting theory of the signifier and text, providing discourse with a determinable, though highly differentiated and reticulated, historical context.[13]

For Foucault modes of context emerge in (as) discourse. Each single text appears amidst an archival reticulum. Thus the theory of discourse carries along with it a fully articulated theory of intertextuality: the system of rules regulating the *epistémè* determines the cultural context of any particular discourse. In Foucault's version of intertextuality, it is not the grammatical or tropological structure of language, nor the historically constituted unabridged contemporary lexicon, nor the unchartable mass of cultural debris embodied in language which constitute irreducible intertextuality; rather it is a *definable*, systematically abridged paradigm—a set of prescribed epistemic structures—that produces an inevitable and inescapable archival network. With Foucault, the context of the discourse, the unconscious intertext, is conjured up only through painstaking descriptive excavation of the archive. In place of the traditional search for sources, the conventional attribution of connecting allusions, or the antiquarian demonstration of influences, Foucault practices an archaeological deployment of systematic rules of formation and transformation that uncovers powerful and unavoidable structural modalities of context. The intertextual materials, which he turns up, are determining elements in the discourse rather than surface aesthetic effects or localized ornaments of an era's style. Even the nondiscursive elements, such as technical processes, pedagogical forms, and institutional procedures, come about as a result of discursive practices.

It is in his method of analysis, which he early names *archaeology* and later renames *genealogy*, that Foucault's project for excavating the archive comes to realization. Such excavation avoids efforts at discovery and purification, practicing instead a set of procedures for rearrangement of selected records, yet not for purposes of totalized reconstructions, but for reporting the rules of formation and transformation that allowed the record as such to emerge. Where conventional history of ideas employs the traditional master concepts of "genesis," "continuity," and "totalization" and where it fixes on the unified discourse of the "author," the "book," or the "oeuvre," archaeology analyzes the discursive rules of formation, exclusion, and transformation, and it examines the discontinuities in specified disciplines and in the sets of disciplines constituting a culture's archive (*AK*, 135–40). When it studies discourse, archaeology does not seek a hidden or overt "intention," "will," or "meaning" in or behind the discourse; it does not refer to a "subject," "mind," or "thought" that evidently gave rise to discourse; nor does it "formalize" laws of textual construction or "interpret" patterns of thematic development. In eschewing forms of intentionality, formalization, and interpretation, archaeology consciously skirts phenomenology, structuralism, and hermeneutics. Its object of analysis is not the author, the linguistic code, the reader, or the individual text, but the limited set of texts constituting the regulated discourse of a discipline. Expanding its analysis, it correlates different disciplinary discourses so as to articulate the general system of rules governing the discursive practices of an era.

To put matters another way, archaeology works toward answering a series of fundamental questions. What is it possible to speak of? What terms are destined to disappear? Which terms enter into current practice? Which ones are censured or repressed? Which ones are considered valid and which questionable? Which are eventually abandoned and which revived? What relations exist between present and past terms or foreign and native ones? What transformations are imposed on terms? Which individuals, groups, or classes have access to such discourse? How are their relations institutionalized? How does any struggle over a discourse operate? Throughout this inquiry, archaeology seeks to describe the rules in a given period and a particular society which define the limits and forms of expressibility, conservation, memory, reactivation, and appropriation. In constructing its history of discourse, archaeology isolates the fact and manner of appearance of discourses; it examines the field where they coexist, prevail, and disappear; and it investigates the transformations enacted there ("HDD," 233–35).

Archaeology carries out a negative as well as a positive program. In its critical aspect, it resembles deconstruction. Deploying *discontinuity* as a methodological wedge, archaeology shows one aspect of its negative operation. Essentially, discontinuity subverts older notions and theories of history. As it differentiates and produces levels of analysis, it foregrounds numerous breaks and limits as they erupt in historical processes and movements. In short, it begets excessive fragmentation in both the object and method of analysis. Because *discourse* per se is an inherently discontinuous activity, archaeology regards *discontinuity* as a positive element rather than some external threat or failure requiring reduction or erasure. Thus archaeology actively courts discontinuity: history becomes effective to the degree that it introduces discontinuity into our very being. As archaeologist, Foucault attempts to restore to the stable ground of Western culture its rifts, instabilities, and flaws. In so doing, he sets our own contemporary grounds trembling. Systematically, he dismantles the traditional devices that construct a comprehensive view of history and that retrace the past as a continuous development. The main conceptual weapon in the assault is *discontinuity*.

At the outset of *The Archaeology of Knowledge*, Foucault situates his enterprise amid similar projects in contemporary psychoanalysis, linguistics, and anthroplogy—all of which unleash *discontinuity* into their respective realms of discourse. Just as these disciplines have *decentered* the "subject" in relation to the laws of his desire, the forms of his language, and the rules of his actions and myths—demonstrating that man cannot explain his sexuality or Unconscious, his system of language, nor the patternings of his fictions or deeds—so archaeology decenters "man" in relation to the (unacknowledged) regularities and discontinuities of his history, showing that man is unable to account for the formation and transformation of his discourse—the operative rules of the *epistémè*. The decentering strategies of archaeology, like those of related contemporary disciplines, deliberately carry forward a critical effort at dislodging "consciousness" as the founding concept and ground of all human sciences. Here Foucault differs importantly from Bloom and White.

Another device in the arsenal of archaeology is *difference*. At times Foucault depicts his general methodological practice as "differential analysis." In particular, when he sets to work the concept of *transformation* and that of *threshold*, Foucault deploys the disruptive powers inherent in difference. In portraying the *epistémè* as neither a sum of knowledge nor a unified mode of thinking but as a space of deviations, distances, and dispersions, Foucault locates his general model of culture amid an active interplay of differences. In place of traditional history, he aims "to substitute the analysis of the field of simultaneous differences (which define at a given period the possible dispersal of knowledge) and of successive differences (which define the whole of the transformations, their hierarchy, their dependence, their level). Whereas one used to relate the history of tradition and of invention, of the old and the new, of the dead and the living, of the closed and the open, of the static and of the dynamic, *I undertake to relate the history of the perpetual difference . . .*" ("HDD," 237; my italics). The theory of difference, as it operates in archaeology, organizes the very field of its practice, accounting for modes of formation, exclusion, and transformation as well as establishing stratified models of the *epistémè* and the archive. Difference underlies the theories of space and time (the simultaneous and the successive). And it directs the methods of inquiry and analysis. Finally, difference serves as a tool to destroy the organizing (dialectical) dichotomies of traditional historiography.

When he reviews Gilles Deleuze's *Différence et répétition* (1969) and *Logique du sens* (1969), Foucault offers something of a manifesto of *difference*:

The freeing of difference requires thought without contradiction, without dialectics, without negation; thought that accepts divergence; affirmative thought whose instrument is disjunction; thought of the multiple— of the nomadic and dispersed multiplicity that is not limited or confined by the constraints of similarity; thought that does not conform to a pedagogical model (the fakery of prepared answers), but that attacks insoluble problems. . . .[14]

This call for a new thought—for the thinking of *difference*—resounds in revolutionary tones reminiscent of early deconstruction. It summons up the heady days of the late 1960s and early 1970s, bringing to mind the *Tel Quel* group, the early Derrida, the born-again Barthes and the nascent Yale and *Boundary 2* groups.

3

Up till now we have not mentioned Foucault's important formulations on *knowledge* and *power*, which more and more color his entire project, including particularly his most recent uses of discourse and archive. Generally speaking, Foucault's texts open to view ever more insistently and thoroughly the negative socio-political dimensions of the archive. Actually, Foucault has always shown concern for powerless and dominated social outcasts—the madman, the patient, the criminal, the pervert—whose exclusions are systematic. It's no quirk that he is fascinated by Sade, Hölderlin, Nietzsche, Artaud, Bataille, and Roussel. When considered from the perspective of the cast-out Other, Foucault's use of the word "discipline" acquires new meaning. The "disciplines" explored by archaeology and genealogy locate and administer knowledge and *power* in numerous exchanges between words and things; disciplines regulate insane "asylums," hospitals, schools, and prisons; they limit and channel thinking; and they direct technical procedures, pedagogical modes, institutional forms, social relations, and economic processes. The disciplines produce discipline. In short, Foucault demonstrates that archival discouse expands, divides, and deploys knowledge and power in the interest of social control. The rules of discourse, particularly the exclusionary ones, direct powerful, though often unnoticed, socio-political practices.

One of the systems of exclusion, which governs Western discourse from the ancient Greeks until now, is the *will-to-knowledge*. As our history unfolds, this system grows stronger, deeper, and more implacable, invading all domains and implanting its machinery of exclusion. An anonymous and polymorphous force, the will-to-knowledge, always susceptible to transformations, selfishly seeks out knowledge for its own instrumental ends; it then summons "truth" as a mask for its operation. As effects of instinct and self-interest, *knowledge* and *truth* possess mainly practical values. Ultimately, the will-to-knowledge (or truth), lawless and violent, creates yet more knowledge and extends the ways and means of control:

The historical analysis of this rancorous will to knowledge reveals that all knowledge rests upon injustice (that there is no right, not even in the act of knowing, to truth or a foundation for truth) and that the instinct for knowledge is malicious (something murderous, opposed to the happiness of mankind). Even in the greatly expanded form it assumes today, the will to knowledge does not achieve a universal truth; man is not given an exact and serene mastery of nature. On the contrary, it ceaselessly multiplies the risks, creates dangers in every area; . . . its development is not tied to the constitution and affirmation of a free subject; rather, it creates a progressive enslavement to its instinctive violence.

("NGH," 163)

There is no knowledge without discourse. Discursive practice forms knowledge. What is knowledge? A disguise rather than a foundation for truth. Dangerous and destructive, the will-to-knowledge suppresses freedom and produces control. The project of Foucault, providing a painstaking analysis of densely regulated discourse, portrays a cultural Unconscious, which expresses not so much various libidinal desires and wishes as a lust for knowledge and its power. Mechanisms of censorship and distortion, however, manifest this drive publicly as a noble will-to-*truth*. In the stages of formation and transformation, revisionary processes insure that this nightmare always appears as dream.

Titled *La Volonté de savoir* (1976), the first volume of Foucault's *The History of Sexuality* focuses on the expanding post-Renaissance discourse of sexology, demonstrating how the "truth" of sex is actually geared to a cultural "knowledge-power" complex. In the historical formation and transformation of this discourse, Foucault perceives a growing practice of power and control, which he aims to keep as *the* topic for the subsequent five volumes of the *History*. For the first time in Foucault's enterprise we grasp how thoroughly his work isolates for view (and has increasingly done so) the operations, the machines, of *power*, which use knowledge to extend social control. The whole play of forces in this domain, when charted, presents an extremely stratified model, almost exceeding the limits of representation. Here discontinuity approaches chaos.

What is *power*? Neither acquired, seized nor shared, power is exercised from innumerable points through a shifting play of relationships, which involve all domains of human existence, including the obvious economic, sexual, intellectual, political, and emotional registers. While power comes from below, being a production of the base not the superstructure, it disseminates across social relationships and, as such, can never manifest a specific matrix. It is not an issue of rulers and ruled. Although it is a matter of calculated aims and objectives, power does not result from the choices or decisions of any particular individuals or groups. Intentional but nonsubjective, power, as manifested in and through interlocking networks and comprehensive systems, has no inventors or directors. Even when it creates resistances, they can only exist within the dispersed play of power relations. There is no escape from power—only a set of possible antithetical stances within this field: adversary, target, revolutionary, compromiser, scapegoat, etc. Like power itself, resistances are spread irregularly across the field:

Just as the network of power relations ends by forming a dense web that passes through apparatuses and institutions, without being exactly localized in them, so too the swarm of points of resistance traverses social stratifications and individual unities. And it is doubtless the strategic codification of these points of resistance that makes a revolution possible, somewhat similar to the way in which the state relies on the institutional integration of power relationships.[15]

This discontinuous force, which disseminates through archival discourse, shows itself as a special and narrow formation of *difference*. It permeates everything as a kind of founding energy, yet it creates divisions and dispersions through incessant disruptive movement. Yet, when contained and analyzed in a specific discourse, such as sexology or penology, power seems less an omnipresent atmospherics of scattered fallout, which passes through all the sources of life, than an ominous weaponry used in limited experiments. As Foucault's perspective shifts from the single discourse to the archive, apocalypse looms ever larger and nearer. Opening the eyes wide always produces such an effect. Power spreads everywhere and seeps into everything. It is productive as well as repressive. There can be no outside or above power.

Every text partakes of the play of knowledge and power. The ideal image of the great literary work, storehouse of cosmic vision and unaging prophecy, rising above and beyond its time and place of production, is a myth. If an ancient text is reactivated in a later time, it enters, once again, into a "game" of knowledge and power. The discourse of the archive is always squarely situated amid such forces at play.

Significantly, Foucault's theories of discourse and archive incorporate into an expanded concept of textuality the entire panoply of historically situated economic, social, intellectual, ideological, moral, institutional, and political thoughts and limitations that constitute and regulate the life of a society. This comprehensive cultural discourse not only determines the production of any new text, but also extends its own contemporary reign and reach through the distribution and consumption of all newly formed texts. In other words, every text emerges out of, through, and back into a complex cultural network. Inescapably and profoundly, textuality functions within the archive; that is to say, intertextuality constitutes textuality. Historical formations, which are usually thought to make up the horizon and "context" of every text, are neither belated nor exterior but prior and interior. The historical "context" allows the text as such to emerge, to be read, to be evaluated, and to be preserved. To the extent that the ordinary term "context" suggests a position outside textuality, it is misleading. "Archive," Foucault's more unfamiliar name, serves as a substitute. Rather than applying "modes of context" to a text in a practice of historical criticism, the archaeologist analyzes "modalities of the archive" as they appear and regulate his target text(s). With Foucault, then, we pass from an imaginary stable outside into the "actual" stratified interiors of intertextuality.

Subversions of Context

I

I have a dream of an intellectual who destroys evidences and universalities, who locates and points out in the inertias and constraints of the present the weak points, the openings, the lines of stress; who constantly displaces himself, not knowing exactly where he'll be nor what he'll think tomorrow. . . .[16]

—Michel Foucault

Unlike deconstructors, Foucault regularly situates discourse within a highly specified epochal enclosure, a particularized intertextual network, which, it seems, cannot be destroyed, subverted, or escaped. In effect, Foucault's intertextuality constitutes and conditions textuality; it apparently limits the free play of the signifier. The extravagances of dissemination and misreading and of infinite intertextuality (as opposed to archival or limited intertextuality) assume no shape in Foucault's archaeologies because all textual interpretations, like all productions, are historically determined and regulated. Before author, text, or reader come onto a historical scene, the epoch in its specificity, its weighty archival configuration, is set. Intertextuality functions here as carefully excavated and plotted, determining "context."

While Foucault credits in full the limiting factors and dense patterns of cultural history, he mourns over the inevitable exclusions and outcasts—everything which is suppressed or silenced. The formation of every archive engenders the production of detritus. Knowledge and power, omnivorous and relentless, produce leftovers. In response, Foucault turns angry, championing people and phenomena on the fringe. Characteristically, Michel Foucault recovers and celebrates the marginal.

Not surprisingly, Foucault dreams of an ideal intellectual who sees beyond rigid archival "evidence" and "truth," who spots constraints and resistances of power and "knowledge," who "destroys" such formations by focusing on existing weak points and present lines of breakage. Taking his opening wherever it appears, this contemporary intellectual stays mobile, ready to displace himself at any time to further the work of destruction.

When he proposes his project of *genealogy*, Foucault outlines a nomadic strategy for a "deconstructive" history. Suspicious of and antagonistic to "knowledge," "truth," "power," and "history," as traditionally determined and used, Foucault seeks to set to work in contemporary history his ideal destructive intellectual. After Nietzsche, Foucault recommends three uses of history ("NGH," 160–64):

(a) Extending traditional monumental history, we practice parodic and farcical exaggeration, pushing everything "sacred" to the carnival-esque limit of the heroic—toward the greatest imaginable men and events.

(b) Collapsing utterly the long line of conventional historical develop-ment, we become everything at once. The multiple and discontin-uous self, incapable of synthesis, uninterested in roots, empathizes with all manner of modifiable men and cultures.

(c) Foregoing the exclusive passion for "truth," we renounce the will-to-"knowledge" and its sacrifice of life. We revere a certain practice of "stupidity."

In this bizarre program, the determinations of context, the limi-tations of "history," are ruthlessly and playfully subverted. The mobile deconstructed self, assigned the status of epic wanderer and picaro, is let loose to dance upon the shards of ancient mon-uments and methods. In place of "history" is parody; in place of "truth" and "knowledge" is "stupidity." History collapses and everything becomes possible. No borders are guaranteed any-more. Context is exploded.

2

In the Yale manifesto, Derrida speculates on the nature of margins, fringes, frames, limits—*borders*—which in practice mark out and distinguish, separate and define, exclude and enclose. This inves-tigation of the *border* interrogates any and every specific deter-mination, line of division, and frame of jurisdiction. Derrida con-cludes: "No border is guaranteed, inside or out" and "Hence no context is saturable any more" ("LO," 78). He echoes here an essay from his *Marges* (1972), which earlier considered the whole question of *context*:

Every sign, linguistic or non-linguistic, spoken or written . . . can be *cited*, put between quotation marks; in so doing it can break with every given context, engendering an infinity of new contexts in a manner which is absolutely illimitable.[17]

Some years later Derrida revises this observation on context:

It would have been better and more precise to have said "engendering *and* inscribing itself," or being inscribed *in*, new contexts. For a context never creates itself *ex nihilo*. . . .[18]

The effect of this reflection is to undermine *context*, depicting it as an arbitrary imposition, a discredited (if formerly revered) universal, and, when transformed, a mobile mechanism useful for breaking up traditional hermeneutics.

The Derridean meditation on borders touches on the subject of *context*. Why? Basically, con-text implies a text and an environment, which necessarily means a difference exists between these entities. They can be delimited. The text is framed and bounded. The context limits the text. Only through a *controlled* application of *difference* can the separation text/context appear and persist. All of which means that the matter of context depends on the operation of difference and the installation of borders. Once borders are overrun and difference is set loose, context multiplies itself to infinity.

We can sketch this process, extending the example of "citation" to the broader theory of *iterability*. According to Derrida, a text or part of a text can be cited in another place at another time; in fact, such re-marking can occur in an infinity of times and places. The re-iterated material, breaking with an old context, can both alter and create numberless new contexts. There is no limit. Context is mobile, not rigid.

Iterability is not dependent on an authoring subject or intention. The activity of iteration is an inherent process of writing (*écriture* and *trace*). Like primitive path-making, it is anonymous and inevitable inscription. It inaugurates difference and subverts stabilizing context. *Iteration* describes the possibility of *writing* itself. Without it there could be no writing.

Pushed to its extreme, the Derridean notion of citation meets the broader theory of intertextuality. To employ any previously used word is to practice "citation." Since every word in our unabridged dictionaries has always undergone usage, possessing its own intertextual history, every word embodies and renews a potential for being cited on each occasion that it is pronounced or written. The appearance of a word extends and reactivates a history. Every word in a text holds this potential. The lines of intertextuality, when multiplied in correlation with citability, surpass all possibility of representation. The dream image of an immense cosmic network only hints at the proper model. Our formula is: the total history of citation (repetition) of each word multiplied by the number of words in a text, equals the quantity of intertextuality. Because we cannot determine the history of citation, our fake formula is useless. Its value lies in its suggestion of the infinity of intertextuality and of the deconstructive potential of citability. Any introduction of "context" severely reduces such boundlessness.

The idea of citation, part of a theory of *iterability*, illustrates the arbitrary nature and constrictive force of context. Whether context is figured as a constitutive moment or period in cultural history or as a regulated practice of interpretation or evaluation, it functions to curtail both textual dissemination and intrepretive free play. It ensures meaning and orderly reading. It promotes and protects tradition. Although the idea of context depends on a concept of intertextuality, it reduces it in the name of law. Context serves as border patrol. Admittedly, there can be no time before the inception of context and no way of escape from its closure. (See Part III, "Split Writing or Producing Undecidables.") Yet the multiplication of contexts, in a free play aimed toward infinity, promises joyful parole. Beyond the subject and his intentionality and past particular moments of tradition and history, the cited or reiterated sign breaches the borders of one enclosure and gets (mis)read into others. Signs live on. Contexts pass away. The play of context is illimitable.

3

In the late 1960s and early 1970s deconstructive theorists conceive *intertextuality* as something of a weapon to be used in the contemporary struggle over meaning and truth.[19] Intertextuality, a text's dependence on and infiltration by prior codes, concepts, conventions, unconscious practices, and texts, appears here as an abysmal ground and as a strategic instrument, which can effectively combat the old law of context. In essence, the theory of the intertext facilitates extremes of dissemination—of the severest dispersions of meaning and truth. Intertextuality subverts context.

As a useful critical device for the work of deconstruction, the theory of intertextuality, whatever its precise configuration, depends upon and involves a panoply of other formulations, especially the idea, taken over from structuralism, of the death of the subject. This strikes at the heart of all varieties of humanism. In effect, intertextuality posits both an uncentered historical enclosure and an abysmal decentered foundation for language and textuality; in so doing, it exposes all contextualizations as limited and limiting, arbitrary and confining, self-serving and authoritarian, theological and political. However paradoxically formulated, intertextuality offers a liberating determinism.

Some theorists, like Heidegger and White for instance, intuit and describe the force of intertextuality as a linguistic determinism, missing, however, its disruptive power and potential for hermeneutic liberation. Here language and trope exert control and set limits. Similarly, the epistemic or archival *discourse* of Foucault functions as a mechanism of control and regulation. The unstable and disseminative energies of intertextuality which one encounters, for example, in Derrida's notions of *trace* and *iterability*, distinguish and characterize a general *deconstructive* formulation of intertextuality. To harness an analogous energy for a project of destruction, Foucault inaugurates his *genealogy*—an enterprise dependent on the revolutionary work of an "ideal intellectual," who plays the fool and practices parody so as to ruin the revered texts and practices of tradition and history. To the degree that the genealogist avoids subversion from within textual work and attempts intervention from some outside, he uses different means to reach similar deconstructive ends. In this event, the liberating linguistic resources of intertextuality remain unexploited. Like Foucault, Bloom limits the deconstructive potentials of intertextuality, but he does so by tying every trope to a specifiable psychological defense lodged in the psyche of the poet. His Map does as much to narrow and constrict as to open and release the forces of intertextuality. Nevertheless, he works toward subverting context by linking every text to an ungovernable "literary Unconscious," an inner linguistic resource like the *trace* or the *archive*, rather than to some external "body of fact" to be brought to bear on isolated texts. When assigned a structural Unconscious, language escapes any thoroughgoing contextualization.

As contemporary ideas and theories of history come more and more to credit the constituting powers of language, the old practice of contextualization or contextual historicism gives way. The tropologies of White and Bloom, like the discourse and archive of Foucault or the trace and *iter* of Derrida, all move in this disruptive direction. The old empirical world of stable fact and event is replaced by a structural Unconscious or buried realm of unstable verbal mirages. The processing of such linguistic units into stable products of representation shows itself as problematical production which imposes limited forms of order and regularity. These constricting formations bear an ideological charge and ethical force. As they emerge, they appear partial, biased, arbitrary, or exclusive. Remainders, unrepresented elements, and other discounted modes of formation emerge as obvious, though omitted or repressed, possibilities.

To escape such narrowness and rigidity and to break up all such fixed and exclusionary forms, contemporary theorists tend to search for and use strategies of expansion and inclusion. Foucault's genealogist, for example, attempts to become everyone in history. Intertextuality, in the hands of deconstructors, seeks to foreground "all" the heterogeneous materials of historical culture. Neither of these projects aims to assert a dominant position above or beyond history; rather they attempt to become immersed or drenched in the richness of it all. In this poststructuralist quest, self and center crumble as do other conventional binding entities. Where traditional Western scholarship has sought to collect, unify, control, extend, and dominate, contemporary intellectual work often tries to have everything carried away and used up. It seeks dispersion, decentering, freeplay, discontinuity, and dissemination.

Traditional ideas of history and context, suspected and discredited, approach an end. Foucault tells us he deliberately produces rifts, instabilities, and flows; he wants to dismantle the old history; and he aims to introduce discontinuity into our very being. Derrida tells us that the play of contexts has no limit; the character of language, its inherent or structural potential to be repeated or iterated, insures the mobility of context. On the one hand, therefore, history—as trope or discourse—shows itself as "willful" imposition; on the other, "textual" conceptualizations of history admit a program of nondiscriminating enrichment and de(con)-struction.

III

CRITICAL READING AND WRITING: STRATEGIES OF DECONSTRUCTION

we might remind ourselves that criticism is as inevitable as breathing, and that we should be none the worse for articulating what passes in our minds when we read a book and feel an emotion about it, for criticizing our own minds in their work of criticism.
—T. S. Eliot, "Tradition and the Individual Talent," *The Sacred Wood*

It is more of a job to interpret interpretations than to interpret things. . . .
—Montaigne, "Of Experience," *Essays*

Interpretation is here construed as an essentially allegorical act, which consists in rewriting a given text in terms of a particular interpretive master code.
—Fredric Jameson, Preface, *The Political Unconscious*

The really difficult task is, as always, the hermeneutic one: to understand understanding through the detour of the writing/reading experience. *Detour* is meant ironically, for there is no other way.
—Geoffrey Hartman, "Past and Present," *Criticism in the Wilderness*

The hermeneutic project which postulates a true sense of the text is disqualified under this regime. Reading is freed from the horizon of the meaning or truth of being, liberated from the values of the product's production or the present's presence. Whereupon the question of style is immediately unloosed as a question of writing.
—Jacques Derrida, "The Gaze of Oedipus," *Spurs*

In Part III we shall survey specific deconstructive readings (*Of Grammatology, S/Z, Glas*), particular strategies of interpretation (Derrida's *split writing*, de Man's *misreading*, Miller's *lateral dance*, Deleuze's and Guattari's *schizoanalysis*), and certain tactics and conceptions of critical writing (Yale-school *allegory*, Barthes' *fragmentation*, Derrida's *double posture*, Hartman's *creative criticism*). Our threefold purpose in Part III is to examine some significant works of deconstructive criticism, to characterize important maneuvers in deconstructive reading, and to explain several influential new forms and notions of critical writing. One of these aims usually dominates in each section, although the others almost continuously surface. At the end we shall offer the reader a convenient review and summary of the interpretive modes and styles of all the central figures discussed throughout *Deconstructive Criticism*, starting with Saussure, Lacan, and Lévi-Strauss.

Marking the Supplement

Among the many early texts published by Jacques Derrida, a handful stand out by virtue of their apparent impact on the subsequent history and direction of deconstruction. In this group are "Freud and the Scene of Writing" (1966), "Structure, Sign, and Play in the Discourse of the Human Sciences" (1967), *Of Grammatology* (1967), "Differance" (1968), "La Double séance" (1970) and "Positions" [Interview] (1971). It is impossible at this writing to assess the wider effects of later writings. This selected list of early published texts omits some of my own favorites, and it is quite obviously open to present doubt and future hindsight. Nevertheless, the importance of the *Grammatology* seems beyond question. In this section we shall examine Derrida's reading of Rousseau in *Of Grammatology*.

Why the *Grammatology*? Among other reasons, the project of Paul de Man initially defines itself in relation to *Of Grammatology* as it swerves from Derrida toward the distinctive theories of rhetoricity, the self-deconstructing text, and misreading. When we take up de Man's project in the third section, we shall discuss these formulations. With its severe critiques of Saussure and Lévi-Strauss and with its dramatic questioning of structuralism and logocentrism, *Of Grammatology* may be imagined to initiate the poststructuralist era. Of course, Saussure's own earlier quest for anagrams and Lévi-Strauss' wily tactics of *bricolage* adumbrate passages beyond strictly structuralist work. Rather than consider again these prophetic forerunners, discussed in detail in Part I and reviewed later at the end of Part III, we now look into the latter half of the *Grammatology*, which offers a close deconstructive reading of Rousseau, particularly his *Essay on the Origin of Languages*. In the development of deconstruction, this reading serves as exemplar.

For convenience we may think of the *Grammatology* as a divided text. The first half presents broad theoretical speculations on the logocentric systematics. The second scrutinizes this metaphysical configuration in the work of Rousseau. The determining links between these two divisions involve the general issues of reading and writing (*écriture*). In the Preface, Derrida stresses that the problems of critical reading "are at all times related to the guiding intention of this book. My interpretation of Rousseau's text follows implicitly the propositions ventured in Part I; propositions that demand that reading should free itself, at least in its axis, from the classical categories of history—not only from the categories of the history of ideas and the history of literature but also, and perhaps above all, from the categories of the history of philosophy" (lxxxix). Throughout *Of Grammatology* Derrida develops innovative strategies for reading—which we shall investigate here and codify in the next section. The problematic of writing, as we know, calls into play *trace*, *differance*, and *spacing*, and it questions the traditional values of sign, truth, and presence. The work of Rousseau is chosen since, more than any other between the late Renaissance and the early Modernist period, it organizes an energetic defense of phonocentric and logocentric notions about writing. In isolating and tracking the specific operations of the *supplement* in Rousseau's text, Derrida initiates a strategy of analysis destined to distinguish the project of deconstruction.

I

What is the *supplement*? Many writers and philosophers throughout our history posit or employ the opposition "nature/culture." According to the traditional account, archaic man, living in an innocent and blissful state of nature, comes upon a danger or insufficiency of one sort or another, bringing about a need or desire for community. In the evolution of man from nature into society, the latter stage of existence is pictured as an addition to the original happy state of nature. In other words, culture supplements nature. Before too long culture comes to take the place of nature. Culture, then, functions as a supplement in two ways: it adds on and it substitutes. At the same time it is potentially both detrimental and beneficial.

Significantly, the structure of the nature/culture opposition repeats itself in other traditional oppositions: for example, health/ disease, purity/contamination, good/evil, object/representation, animality/humanity, and speech/writing. Temporal priority distinguishes the first term in each pair; the second entity comes as a *supplement* to the first. In the case of speech/writing, for instance, the conventional explanation relates how writing comes late in the history of man, arriving as a double-edged supplement that offers gains and losses to man. It protects yet menaces. Traditionally, the first term in each opposition constitutes the privileged or better state or entity. Nature over culture.

But Derrida suggests that nature untouched by the force of *supplementarity* possesses no truth-value: there is no original unsupplemented nature—only a desire for it or a myth creating it. Inverting the nature/culture opposition and thus overturning this metaphysically pure idea, Derrida notes the emergence of an undecidable concept (the *supplement*), tracing its pervasive operations throughout the text of Rousseau. The effect is to deconstruct nature and culture, showing that culture does not supplement nature but that ~~nature~~ is *always already* a supplemented entity.

Since the concept "nature" is in question, we may write it, then cross it out, yet keep both it and the deletion, indicating the equivocal status of the term. Following Heidegger, Derrida occasionally employs this strategy of crossing out but keeping a word—of putting it *under erasure* ("sous rature"). In questioning one or another notion of "natural origin" or of "unsupplemented purity," Derrida frequently invokes the *always already* structure. Essentially, the *always already* works to insert the *supplement* into any seemingly simple or pure metaphysical conceptualization.

When Rousseau describes an event or phenomenon, he invariably ends up relying on the supplement. Although nature is declared to be self-sufficient, it needs and drags in culture. Education, for instance, aids the insufficiencies of the untrained intellect: there is a lack in natural man, which instruction and learning overcome. Masturbation, considered as a supplement to normal sex, assists people in compensating for dearth. Writing fulfills a similar role, making up for the limitations of speech. Typically, Rousseau is ambiguous about the numerous supplements that infiltrate his texts. On the one hand, for example, he openly deplores education, masturbation, and writing; on the other hand, he himself is a self-proclaimed educator (*Emile*), master masturbator (*Confessions*), and ambitious writer (*La Nouvelle Héloïse*). At length Derrida exposes an intricate chain of supplements at work in Rousseau's discourse. He illustrates Rousseau's persistent ambivalence and, more importantly, his insistent reliance on the logic of supplementarity.

Derrida reveals that the apparent addition/substitution of the supplement actually *constitutes* the seemingly unsupplemented entity. Thus sex and masturbation *both* depend on an imagined sexual object, on an unconsummated desire, and on a sense of self and other. Consciousness of self and other sets up the possibility of masturbation and sex. Often enough, masturbation precedes "normal" sex. In what sense, then, is such activity an addition? A fall from "normal" plenitude? Is it not a most natural practice? Writing and speech both require the possibility of articulation—of marking. Is not the possibility of writing (*écriture*) the necessary condition of speech? Intelligence, "natural" or "cultivated," presumes the ability to learn by oneself and from others. Do we not observe that education—the potential and actual process of taking in and organizing information—that education characterizes the mode of being of natural man? It operates at the "origin."

Supplementarity names the condition of humanity. Or, more precisely, the operation of the supplement is a precondition of man. All that man is is constituted by the force of supplementarity. The supplement, if you will, is an essential accident or an originary accessory. The possibility of society, education, speech, sex, and humanity are, strictly speaking, supplementary possibilities. So too are economics, politics, and history. The logic and economy of supplementarity demonstrate that the outside and the belated are really the inside and the primordial. In the state of "nature," the supplement has always already started. Nothing is uncontaminated by supplementarity. In a manner of speaking, man's departure from "nature" toward culture is instantaneous and interminable.

A mishmash of formulations on the supplement, cut from the *Grammatology*, brings us nearer to sighting its "relation" to "nature":

the supplement comes *naturally* to put itself in Nature's place. (149)

It is the strange essence of the supplement not to have essentiality: it may always not have taken place. Moreover, literally, it has never taken place: it is never present, here and now. If it were, it would not be what it is, a supplement, taking and keeping the place of the other. (314)

Man *calls himself* man only by drawing limits excluding his other from the play of supplementarity: the purity of nature, of animality, primitivism, childhood. . . . (244)

If we consider the *concept* of animality not in its content of understanding or misunderstanding but in its specific *function*, we shall see that it must locate a moment of *life* which knows nothing of symbol, substitution, lack and supplementary addition. . . . A life that has not yet broached the play of supplementarity and which at the same time has not yet let itself be violated by it: a life without differance. . . . (242)

The same is here called supplement, another name for differance. (150)

Blindness to the supplement is the law. And especially blindness to its concept. . . . The supplement has no sense and is given to no intuition.
(149)

The supplement is maddening because it is neither presence nor absence. . . . (154)

the indifferent process of supplementarity has always already *infiltrated* presence. . . . (163)

supplementarity, which *is nothing*, neither a presence nor an absence, is neither a substance nor an essence of man. It is precisely the play of presence and absence, the opening of this play that no metaphysical or ontological concept can comprehend. (244)

Rousseau is not alone in being caught in the graphic of supplementarity. All meaning and therefore all discourse is caught there, particularly and by a singular turn, the discourse of metaphysics. . . . (246)

Writing will appear to us more and more as another name for this structure of supplementarity. (245)

This graphic of supplementarity is the origin of languages. . . . (235)

Through this sequence of supplements a necessity is announced: that of an infinite chain, ineluctably multiplying the supplementary mediations. . . . (157)

This dozen pieces, a baker's dozen, comments already on the supplement. It adds one layer of alteration—my cutting through ellipses. If you yourself design a form or meaning from all this, you will inevitably compensate me and heap on one or more layers. My supplement instigates yours and so on. An infinite chain describes the structure of supplementarity.

In commenting on this string of citations, which themselves bear a supplementary relation to one another, we supplement this already several times supplemented ensemble. There is no escape, obviously, from supplementarity. Thus the pure entity, the uncontaminated thing, the immediate presence, the pristine object and the undivided origin come forth necessarily as fictions—under pressure from an infiltrating chain of supplements, which appear at or in all moments of "primordial" ge~~nes~~is. Ensemble is a model for supplementarity.

The most disturbing aspect of the supplement is its lack of substance and essentiality: it cannot be touched, tasted, heard, smelled, seen or intuited; it cannot be thought—within the logocentric systematics. As such it exhibits kinship with the *trace*, with *differance*, and with *écriture*. It too is an *undecidable*. To understand such undecidables, now numbering about three dozen in Derrida's canon, we may think of them as nonsynonymic substitutions of *differance*, keeping in mind that none of these concepts overlaps any other. Like *differance*—the *trace, écriture, dissemination, spacing, iterability, border*, and *supplement* remain distinct.

Outside the grasp of classical metaphysics, the supplement operates, unacclaimed, in the texts of writers and philosophers. Derrida marks it in Husserl and Lévi-Strauss as well as in Rousseau. Significantly, this undecidable escapes any appropriation into the binary oppositions of philosophy and literature, yet it dwells amidst such oppostions, resisting and disorganizing them while refusing inclusion as a third term. The supplement disrupts Rousseau's text; he describes it without declaring it; he dwells within its necessity.

2

When Derrida urges that "reading should free itself, at least in its axis, from the classical categories of history," he recommends that logocentric concepts, like nature, speech, animality, presence, being, origin, self, and truth, not serve as unquestioned supporting structures or stable centers for thematic, historical, psychological, or philosophical analysis. In his own study, he is able to show a *regulated* system of contradictions running through Rousseau's text. This particular reading could not happen using unexamined traditional categories and practices. The supplement is a production of deconstruction—which in a certain way operates outside the thinking of the logocentric epoch.

From time to time in the *Grammatology* Derrida turns from critical analysis to metacritical advice and speculation. Taken together, these moments, which generate a theoretical ensemble on reading, offer insights into the practices and problematics of early deconstruction. From the vantage of the 1980s *Of Grammatology* appears in some ways a conservative effort. Among other examples of this critical strand are the instances of Derrida arguing at length and with care about the dating of Rousseau's *Origin*— a matter of interest mainly to Rousseau scholars—and quibbling in his notes with other scholarly works on Rousseau. The most important conserving aspect of Derrida's whole enterprise is his dedication to working laboriously and scrupulously within the closure of the logocentric systematics. As part of this endeavor, he admits and promotes the values of careful reading, particularly in the phenomenological and structuralist modes. At the same time he seeks progress beyond such traditionalist practices. Generally speaking, this double strategy suggests using the resources of tradition so as to dramatize its closure and to begin its breakdown. For Derrida such a procedure is necessary; it is not a matter of choice. Using the terms of "Structure, Sign, and Play," we can say that deconstruction practices two interpretations of interpretation. It aims to decipher the stable truths of a work, employing conventional "passive" tactics of reading; and it seeks to question and subvert such truths in an active production of enigmatic undecidables.

Significantly, undecidables emerge from within deciphered texts; they are not alien importations. Thus the materials for deconstruction reside within the tradition. In other words, the text offers itself to deconstruction quite naturally. Derrida's rigorous reading of Rousseau presses home this point. So it is that the revolution of deconstruction requires as much conventional work as messianic daring. The quick fix and the sudden escape are the mirages of the misguided and the reckless who set out forgetful of historical necessities. Their blindness (mis)leads them.

About the role of conventional commentary Derrida insists: "To recognize and respect all its classical exigencies is not easy and requires all the instruments of traditional criticism. Without this recognition and this respect, critical production would risk developing in any direction at all and authorize itself to say almost anything" (158). Deconstructive reading, respecting traditional criticism, neither supersedes its object (the text) nor plays fast and loose with it. Rather the text undergoes conscientious scrutiny. Of the limitations of the old reading Derrida observes: "But this indispensable guardrail has always only *protected*, it has never *opened*, a reading" (158). In the past, critical reading worked within and with the elements of the logocentric system, foregoing its own potentially corrosive powers of criticism by repeating endless variations on given precepts. Fine-tuning the myriad mechanisms of logocentrism, traditional commentary never opened these precepts to criticism. In the past, as Derrida construes it, reading was more often refinement of the given than inquiry into founding mechanisms.

After admitting the values of traditional criticism and suggesting their limited though indispensable role in deconstruction, Derrida reviews the theory of textuality. This conjunction is no accident. He points out that deconstruction first assumes a theory of language (textuality) then initiates a reading. Thus methodological considerations "are closely dependent on general propositions that we have elaborated above; as regards the absence of the referent or the transcendental signified. *There is nothing outside of the text*"

(158). The point is that deconstructive reading not only questions the old commentary's refined repetition or doubling of the work, but also refuses the traditional violation of the text that links it to an outside. No connection exists between "real" biographical events, "authentic" history and phenomena, "actual" metaphysical entities, and the text at hand. Deconstruction stays within the text because there is nothing else: biography, history, and metaphysics are always already written. Written into the (inter)text.

Deconstructive reading neither escapes nor avoids biography, history, and metaphysics. Its target texts cohabit with them. Historical totalities of all kinds and philosophical structures of all orders organize, envelop, and blend within the text by virtue of the already-thereness of language and culture. Every reading dredges up and carries off an "unformed mass of roots, soil, and sediments of all sorts" (161). But these elements never touch ground; they are always already written. The text to be *desedimented* resides among numerous eras, and reading must resign itself to the fact of such intertextuality.

What about the author? about Rousseau? Derrida frequently stresses that Rousseau describes the *supplement*, which disrupts and undermines his text, but he doesn't declare it. It is a blind spot in his writing. Broadly speaking, a writer works in a linguistic and cultural system which his own discourse cannot completely dominate. Up to a point he goes along with the constituted codes. Deconstructive reading, therefore, "must always aim at a certain relationship, unperceived by the writer, between what he commands and what he does not command of the patterns of the language that he uses" (158). The intention of the author, conscious or unconscious, does not guide Derridean deconstruction. Often enough, a strand of thought, left undeveloped in an author's text, provides Derrida with material to deconstruct a pattern of concepts or a textual system. The author is a name.

The formula for deconstructive reading is: repeat and undermine. The conventional repetition of the text, minutely and laboriously accomplished, establishes the foothold of deconstruction within the resources of the text and the tradition. The subversion of the text, predicated on the rich possibilities of textuality and intertextuality, makes insecure the seemingly stable text and tradition through the *production* of undecidables. "It is certainly a production," stresses Derrida,

because I do not simply duplicate [repeat] what Rousseau thought of this relationship [between the supplement and the metaphysical systematics]. The concept of the supplement is a sort of blind spot in Rousseau's text. . . . But the production, if it attempts to make the not-seen accessible to sight, does not leave the text. . . . It is contained in the transformation of the language it designates, in the regulated exchanges between Rousseau and history. We know that these exchanges only take place by way of the language and the text. . . . (163–64)

Deconstruction is production. It is not self-effacing repetition or doubling commentary, although it uses such methods along the way. It always works within the text and the intertext. But there it produces the imperceptible: the trace of—the *supplement*, for example.

The production itself of deconstruction is necessarily a text. And each such work of critical writing contains its own blind spot. *Aporia* is an accepted aspect of the deconstructive enterprise. Every deconstruction opens itself to further deconstruction (24, 164). Implicitly, the final production of a deconstructive reading can never be final; it is rather a finale subject to a new erasure.

Split Writing or Producing Undecidables

At the conclusion of "The Ends of Man," a conference presentation delivered in America during the fall of 1968, Jacques Derrida outlines various options for deconstructing the logocentric systematics. He notes that this system regularly transforms transgressions into "false sorties." And he observes that we have, from the inside where we are, two potential strategies. First, deconstruction can attempt its work without changing ground and by repeating the original problematics, using against the system its own resources. (This approximates Heidegger's strategy of destruction.) Seond, deconstruction can change ground and abruptly step outside, affirming total discontinuity and difference. The danger of the first strategy is to confirm and consolidate, in an ever more secure and profound manner, that which is being challenged. With the second the risk is to re-situate the new ground on the older one, remaining even more naively and blindly within the logocentric enclosure, notably through the insistence and agency of (old) language.[1]

Whatever the risks and dangers, the necessity of a "change of ground" cannot be dismissed. Derrida recommends that both forms of "deconstruction" be employed. "A new writing must weave and intertwine the two motifs. That is, several languages must be spoken and several texts produced at the same time" (205). He closes his reflection with the suggestion that "it is perhaps a change of style that we need" (206).

Not long after this time, Derrida and other French deconstructors initiate a new writing, as in *La Dissémination* and *Glas* and *S/Z* and *The Pleasure of the Text*. Looking back from the 1980s, the deconstructive texts of the 1960s seem stylistically conservative. Derrida's *Of Grammatology*, *Writing and Difference*, and *Speech and Phenomena*, all written in the 1960s, rely for the most part on conventional modes of scholarly writing and organization. In later sections we shall sample some of the new writings, which aim to transform the terrain from within and from without. And to fashion a new style.

Published in the autumn of 1971, Derrida's interview with J.-L. Houdebine and Guy Scarpetta, titled "Positions," presents his most economical and lucid account of the strategies of deconstructive reading. Its codification below assumes familiarity with the previous section of our text.

The place where a reader notices a displacement or reversal in a textual chain or system often constitutes the site of a philosophical or thematic opposition. Disclosing such a crevice, the deconstructor systematically and tenaciously inverts the opposition to reveal the actual hierarchical relation of the dichotomous terms. At this point she steadfastly disallows any reconstitution, sublimation, or synthesis (any Hegelian *Aufhebung*) of opposing terms. This strategic inversion and stubborn exposé produce an unexpected gap, forcing the emergence of a new concept, which nameless *mark* neither neutralizes nor reforms the old opposition. Rather, it functions as a disorganizing structural force that invisibly inhabits and transgresses the opposition somewhat like the Unconscious of Freud, which secretly dwells amidst the subconscious and conscious domains of each person's psyche. The purpose of the deconstructor is to produce such *undecidables* and to track their insistent operations throughout the text. In this work the critic does not track literary or metaphysical theme since the new concept is always subtracted from, then added to, theme.

The *split writing* of deconstruction, its *double science*, consists of deliberately *inverting* traditional oppositions and *marking* the mysterious and disorienting play of hitherto invisible concepts that reside, unnamed, in the gap between opposing terms. (Between "nature" and "culture," for example, dwells the *supplement*.) In this double gesture, deconstruction avoids simply defusing oppositions or reforming them; in other words, deconstruction actively resists the inclusion of the new concept into the old dichotomy.[2] Yet, since deconstruction works with language, it cannot escape such re-appropriation; finally its productions, in turn, fall prey to further deconstruction. As analysis, deconstruction is interminable.

Deconstruction exceeds the limits established by traditional hermeneutics. It does not reproduce or recreate through the effaced doubling of commentary or interpretation the conscious or intentional meaning made by the writer in interaction with her world and time. Since there is nothing beyond text, deconstruction works always from inside. Yet this labor is not interpretation or commentary inscribed by critics who serve as transparent mediums—purveyors of truth; it is production of hidden and mirage-like "semiological" structures that reveal the radical and prolific play of differance in texts. (The old reading celebrates identity.) Deconstruction is the free, systematic, and painstaking practice of *erasure* and *split writing*. Without end. All the while, the old never disappears under the new reading and writing. Transformation suggests death, but signals rebirth.

The deconstructive intervention into a particular text or into the wider discourse of a discipline is, to a certain extent, historically determined. Thus the standpoint of the deconstructor is never simply a free choice; it exists as an historical possibility.

(The *incision* of deconstruction, which is not a voluntary decision or an absolute beginning, does not take place just anywhere, or in an absolute elsewhere. An incision, precisely, it can be made only according to lines of force and forces of rupture that are localizable in the discourse to be deconstructed. The *topical* and *technical* determination of the most necessary sites and operators—beginnings, holds, levers, etc.—in a given situation depends upon an historical analysis. This analysis is *made* in the general movement of the field, and is never exhausted by the conscious calculation of a "subject.") (*Pos*, 82)

Though parenthetical, this remark deserves the emphasis here of last place. For too often Derridean deconstruction shows up in other representations as an extreme Nietzschean lawlessness of reading and writing *outside* all bounds of history and tradition. Between the two interpretations of interpretation announced in "Structure, Sign, and Play," there can be no effective choice. Despite his ambiguity in this most influential early essay, Derrida almost everywhere else urges both interpretations. Nevertheless, the radical misreading of Derrida, championing a single-minded

Nietzschean program for joyous freeplay, has become canonical in some quarters. (For tactical purposes we celebrated this project at the close of chapter 2.) For Derrida the deconstructor's entry into a textual field never occurs from an absolute elsewhere (an outside) nor from just anywhere (*any* inside); it often starts at a *given* point of weakness in the discourse. But in every case its determination exceeds the will or wisdom of the subject, who comes into the field at a particular moment or conjunction of development and history. His personal engagement then is neither an instance of absolute beginning nor an issue of choice. The scene of breakthrough is always already inscribed in a chain of historical oppositions and determinations. Freedom has to be conditional— not simply assumed. Split writing operates with history. And against.

Allegory and (Mis)Reading

Paul de Man's highly influential theory of rhetoricity *follows* from his obsessions with reading. He insists in the Foreword to *Blindness and Insight* that "prior to theorizing about literary language, one has to become aware of the complexities of reading" (viii). In the Preface to *Allegories of Reading* he reveals that he started the book as a historical study and ended up with a theory of reading: "I had to shift from historical definition to the problematics of reading" (ix). The difficulties of reading precipitate and direct de Man's theories of language, literature, and criticism. "What emerges is a process of reading in which rhetoric is a disruptive intertwining of trope and persuasion or—which is not quite the same thing—of cognitive and performative language" (*AR*, ix). The vertiginous aberrations characteristic of literary language are productions of critical reading. To grasp de Man's deconstructive project is to understand his experiences of reading, which generate particular ideas of rhetoricity and misreading as well as specific notions of the literary text as self-deconstructive and critical writing as allegorical. Let us disentangle this knotted pattern.

I

To open our examination of de Man's theory of critical writing, we begin with an inordinately dense passage taken from an essay on Nietzsche's "Rhetoric of Tropes." When he reads a literary text, de Man makes several discoveries:

The wisdom of the text is self-destructive . . . , but this self-destruction is infinitely displaced in a series of successive rhetorical reversals which, by the endless repetition of the same figure, keep it suspended between truth and the death of this truth. A threat of immediate destruction, stating itself as a figure of speech, thus becomes the permanent repetition of this threat. Since this repetition is a temporal event, it can be narrated sequentially, but what it narrates, the subject matter of the story, is itself mere figure. A non-referential, repetitive text narrates the story of a literally destructive but nontragic linguistic event. We could call this rhetorical mode . . . allegory— (*AR*, 115–16)

The dramatic states of "suspension" and "repetition" announce the impossibility of reading—the necessary *unreadability* of the text. Reading uncovers and confronts a language that vacillates uncontrollably between the promise of referential meaning and the rhetorical subversion of that promise. Truth is permanently threatened. A disruptive tropological language endlessly repeats the threat. Whatever wisdom the language of the text offers is undermined through a continuous slide or displacement from figure to substitute figure. A process of tropic reversals, seeming linguistic misfortunes, marks the experience of reading. However disorienting, this experience can be related—told. Critical writing is, in fact, narration of reading experience. As story, the critical text itself relies unavoidably on figurative language; it repeats the confusions between figural and referential dimensions; it remains suspended, while spread across a diachronic narrative, between truth and the death of truth. The rhetorical mode of critical writing, a textual plot of another text's tale, a figure of a figure, is *allegory*. In de Man's view, "the allegorical mode is accounted for in the description of all language as figural and in the necessarily diachronic structure of the reflection that reveals this insight" (*BI*, 135). To the extent that critical narrative is diachronic and figural (fictitious), it is allegorical.[3]

For de Man critical writing can never be simply description, repetition, identification, or representation of a literary text. Between the critical and the literary text a space for difference or trope intervenes. The only accurate way for criticism to describe, repeat, represent, or be identical with a poem would be to recopy it. Criticism deviates from the text. (Moreover, the text deviates from itself.) Even paraphrase, the mainstay of the critical faith, has for its actual purpose "to blur, confound, and hide discontinuities and disruptions in the homogeneity of its own discourse."[4] As it relates (to) the poem, critical writing manifests itself as a distinct and distant sequence of images, an allegory, of reading.

Since all language is rhetorical, it appears inevitable that literature assume no priority over criticism or vice versa. The precise way to make this point is to say: literary language is characterized by rhetoricity and, accordingly, any language in *any* text is "literary" to the extent that it is rhetorical. "Literature as well as criticism—*the difference between them being delusive*—is condemned (or privileged) to be forever the most rigorous and, consequently, the most unreliable language . . ." (*AR*, 19; my italics). Any prior or absolute distinction between literature and criticism partakes of delusion because "the criterion of literary specificity does not depend on the greater or lesser discursiveness of the mode but on the degree of consistent 'rhetoricity' of the language" (*BI*, 137*n*). Thus critical writing always stays caught up and suspended within its own linguistic play of truth and falsehood. Criticism is (allegorical) *text*.

2

De Man formulates his experiences of unreadability into a theory of *misreading*. The elucidation of misreading touches near the heart of his enterprise: "we reach the conclusion that the determining characteristic of literary language is indeed figurality, in the somewhat wider sense of rhetoricity, but that, far from constituting an objective basis for literary study, *rhetoric implies the persistent threat of misreading*."[5] But de Man puts this observation yet more directly: "the specificity of literary language resides in the possibility of misreading and misinterpretation" ("LL," 184). In other words, if it ruled out or refused all misreading whatsoever, a text would not be literary. A text is literary to the degree that it permits and encourages misreading. Consequently, any criticism or interpretation that aims to achieve "controlled" or "correct" readings is seriously deluded.

Because misreading is a necessary and inevitable constituent of literary criticism, the history of criticism constitutes itself as a systematic narrative of error. To give two examples, Rousseau and Nietzsche have been misread throughout critical history. In particular, "the established tradition of Rousseau interpretation . . . stands in dire need of deconstruction" (*BI*, 139). Here we perceive the grounds for a new critical project: to revise the traditions of Rousseau and Nietzsche interpretation, which is what de Man initiates in the essays of *Allegories of Reading*. Straight-

forwardly, de Man generalizes his overall conception of misreading as he considers Nietzsche: "Perhaps we have not yet begun
to read him properly. In the case of major authors, this is never
a simple task. There are likely to be long periods of continual
misinterpretation." And "As long as we are not sufficiently aware
of this, we risk to produce the wrong kind of misreading. For
there can be more or less valid misreadings. . . ."[6] If misreading
is a constituent of "literary" texts, then, paradoxically, the extent
or range of misreadings of a text certify its literariness. Indeed,
"By a good misreading, I mean a text that produces another text
which can itself be shown to be an interesting misreading, a text
which engenders additional texts" ("NTR," 51). To sum up, all
interpretation, given the rhetoricity of language, is misreading;
when a text is densely rhetorical, it will generate numerous misreadings. Any critical reading that tries to contain the inevitable
misreadings itself affirms the inevitability of misreading in spite
of its very desire to circumscribe the random play of grammatical
structures and the dizzying aberrations of rhetorical figures. Necessarily, the critical readings of an author or of a text exist in the
mode of error.

This theory of misreading is applicable in all cases, though de
Man's demonstrations have been mainly with major critics in his
early essays collected in *Blindness and Insight* and primarily with
Rousseau and Nietzsche in his later studies gathered in *Allegories
of Reading*. For these latter authors themselves the operation of
the misreading phenomenon is likewise inevitable. Of Rousseau,
de Man notes: "Just as any other reader, he is bound to misread
his text. . . . The error is not within the reader; language itself
dissociates the cognition from the act *Die Sprache verspricht*
. . ." (*AR*, 277). In short, any reading by an author (as well as
by a critic) is ultimately unable to control or delimit the text. The
phenomenon of misreading can never be contained or erased.

One recurrent manifestation or version of misreading is of particular interest to de Man during the late 1960s and early 1970s.
Through examination of selected leading critics (Lukács, Bin-
swanger, Blanchot, Poulet, and Derrida), he reveals that each critic
unwittingly manifests a discrepancy between his explicit theories
of literature and his actual interpretations. Paradoxically, these

critics "seem to thrive on it and owe their best insights to the assumptions these insights disprove" (*BI*, ix). This *blindness/insight* pattern is "a constitutive characteristic of literary language in general" (*BI*, ix). The basic point is that both literary and critical texts exhibit the misreading experience. Texts are unreadable for both the author and the critic of the text. Neither the author nor the critic can "read" his own or anyone else's text.

When de Man declares that "There is no need to deconstruct Rousseau; the established tradition of Rousseau interpretation, however, stands in dire need of deconstruction" (*BI*, 139), the implication is that Rousseau himself is enlightened. "On the question of rhetoric, on the nature of figural language, Rousseau was not deluded and said what he meant to say" (*BI*, 135). Yet we must refine this early formulation in light of later reading experiences. Given the random operation of grammar as a determining element in the rhetoricity of language, the possibility of the author's *total* enlightenment or control is relinquished: "Just as any other reader, he is bound to misread his text. . . ." In de Man's deconstructive project the conception of the text as self-deconstructing ultimately subsumes the phenomenon of the author as self-deconstructor: "A literary text simultaneously asserts and denies the authority of its own rhetorical mode. . . . Poetic writing is the most advanced and refined mode of deconstruction . . ." (*AR*, 17). In essence, *literary* texts deconstruct themselves; they are always already deconstructed whether the author (or critic) realizes it or not. Each author, to be sure, exhibits individual degrees of understanding and awareness about the unsettling rhetoricity of language. Nevertheless, an author is finally never free to hem in the randomness of grammar, the play of figures, and the aberrations of semantic references.

3

For de Man the cognitive elements of literary texts reside in the language, not in the author. (When de Man writes his criticism, the "agent" occasionally disappears from his sentences: language displaces author.) The issue, therefore, of whether the author is or is not blinded by language is, in a sense, irrelevant. To the degree that a literary text reveals or acknowledges the rhetoricity of its mode, it affirms the inevitability of misreading. "It knows and asserts that it will be misunderstood. It tells the story, the allegory of its misunderstanding . . ." (*BI*, 136). For example, "Rousseau's fictional as well as his discursive writings are allegories of (non)signification or of unreadability, allegories of the deconstruction and the reintroduction of metaphorical models" (*AR*, 257). We discover here that the mode of allegory characterizes both secondary works and primary texts. (Allegory is not a consequence of authorial intention.) And again, criticism emerges as the story of a story told in a figurative language about figurative *language*. Thus the traditional critical demand for meaning or truth, suspended by de Man, gives way to redoubled unreadability. And deconstruction becomes the deconstruction of a deconstruction. Oddly, the only force that lightens this abysmal labyrinth of writing and (mis)reading is the lure, the promise, of truth. De Man never renounces referentiality; he problematizes it, undermines it, explodes it—yet preserves it.

Among all the deconstructive close readers, de Man pays least attention to intertextuality. Rarely does he focus on the pressing influences of forerunners or on the determining cultural forces operating upon or in texts. He does sometimes highlight the past and current critical responses to texts. Such critical heritages always need to be cleared away, and they are often scorched by implication, if not directly. So tangled up does de Man get in the epistemological abysses of figurative play that he never quite arrives at history. He tells us in the opening lines of *Allegories of Reading* that the complexities of reading keep him from history.[7] (He suspects that Derrida's *historical* notion of "logocentrism" is a fiction—a productive narrative frame for *reading* [*BI*, 137–39].) This absence of intertextual materials and determinants distinguishes de Man's critical writing, as does his labyrinthine wanderings amid figural turns and returns. The blind alley is almost the whole of the diminished truth for him. Deconstruction insists on performing what cannot be performed—reading texts. Necessarily, then, allegory aptly characterizes critical (mis)reading and writing. Meanwhile, the historical dimension rests on the back burner.

Actually, though, de Man does not believe in history. Or, to be more accurate, de Man regards history writing as fiction. The stark conclusion to his essay in the Yale manifesto "warns us that nothing, whether deed, word, thought or text, ever happens in relation, positive or negative, to anything that precedes, follows or exists elsewhere, but only as a random event whose power, like the power of death, is due to the randomness of its occurrence" (*D&C*, 69). Such total discontinuity or randomness, introduced earlier through grammar into the theory of language (rhetoricity), now disrupts and disallows any history. That we recuperate and integrate things and events in historical (and aesthetic) systems does not deny the fallaciousness of all such fabricated continuities; it merely affirms a necessity. Significantly, this necessity results from language: the making of continuities is not our doing as subjects; we ourselves are its products. "No degree of knowledge can ever stop this madness, for it is the madness of words" (*D&C*, 68).

Critical reading, like the making of history, is monumentalization. Randomness is brought to order. Language is the agent. We are bystanders. Allegory triumphs. "Reading as disfiguration"—as activity that accepts randomness—"to the very extent that it resists historicism, turns out to be historically more reliable than the products of historical archeology" (*D&C*, 69). Though perhaps too self-consciously paradoxical, this statement justifies and explains de Man's critical practice. To read closely in the deconstructive or *disfigurative* manner produces more reliable history than the history of historicists and archeologists, who champion carefully forged lies of order and continuity. While de Man never deliberately gets to history (in the old sense), he does so inevitably through the work of *disfiguration*.

The Lateral Dance

> In spite of the bewildering array of possibilities in literary method-
> ology, the methods available may . . . be reduced to two distinctly
> different sorts. One kind includes all those methods whose presuppo-
> sitions are in one way or another what I would call "metaphysical." The
> other kind includes those methods which hypothesize that in literature,
> for reasons which are intrinsic to language itself, metaphysical presup-
> positions are, necessarily, both affirmed and subverted.[8]
>
> —J. Hillis Miller

For J. Hillis Miller there exists two types of critical interpretation—the metaphysical and the deconstructive. Since they cannot be synthesized, one must choose between them. After choos-
ing deconstruction in the late 1960s, Miller proceeds to read texts
under the avowed influence of Jacques Derrida and Paul de Man.
In his practice, he employs their theories of misreading and split
writing, though he uniformly favors rhetorical analysis over the
production of undecidables. Generally speaking, Miller relies on
the notions of the self-deconstructing text and the allegorical modality of critical writing. Let us explore in some detail Miller's
forthright formulations on critical reading, his interpretive strategies for breaking down the logocentric systematics, and his project's difference from those of de Man and Derrida.

I

For Miller all interpretation is misinterpretation. To read is to
connect elements and construct patterns out of the diffuse materials
in a writing. As a reader works through the chain of words in a
text, he or she imposes meaning in an act of willed mastery. Texts
are unreadable—or undecidable—in that they allow a host of potential misreadings. To reduce a text to a correct or single homogeneous reading is to restrain the free play of its elements.
"This does not mean," emphasizes Miller, "that the narrator or
the reader is free to give the narrative any meaning he wishes, but

that the pattern is subject to 'free play,' is formally 'undecidable.'
Meaning emerges from a reciprocal act in which interpreter and
what is interpreted both contribute to the making or the finding
of a pattern. . . ."⁹ Consequently, "there are obviously strong
and weak critical misreadings, more or less vital ones" ("DD,"
24). But always *misreadings* because an interpretation can neither
reach the "original" meaning of a text, nor contain all the potential
readings. There can never be "objective" interpretation—only
more or less vital misreadings.

One of Miller's tactics in reading a text is to trace the meaning
of a key word back to its etymological "roots." In so doing, he
shifts the apparent stability of the master term out of a closed
system and into an ongoing bifurcating labyrinth. The effect of
such semantic dissemination is to deracinate the text, revealing
the inexhaustible possibilities for interpretation and the futility of
logical and dialectical orderings. After he reads an exemplary
poem, he concludes: "Such a poem is incapable of being encom-
passed in a single logical formulation. It calls forth potentially
endless commentaries, each one of which, like this essay, can only
formulate and reformulate its *mise en abyme*."¹⁰

How does a literary critic read a text? "The reader is forced
then to shift sideways again seeking to find somewhere else in the
poem the solid ground of that figure, seeking, and failing or falling, and seeking again" ("SR," 18). The creation of a critical
reading is the production of a failure. Trying to ground her interpretation in some element of the text, the critic always discovers
the collapse of the ground into the free play of figure. She is
compelled, then, to move down the chain of words, seeking a still
point, which—in time—gives way again to the play of figure.
Thus the reader moves on, once again, to find another more stable
foundation: "The reader must then seek the literal base elsewhere,
in a constant lateral transfer with no resting place in the unequiv-
ocally literal, the mimetic, the 'exact rock,' cured at last" ("SR,"
19). Miller characterizes the productions of such reading acts as
mises en abyme, and he depicts the process of reading itself as *lateral
dance*.

The name of this incessant movement from one displaced figural
point to another is *allegory*. "Story-telling, the putting into lan-

guage of man's 'experience' of his life, is in its writing or reading a hiatus in that experience. Narrative is the allegorizing along a temporal line of this perpetual displacement from immediacy" ("AT," 72). The theory of allegory, borrowed from de Man, insists on the crucial role of *difference* and *spacing* in all reading and writing. All experiences of critical reading and writing differ from their objects and from themselves as they take form in narration. This slippage results from insistent temporality and rhetoricity (or textuality). In place of the "same" is difference, of presence, absence. The possibility of a safe critical discourse, a metalanguage, above or beyond time or rhetoric, secure from allegory, is denied.

When he reads a novel by Thomas Hardy, Miller gives full voice to his general theory of the *lateral dance* (here I conflate three important paragraphs):

Each passage is a node, a point of intersection or focus, on which converge lines leading from many other passages in the novel and ultimately including them all. No passage has any particular priority over the others, in the sense of being more important or as being the "origin" or "end" of the others. . . . Moreover, the chains of connection or of repetition that converge on a given passage are extremely complex and diverse in nature, and no one of these chains has archeological or interpretative priority over the others.

. . . The reader can only thread his way from one element to another, interpreting each as best he can in terms of the others. It is possible to distinguish chains of connection that are material elements in the text. . . . None of these chains, however, has priority over the others as the true explanation of the meaning of the novel. Each is a permutation of the others rather than a distinct realm of discourse. . . .

. . . The reader must execute a *lateral dance of interpretation* to explicate any given passage, without ever reaching, in this sideways movement, any passage that is chief, original, or originating, a sovereign principle of explanation. ("FR," 58–59; my italics)

The metaphor of the dance reveals for us the moves in the act of interpretation. Insofar as a text is a spatialized tapestry of myriad interlocking threads (for example, words, images, characters, themes), it is constituted as level, meaning that no spot or passage can rise above any other. Nothing may be privileged: there can be no origin, no end, no focus, no priority element, no sovereign principle. To the extent that a text is a temporal chain of inter-woven elements, the reader can only transfer elements from one sequence to another, stopping now and then—at will—to confer meaning through an arbitrary act of interpretation. There can be no "true" explanation or meaning of the text—only more or less vital patterns of textual connections. Thus, the dance of decon-struction is structured, like all dance, as repetition, yet such rep-etition is ultimately liberated and hollowed out by difference. The parallel here with contemporary dancing is remarkably strong: after the waltz we have the swinger's solo; and at the disco the music never stops, the dancers merely walk off when they've had enough.

2

For some American critics, unhappy about recent developments in critical and literary theory, Miller serves as *the* model, a fall guy or point man, for the school of deconstruction. Seemingly, he undermines traditional ideas and beliefs about language, literature, truth, meaning, consciousness, and interpretation. In effect, he assumes the role of unrelenting destroyer—of nihilistic magi-cian—who dances demonically upon the broken and scattered fragments of the Western tradition. Everything he touches soon appears torn. Nothing is ever finally darned, or choreographed for coherence, or foregrounded as (only) magical illusion. Miller, a relentless rift-maker, refuses any apparent repair and rampages onward, dancing, spell-casting, destroying all. As though he were a wizard, he appears in the guise of a bull-deconstructor loose in the china shop of Western tradition.

But, of course, this portrait is a distorted image. Miller under-stands himself and the great tradition otherwise. "The so-called 'deconstruction of metaphysics' has always been a part of meta-physics, a shadow within its light, for example in the self-sub-version of Plato in *The Sophist*."[11] All texts contain both the traditional materials of metaphysics and the subversion of these materials. "This subversion is wrought into the conceptual words, the figures, and the myths of the Occident as the shadow in its light. . . ."[12] As an important consequence, "Deconstruction is not a dismantling of the structure of a text but a demonstration that it has already dismantled itself" ("SR II," 341). Miller pictures himself as moving always into this land of shadows, seeking to go beyond the blinding light to the dark underside of history in order to make the ever-present darkness visible in the texts of the tradition.[13] Accordingly, the deconstructive critic plays the old role of handmaiden to the text, though the maiden is now a shady fairy godmother wielding apparently boundless negativizing powers.

While the subversion of logocentric metaphysics has always been a part of the tradition, "the putting in question of metaphysics has taken a novel turn in modern times with new concepts of language, new ideas of structure, and new notions of interpretation" ("SH," 298). The shadowmen of our tradition are known, if not loved. "One knows the familiar litany of the names of these doubters, underminers of the Occidental tradition in its economic and political theory, in its ethical and ontological notions, in its concept of human psychology, and in its theory of language: Marx, Nietzsche, Freud, Saussure" ("TD," 8). We can add to this tradition many other practitioners of "deconstruction" from earlier eras and from our own time. In Miller's novel view such subversives are not revolutionaries. "Rather than the notion of revolution one needs the more enigmatic concept of repetition (repetition as displacement or decentering) to describe the effect of these writers on the culture to which, like all of us, they belong. By resurrection, rearrangement, re-emphasis, or reversal of old materials they have made a difference" ("TD," 8). The tradition of *difference* within our culture, as Miller depicts it, appears a conserving force, which ultimately renews and preserves the culture by retrieving repressed materials. This archeological thrust of deconstruction, initiated earlier with Derrida, is too rarely recognized or admitted. Thus does an imaginary bull metamorphose into a fox who raids the resources, circumspectly—precipitating rearrangement of the old guard.

For Miller, as for Derrida, there can be no escape outside the tradition. Alternative schemes inevitably turn out to be modified versions of ancestral metaphysics. The protean power of the logocentric systematic to re-form itself results because "our languages contain no terms, no concepts, and no metaphors which are not inextricably implicated in the patterns of metaphysical thinking" ("TD," 10). There is no effort in Miller's project to step abruptly outside the historical enclosure. The breakdown of the system occurs from the inside. Such a deconstructive enterprise is possible because language embodies "a clash of incompatibles which grates, twists, or bifurcates the mind . . ." and because it already incarnates "the immense anacoluthon of Western literature, philosophy, and history as a 'whole'" ("ABW," 56). The system contains the materials for its own subversion.

3

What, in summary, are the means and ends of deconstruction in Miller's project?

[1] Deconstruction as a mode of interpretation works by a careful and circumspect entering of each textual labyrinth. The critic feels his way from figure to figure, from concept to concept, from mythical motif to mythical motif, in a repetition which is in no sense a parody. It employs, nevertheless, the subversive power present in even the most exact and unironical doubling. [2] The deconstructive critic seeks to find, by this process of retracing, the element in the system studied which is alogical, the thread in the text in question which will unravel it all, or the loose stone which will pull down the whole building. [3] The deconstruction, rather, annihilates the ground on which the building stands by showing that the text has already annihilated that ground, knowingly or unknowingly. Deconstruction is not a dismantling of the structure of a text but a demonstration that it has already dismantled itself. ("SR II," 341)

This passage, a compact depiction of Miller's deconstructive procedures, explains three matters plainly: the means, the ends, and the effects of his deconstructive criticism. To begin with, the deconstructive interpreter carefully traces and repeats certain elements in the text, which may include the figures, the concepts, or the motifs in a work. As he repeats the selected elements, the critic unleashes the disruptive powers inherent in all repetition. In other words, the critic through seemingly innocent repetition foregrounds and sets in motion the operations of *difference*, calling into play a disorienting chain of substitutions and displacements that ultimately destabilize and decenter the text. Since he cannot repeat all textual elements, the deconstructor must find and employ that element or those few which will undermine most effectively the whole text. In the work of deconstruction, the critic comes upon his materials only in the text; consequently, the deconstruction of the text is discovered to be already underway before the intervention of the critic. "The critic cannot by any means get outside the text, escape from the blind alleys of language he finds in the work" ("SR II," 331).[14]

Still, the project has not yet been fully disclosed. The deconstructor does not simply enter a work with an attentive eye for the loose thread or the alogical element that will decenter the entire text; he intends *beforehand* to reverse the traditional hierarchies that constitute the ground of the text. The underlying program of *split writing* precedes the actual productions of deconstructive misreading. "'Deconstruction' as a procedure of interpreting the texts of our tradition," reveals Miller, "is not simply a teasing out of the traces of that dialogical heterogeneity. . . . Deconstruction rather attempts to reverse the implicit hierarchy within the terms in which the dialogical has been defined. It attempts to define the monological, the logocentric, as a derived effect of the dialogical rather than as the noble affirmation of which the dialogical is a disturbance, a secondary shadow in the originating light" ("ABW," 59–60). The role of the deconstructor as shadowman reemerges in the end: the project of deconstruction for Miller is to redefine Tradition by putting the "tradition of difference" in place of the dominant "tradition of metaphysics." In the short run, the deconstructive critical project works to widen the rift between the two traditions as a way to demonstrate the repression of the outlawed tradition while challenging the misguided caretaking of the canonized tradition. Ultimately, the practice of deconstructive analysis has for its goal the deconstruction not only of individual texts but also of the general system of traditional metaphysics.

Yet "deconstructive discourse can never reach a clarity which is not vulnerable to being deconstructed in its turn" ("DD," 30). Or, in Miller's words from the Yale manifesto, "the 'deconstructive' reading can by no means free itself from the metaphysical reading it means to contest" (*D&C*, 225). Unable to go beyond language, the deconstructor is compelled to use the concepts and figures of the metaphysical tradition. Thus he cannot construct a trope-free critical discourse; neither can he get to an undifferentiated literal bottom in the texts he reads. Impasse, endpoint, allegory, *aporia*. The outside is only an alluring illusion.

With his abiding concern for coping with logocentrism and for employing the energies of differance, Miller bears almost no resemblance to de Man. His regular insistence on the self-deconstructive and allegorical structures of writing and his obsession with tracking figural oscillations distinguish his methods from Derrida's. In other words, Miller's enterprise, an original blend, differs markedly from his two colleagues'. Unlike de Man, he stays ever attentive to and involved with history. For him critical reading by nature is archeological activity. There can be no back burner for history. Unlike Derrida, Miller denies the attractive illusion and paradoxical necessity of a revolutionary "change of ground." In effect, he does not believe in *split writing*. Or his disbelief vacillates. The logocentric systematics, embodying its nihilistic shadow, carries *within* itself the resources for deconstruction. The monstrous future, the coming new paradigm, the non-logocentric and apocalyptic outside—which play a role in Derrida's early vision of deconstruction—hold no place in Miller's program. He proclaims no new day, implies no messianic hope, propounds no monstrous future.

The hysterical and radical Nietzschean joy, characteristic of much early French deconstruction, suggestive of revolutionary endeavors, appears infrequently in Miller's works; when it does, the manic tone veers toward depression and the radical edge gets blunted. "Deconstruction attempts to resist the totalizing and totalitarian tendencies of criticism. It attempts to resist its own tendencies to come to rest in some sense of mastery over the work. It resists these in the name of an uneasy joy of interpretation, beyond nihilism, always in movement, a going beyond which remains in place . . ." (*D&C*, 252–53). The joy of a beyond, of the inconceivable yet promising outside, makes Miller "uneasy"; for him any "beyond" is already "in place" inside. Repetition replaces revolution. Deconstruction has always been with us. Plato did it in *The Sophist*. That's history. No going beyond it.

From Codes to Lexias
or Packets of Notation

In its English translation, Roland Barthes' *S/Z* boasts a sweeping dustjacket assessment by Susan Sontag: "*S/Z* demonstrates once again that Roland Barthes is the most inventive, elegant, and intelligent of contemporary literary critics." And it bears a prefatory Note by Richard Howard, which concludes provocatively: "Barthes's essay is the most useful, the most intimate, and the most suggestive book I have ever read about why I have ever read a book." Finally, Howard himself begins by citing some laudatory comments on *S/Z* from a British reviewer. Quite simply, *S/Z* (1970) is one of the most celebrated masterworks of contemporary criticism. Often it serves as *the* model of practical structuralist analysis. More recently, it has been regarded as something of an early "deconstructive" text that pushes past various limitations of structuralism. Our commentary furthers this view.

Taking *Sarrasine*, a little-known Balzac novella of roughly 13,000 words, Barthes performs an innovative analysis of approximately 75,000 words. In effect, he saturates an apparently humdrum realistic tale in a fecund reading. His commentary functions on four levels. First, 561 lexias (variable units of reading) are etched out and examined consecutively for connotative significance. Second, five codes—the cultural, hermeneutic, symbolic, semic, and proairetic (narrative)—are regularly invoked to orient and organize the numerous unfolding connotations of the lexias. Third, ninety-three causeries, reflecting sometimes on the lexias and codes and sometimes on more general literary and critical matters, are deployed much like conventional book sections. And, fourth, two appendices, one a chronological list of action sequences and the other a topic outline keyed to the causeries, are offered in a gesture, a sketch, of summation.

Of these analytical strata, the structuralist one of codes frequently provokes the most admiration. The lexias in this understanding serve as "codemes"; the appendices as backup tabular notes and data sources; and the brief expositions as elucidations and essayistic extensions of the codes.

Barthes rather obviously plays with the codes from the outset. He uses them yet subverts them. It's a case of double writing. Having defined each code once, Barthes redefines them to suggest their "function":

> there will be no other codes throughout the story but these five, and each and every lexia will fall under one of these five codes. Let us sum them up in order of their appearance, *without trying to put them in any order of importance*. Under the hermeneutic code, we list the various (formal) terms by which an enigma can be distinguished, suggested, formulated, held in suspense, and finally disclosed (these terms will not always occur, they will often be repeated; *they will not appear in any fixed order*). As for the semes, we merely indicate them—without, in other words, trying either to link them to a character (or a place or an object) or to arrange them in some order so that they form a single thematic grouping; *we allow them the instability, the dispersion, characteristic of motes of dust, flickers of meaning*. Moreover, we shall refrain from structuring the symbolic grouping; *this is the place for multivalence and for reversibility*; the main task is always to demonstrate that this field can be entered from any number of points, *thereby making depth and secrecy problematic*. Actions (terms of the proairetic code) can fall into various sequences which should be indicated merely by listing them, since the proairetic *sequence is never more than the result of an artifice of reading.* . . . Lastly, the cultural codes are references to a science or a body of knowledge; in drawing attention to them, we merely indicate the type of knowledge (physical, physiological, medical, psychological, literary, historical, etc.) referred to, *without going so far as to construct (or reconstruct) the culture they express.*
>
> (19–20; my italics)

At the outset Barthes founds a set of totalizing codes, telling us that each and every lexia will attach to one code, but at the same time he refuses to organize the elements of the codes. The result is a critical narrative portioning out materials into five "homogeneous" heaps. But the ensembles are neither ordered nor structured. They are deposited. Instead of revealing the deep frame or law of the text, the codes actually point up the textual or already-written nature of the lexic materials: the codes establish textuality and intertextuality—not deep structure. Barthes is clear:

> if the text is subject to some form, this form is not unitary, architectonic, finite: it is the fragment, the shards, the broken or obliterated network. . . . (20)

> they [the coded elements] are so many fragments of something that has always been *already* read, seen, done, experienced; the code is the wake of that *already*. Referring to what has been written, i.e., to the Book (of culture, of life, of life as culture), it makes the text into a prospectus of this Book. (20–21)

The codes tear out, collect, and tag miniscule tufts of the cultural intertext. In the target text everything is *always already* written so that the analysis of the book necessarily partakes of the greater archival Book. The book and its codes are inevitably shards and bits of this other Text. Unity of any sort does not come to bear.

(When we consider that Barthes' observations pertain to a text by Balzac, we grasp the historical import of his reading. Barthes deconstructs *realism* by undermining the old concepts of *mimesis, authorship*, and *reading* as well as the conventional notions of aesthetic *form, meaning*, and *style*.)

Barthes dallies with the codes. He works with them only up to a point. They function economically in the process of *structuration*: they aid the reading activity. But they are not allowed to build structure. The ludic motion of the reading, not the law of the tale, is Barthes' game. He wants to produce, to write, to disseminate the text, not consume it, not determine it, not close it. No matter how plural the text, whether triumphantly or parsimoniously so, the interpretive ideal orients reading toward triumphant dissemination. Excess of meaning rather than truth is the goal.

What of the lexias? Their deliberate arbitrariness and over-abundance constitute and deconstitute the codes. "We shall therefore star the text, separating, in the manner of a minor earthquake, the blocks of signification . . . into a series of brief, contiguous fragments. . . . This cutting up, admittedly, will be arbitrary in the extreme . . ." (13). The critical text itself necessarily becomes diced into bits. Each of the 561 lexias receives a paragraph. Each of the ninety-three causeries also gets a paragraph. Four modes of type alternate to keep the levels of analysis visually distinct. Despite such apparent clarity and organization, "each lexia does not aim at establishing the truth of the text (its profound, strategic structure), but its plurality (however parsimonious); the units of meaning (the connotations), strung out separately for each lexia, will not then be regrouped, provided with a metameaning . . ." (14). Grouping and metanaming, functions of structural coding, are refused. Truth is renounced. The cracks of the quake are foregrounded. Straightforwardly, the overall style and strategy of interpretation are admitted and accurately depicted:

The commentary, based on the affirmation of the plural, cannot therefore work with "respect" to the text; the tutor text will ceaselessly be broken, interrupted without any regard for its natural divisions (syntactical, rhetorical, anecdotic); inventory, explanation, and digression may deter any observation of suspense, may even separate verb and complement, noun and attribute; the work of the commentary, once it is separated from any ideology of totality, consists precisely in *manhandling* the text, *interrupting* it. (15)

This account of commentary centers on the lexia—the agent of interruption, the force of breakage. Unlike the codes, which systematize and unify, the lexias, the series of arbitrary pieces displayed step-by-step, effect slow-motion *decomposition* and forcefully institute *re-reading* as play. For the peculiar consequence of Barthes' lexic cutting is that the *entire* Balzac text is (re)cited word-by-word over the course of the commentary. Nothing is omitted. But everything is interrupted—shattered.

The deployment of the lexias depends on a strategic theory of semantic *notation*—of connotation and denotation. By arbitrary definition each lexia carries at most three or four meanings. A lexia, then, may be a few words or a string of sentences: the determining factor is the external limit on meanings or quantity of notation.

Generally speaking, we think of a word as having both a definite meaning, which we can locate in a dictionary, and an expanded (yet limited) meaning, which we can determine by context. Barthes turns this old formulation around. For him denotation is the last connotation. When the play of meanings closes, when connotation is regulated, denotation emerges. Most reading, in Barthes' view, works through connotation toward denotation. That is to say, reading seeks truth, objectivity, law. Whether in the name of denotation or connotation, this quest for the stable center provokes Barthes' derision. Yet, strategically speaking, the old concept of connotation allows for *some* plurality of meaning and, therefore, it promises some tactical returns for contemporary critical reading. Among other things, connotation possesses the power to relate meaning to other anterior and exterior sites of meaning; it refuses to fix itself anywhere (recourse to the dictionary is not sufficient); it disrupts univocal communication; and it permits restricted dissemination. As a tool, then, connotation opens access to the limited "plural texts" (the classics) of our tradition. Admittedly, it is inadequate to the modern limit-text— say *Finnegans Wake*—where licentious dissemination creates a different order of reading. Using connotation, the plural of the classic text can be produced in reading. As a device, connotation has value. Denotation, its unavoidable other, must therefore be maintained in a theatrics, an illusion, of truth.

Both codes and lexias package meaning. They are sculpted systems of notation useful in interpretation. In its innovative drift from codes to lexias, from totalization to fragmentation, *S/Z* furthers the drive beyond structuralism to "deconstruction." The reading of the text, its manhandling, happens on the level of lexias. Nevertheless, both codes and lexias arbitrarily and artificially frame units of meaning so that, despite mounting breakdown, such conveniences of order find a place in critical writing. By refusing to *structure* the codes and to formalize the lexias, Barthes undermines his own constructions. In short, he works *with* and *against* the resources of critical tradition. His is a double gesture.

What we call "causeries," Richard Howard labels "divagations." Both terms designate the ninety-three wandering discussions or mini-essays which chronologically precede the readings of patches of lexias and the assignings of code names. These "essays" serve various peculiar functions. They force the grouping or apportionment of lexias. Still, some of the divagations come before no collections of lexias; others precede anthologies of two dozen or more lexias. In brief, the causeries may gather and comment on many, a few, or none of the lexias. There exists no necessary connection between lexias (and their codes) and the incidences (and topics) of the causeries. Effectively, such wandering or randomness destabilizes yet energizes the critical text. Since many, the majority, of the divagations present penetrating and startling observations and insights, the pleasures of reading them amply compensate for the uncertainty of their status. Hellbent for order, any reader can filter these numerous reflections for recurring themes and other comforting regularities. Potentially, they proffer order. One can fashion a well-made text from *S/Z*. The surplus of the text, produced by the numerous "uncertain" causeries, transgresses the canons of coherence. Barthes attaches a lengthy and detailed Summary of Contents, promising to bring order to his excessive reflections. But his six dozen categories and subcategories only reduplicate the already twisted strands of surplus. Combined with the fragmentation of the lexias and the subversion of the codes, the dalliance of the divagations tends toward the fractured writing characteristic of later French deconstruction.

Just as Barthes' theory of the plural or disseminated text connects with his formulations on reading, so his polyphonic reading relates to his theory of critical writing. These lines of thought come together in several passages of *S/Z*:

In fact, the meaning of a text can be nothing but the plurality of its systems, its infinite (circular) "transcribability": one system transcribes another, but reciprocally as well: with regard to the text, there is no "primary," "natural," "national," "mother" critical language: from the outset, as it is created, the text is multilingual; there is no entrance language or exit language. . . . (120)

this is in fact the function of writing: to make ridiculous, to annul the power (the intimidation) of one language over another, to dissolve any metalanguage as soon as it is constituted. (98)

The language of critical writing, transcribing the plurality of meanings in a text, partakes of the language of the text—of the system of language. Critical language is neither inferior nor superior to "literary" language. There can be no privileged (meta)language, providing a sure way into or out of the text. Writing works to level the violence and eminence of any special language. All language is polyglot, with nowhere an isle of purity beyond the reach of contamination and mongrelization. Critical writing, a practice of transcription, emerges from the immense dictionary of all language. As such, it is fragmentary and heterogeneous borrowing.

In *L'Empire des signes* (1970), Barthes admires the Japanese custom of attending to wrapping while disregarding contents. The surface of the present, not its hidden gift, elicits appreciation. The preparations and the requisites of meaning, ritual and arbitrary, hold more interest and importance than the impatient possession of its truth. Whether the volume is ultimately empty or overfull seems less pressing than that its packaging be enjoyed. The writing of *S/Z* celebrates this non-Western tradition. Thus the lexia, a haiku of criticism, a delicacy of *S/Z*, is less violent manhandling than frail handiwork in miniature. A package of notation. Without hidden truth. A ritual of reading. Bonsai cultivated.[15]

Of Spaced Columns and Supplementary Fonts

mais la déconstruction n'est pas une opération critique, le critique est son objet; la déconstruction porte toujours, à un moment ou à un autre, sur la confiance faite à l'instance critique, critico-théorique c'est-à-dire décidante, à la possibilité ultime du décidable; la déconstruction est déconstruction de la dogmatique critique. . . .[16]

[but deconstruction is not a critical operation, the critical is its object; deconstruction always bears, at one moment or another, on the confidence given the critical, critico-theoretical, that is to say, deciding authority, the ultimate possibility of the decidable; deconstruction is deconstruction of critical dogmatics. . . .]

—Jacques Derrida

At one moment or another deconstruction turns on criticism and on itself. It becomes metacritical scorching of critical confidence. The decidable melts down into the undecidable. A chain reaction sets off relentless decompositions here, there, then seemingly everywhere. Textual dispersion results. Security falters.

Offered during a conversation on *Glas* (1974), this observation or reminder by Jacques Derrida characterizes an important aspect of deconstruction—an aspect that, in particular, destabilizes the work of critical reading in *Glas*. *Glas* bears to critical discourse a relation like that which *Finnegans Wake* holds with the novel. Excesses of innumerable sorts court unreadability. It is difficult, then, to say we have "read" *Glas*; the relationship is more one of "getting to know you" than "you're mine." Let us pursue such knowledge in an initial embrace.

Glas literally monumentalizes *split writing*. Two columns run continuously down each page and throughout the book. A space clearly separates the left and the right columns. The left column concerns Hegel, the father, philosophy, the status of knowledge and the psychology of the family. The right dwells on Genêt, the mother, literature, the ways of sex and the effects of castration. Fragmented and chaotic, both texts forbid access, although gradually the left seems almost coherent and focused when measured against the scattered and capricious right. On one side, the text reflects upon Mind; on the other side upon Body. The eagle and the flower symbolize these respective domains. Less simply, the book, seeming a parodic scan of the bicameral mind, shuttles between a barely tolerable neurosis and a progressive schizophrenia. Or, to toss out still another model, *Glas* moves between the Whole of Hegel's Absolute Knowledge and the Part of Genêt's Fetishized Objects.

To thematize, symbolize, or so model *Glas* is to court sure reduction. The uncomforting fact is that within each column numerous stolen citations, puns, themes, styles, and variable units of composition disrupt the reading. For example, conventional paragraphs get part of their middles shifted to make room for other invading paragraphs. Such incisions regularly interrupt each column. The enigmas of how to read these new spaces of writing present themselves on the opening pages and throughout the text. (This difficulty was posed earlier by "Tympan" in *Marges*.) To accommodate Derrida's sumptuous "compositions," various type sizes and styles continually decorate and alter the page. Visually, these supplementary fonts consecrate the poetics of fracture in evidence amidst the most radical enterprises of contemporary critical writing. What *S/Z* starts, *Glas* finishes. Derrida somberly realizes but playfully accepts the sacrifice of readability. His double posture is strategic and theatrical. Our operation of reading, a castrating procedure, perhaps provokes his tactical divisions:

Si j'écris deux textes à la fois, vous ne pourrez pas me châtrer. Si je délinéarise, j'érige. Mais en même temps, je divise mon acte et mon désir. Je—marque la division et vous échappant toujours, je simule sans cesse et ne jouis nulle part. Je me châtre moi-même—je me reste ainsi—et je "joue à jouir."

Enfin presque.

(Ah!) tu es imprenable (eh bien) reste.

Entrave, donc, deux fois.

Car si mon texte est (était) imprenable, il ne sera(it) pas pris, ni retenu. Qui serait puni, dans cette économie de l'indécidable? Mais si je linéarise, si je me mets en ligne et crois—niaiserie—n'écrire qu'un texte à la fois, cela revient au même et il faut encore compter avec le coût de la marge. Je gagne et perds à tous les cas mon dard.

double posture. Double postulation. Contradiction en soi de deux désirs inconciliables. Je lui donne ici, accusé dans ma langue, le titre de DOUBLE BANDE, le (la, les) mettant pratiquement en forme et en jeu.[17]

[If I write two texts at once, you cannot castrate me. However much I delinearize, I erect. At the same time, I divide my act and my desire. I—show off the division and always escape you, I sham without intermission and come nowhere. I castrate myself—I hold myself thus—and I "play at coming."
Well, almost.

(Ah!) you are impregnable (well) holding.

Checked, then, twice.

For if my text is (were) impregnable, it will (would) not be taken, nor held. Who would be punished in this economy of the undecidable? But if I lineate, if I set going a line and believe—nonsense—I am writing only one text at a time, it amounts to the same thing and it is still necessary to reckon with the cost of the margin. I gain and lose in each case my forked tongue.

double posture. Double postulation. Contradiction in-itself of two irreconcilable desires. I present it here, imputed in my language, the style of DOUBLE BAND, actually putting it (them) into form and into play.]

The spaced columns forbid any identity between Hegel and Genêt. Everything divides them. They are not related or regulated through balances, equalities, oppositions, or inversions. It's a *two-fold band*. Impregnable. Their implied relations stay undecidable. The two texts go separate ways. Yet telling conjunctions "happen" from time to time. (The Last Supper is discussed opposite the above citation.) The constant temptation to align these pillars under some common dome, to link the two, in a chiasmal pattern, for instance, vexes old modes of interpretation and subverts them through unrelenting division. Derrida refuses to harmonize his design. Sometimes the twin texts admit a parallel or resemblance. Such aleatory effects sustain the illusion of and search for unity. *Glas* has and eats its dadaistic cake. The spaces and fissures within and between the columns deal up a deluge of differences.

The first sentence of *Glas* asks: "quoi du reste aujourd'hui, pour nous, ici, maintenant, d'un Hegel?" (what remains today, for us, here, now, of a Hegel?). The final sentence, a fragment, seems an answer: "Aujourd'hui, ici, maintenant, le débris de" (Today, here, now, the debris of). And, in fact, *Glas* generates an overwhelming sense of richness gone bad, of surplus turned into debris, of exhaustion made final, of the here and now (full presence) become empty. At the same time it everywhere interrupts its entropic patterns and melancholy undertones, manhandling concepts, words and texts licentiously and gaily. The intimacy of the effort makes the project seem a family affair. Between Hegel (the father) and Genêt (the mother), Derrida (the son) resists obedience and silence (castration) in a kind of sprouting decelebration (independence) of parentage. This grim ritual of resistance becomes at once a bacchic revel and a defensive incorporation. Genêt as well as Hegel, badly abused, becomes enthroned in a dark chamber. A crypt.

What remains after such deconstruction? To such a "quoi du reste" Derrida replies not "je ne sais quoi" but *Glas*. A doubled self-consuming production whose modes exceed the debris and the abyss of previous deconstructions. A *supplement* to personal and cultural history.[18] Such supplementarity extends to and constitutes mind and body, father and mother, philosophy and literature, knowledge and sex, the family and castration—the two texts of *Glas*. All cross one another. All are undecidable. All disseminate. Strange hybrid formulations come to mind.

The *gl* of *glas* rings out across Derrida's Joycean writing. Caught deep in his throat, it mimics the sound tolled by the death knell (*glas*). It separates (*glose*) and joins (*glu*). As *glace*, it is icing on the cake and flaw in the gem, mirror and window. Like gleet, the *gl* makes up bodily discharges like phlegm and mucus (*glaire*). Overall, a sure cry (*écriture comme glapir et glatir*). The effect of Derrida's verbal play here is to foreground the materiality or physicality of language: language's wicked asemia and wit, generating relentless disruptive surfaces, continually surpass the reader and the author. More than the excess of themes, or the surplus of interruptions, or the multiplying bifurcation of compositional units, this textual play of signifiers presses home the interminable qualities of writing and analysis. Or rather, it arrests and checks any passage beyond language.

In several analyses and assessments of Derrida's book, Geoffrey Hartman, a Yale critic, has cast *Glas* as a precarious limit-text, which jeopardizes the fundamental stakes of criticism:

It is not only hard to say whether *Glas* is "criticism" or "philosophy" or "literature," it is hard to affirm that it is a book. *Glas* raises the specter of texts so tangled, contaminated, displaced, deceptive that the idea of a single or original author fades. . . .[19]

The result for our time may be a factional split between simplifying types of reading that call themselves humanistic and indefinitizing kinds that call themselves scientific. The fate of reading is in the balance.[20]

The notions of author and book, now inadequate, give way under the extremist critical (*inter*)*text*—tangled, contaminated, displaced, deceptive. The categories criticism, philosophy, and literature collapse; borders are overrun. Traditional forms of critical discourse dissolve. The promise of deconstruction is fulfilled for now with *Glas*. For Hartman, like Miller, a choice forces itself upon criticism: a simplifying humanism versus an indefinitizing deconstruction. The future of critical reading and writing hang in the balance. *Glas* is a forceful *summa*. While Miller chooses deconstruction, Hartman chances a poise of balance. There are several ways to

decipher his "The fate of reading is in the balance." It is characteristic of Hartman to pun on his strategy. In this, he resembles
Derrida more than all other deconstructors. Wordsmith, worried,
Hartman realizes that *Glas* is the moment when deconstruction
turns on criticism and deconstructs its limits and its substance.

Divagation on the Analytics of Desire

As poststructuralism develops and expands from the late 1960s on, deconstruction appears to occupy an ever more distinctive place within this general movement. Its theories of language and text, in particular, increasingly distinguish it from other post-structuralist projects. While Foucault, for example, shifts gradually from *discourse* toward *power* as theoretical foundation and focus, Derrida and other deconstructors specify more fully and more boldly the scope of *textuality* and the (de)formations of *differance* and *rhetoricity*. One noteworthy current within the broad movement of poststructuralism explores the possibilities and potentialities of *desire* as a foundation for a project of criticism. Among those whose works relate, more or less centrally, to such an enterprise are Roland Barthes, Gilles Deleuze, Félix Guattari, Julia Kristeva, and Jean-François Lyotard. Like *power* for Foucault, *desire* for some poststructuralists emerges as a mysterious and disruptive, all-pervading productive force of libido. It is an "undecidable," occupying a space analogous to *differance* in Derridean deconstructive theory. As Guattari portrays it, "desire is everything that exists *before* the opposition between subject and object, *before* representation and production."[21] And he follows up, declaring "Desire is not informed, informing; it's not information or content. Desire is not something that deforms, but that disconnects, changes, modifies, organizes other forms, and then abandons them" (69).

Significantly, *desire* manifests itself not just in textual forms, but in psychological, social, and institutional formations. Through and beyond discourse, it changes, modifies, and organizes the world and, consequently, it produces inevitable political effects—which call for a vigilant political criticism. Such criticism begins by setting *desire* free from the timid constraints of traditional psychoanalytical theory. As a result, the poststructuralist analytics of *desire*, mostly an affair of French criticism thus far, tends toward a critique of psychoanalysis and toward a committed political criticism, all the while exceeding the strictly textual project of deconstruction.

Under pressure from theorists of *desire* and *power*, deconstructors sometimes assign to their textual enterprise powers and potentialities for "real world" praxis and political impact. Such avowals insist, nevertheless, on the fundamental role of textual work. In the late 1970s Derrida, for instance, writes:

la nécessité d'une déconstruction. Selon la conséquence de sa logique, elle s'attaque non seulement à l'édification interne, à la fois sémantique et formelle, des philosophèmes, mais à ce qu'on lui assignerait à tort comme son logement externe, ses conditions d'exercice extrinsèques: les formes historiques de sa pédagogie, les structures sociales, économiques ou politiques de cette institution pédagogique. C'est parce qu'elle touche à des structures solides, à des institutions "matérielles," et non seulement à des discours ou à des représentations signifiantes, que la déconstruction se distingue toujours d'une analyse ou d'une "critique."[22]

[the necessity of a deconstruction. According to the consequence of its logic, it makes an attack not only upon the internal construction, both semantic and formal, of philosophemes, but upon what one would assign to it wrongly as its external place, its extrinsic circumstances of use: the historical forms of its pedagogy, the social, economic, or political structures of this pedagogical institution. It's because it meddles with solid structures, with "material" institutions, and not solely with discourses or with signifying representations, that deconstruction is always distinct from an analysis or a "critique."]

Deconstruction does meddle with social structures and cultural institutions in its attacks on the philosophical formations of culture. Yet such disturbances are not external to textual analysis. Economic, educational, and political institutionalization grow out of cultural practices established in philosophical systems—which constitute the "materials" of deconstructive work. Early and late deconstruction works within and against traditional metaphysical formations, scrutinizing such cultural resources and forms for a project of interrogating and breaching established borders.

One of the most important and influential of French poststructuralist works on *desire* is Gilles Deleuze's and Félix Guattari's

Anti-Oedipus (1972). Boisterous and bizarre, this challenging book begins to have an impact on American poststructuralism during the late 1970s. Fredric Jameson, in particular, explores and employs its theories productively.[23] Others should follow. With its overriding aim of establishing a new mode of analysis—schizoanalysis—*Anti-Oedipus* solicits our interest, for it presents strategies of reading different from, though analogous to, certain key stages of deconstruction. In order to contrast the stategies of schizoanalysis with deconstruction, we shall first review an ensemble of topics necessary for a working familiarity with the project of Deleuze and Guattari. Proceeding indirectly, we shall start by discussing the related conceptualizations of the libido, the Unconscious, and schizophrenia and will then examine the linked theories of Oedipus, social-libidinal production, and capitalism. After that we shall conclude with a contrast of the schizoanalytic and deconstructive projects, focusing on the matter of interpretive strategy.

I

Destroy, destroy. The task of schizoanalysis goes by way of destruction—a whole scouring of the unconscious, a complete curettage.[24]

—Gilles Deleuze and Félix Guattari

Deleuze's and Guattari's *Anti-Oedipus* scours old notions about the inside and the outside of existence, about psychological and sociological domains, offering new understandings of the Unconscious and the social body, promoting visions of revolutionary psychological formations and new earths to inhabit. Along the way the book dethrones conventional psychoanalysis and Marxism and develops a new analytics provocatively and self-consciously named *schizo*analysis.

During the course of development of human societies, three distinct forms of culture emerge: primitive (tribal), barbarian (despotic), and "civilized" (capitalistic). Each exhibits different modes of libidinal activity, economic production, political grouping, familial patterning, and linguistic practice. Capitalism, now about two centuries old, alters or breaks the old forms and modes of culture, yet sometimes it returns, in extreme moments, to barbaric and primitive ideas and usages. Within this overall historical frame, *Anti-Oedipus* focuses upon contemporary capitalist culture, situating it for clarification and understanding amid the older cultural formations.

In particular, the cultural understanding and sanctioned application of libidinal energy undergo changes during the course of history. Generated in the Unconscious, the disruptive productions of desire experience social codings and overcodings. A system of rules and axioms regulate desire. *Desire* itself, a disjunctive flow, attaches to and invests the social body through its loves and sexuality. It functions as a machine and as production, linking the Unconscious to the social field. The libido is machinelike in the sense that it consists of flows and breaks. Just as the mouth breaks the flows of air and milk, the penis the flows of urine and sperm, and the anus the flows of feces, so the various desiring machines cut into the flows of libidinal energy. Such mechanisms are "machines in the strict sense, because they proceed by breaks and flows, associated waves and particles, associative flows and partial objects, inducing—always at a distance—transverse connections, inclusive disjunctions, and polyvocal conjunctions, thereby producing selections, detachments, and remainders . . ." (287). All these processes are means of production. *Desire* is production. This machinic production invests the social field and elicits coding.

Desiring machines and productions operate on a molecular, not molar, level. The particles or elements carried in the flow or, better yet, flow-break of desire are *partial objects*. The smallest constituent units of the Unconscious, molecules of desiring chains in flux, partial objects enter into ephemeral relations and combinations—without ever constituting totalities or unities. "We live today in the age of partial objects, bricks that have been shattered to bits, and leftovers. We no longer believe in the myth of the existence of fragments that, like pieces of an antique statue, are merely waiting for the last one to be turned up, so that they may all be glued back together to create a unity that is precisely the same as the original unity. We no longer believe in a primordial totality that once existed, or in a final totality that awaits us at some future date . . ." (42). The autonomy of partial objects, the most minimal and *trace*-like elements of the Unconscious, corpuscles or waves constituting a libidinous flow-break, generates and insures a free play of particles in which multiplicity and fragmentation, not unity or totality, form heterogeneous conjunctions and inclusive disjunctions. Such aleatory combinations and fabrications are always selective and incomplete. Machinic connections, powerful and intense, continuously produce and proliferate free multiplicities because, despite every break or interruption, the flows never cease.

When the Unconscious attaches to or invests a social field, it mobilizes an interplay of overinvestments, counterinvestments, and disinvestments. All these oscillations happen between two extreme poles. One extreme involves large aggregates or molar structures that subordinate molecules while the other includes micro-multiplicities or partial objects which subvert structures:

The two poles are defined, *the one* by the enslavement of production and the desiring-machines to the gregarious aggregates that they constitute on a large scale under a given form of power or selective sovereignty; *the other* by the inverse subordination and the overthrow of power. *The one* by these molar structured aggregates that crush singularities, select them, and regularize those that they retain in codes or axiomatics; *the other* by the molecular multiplicities of singularities that on the contrary treat the large aggregates as so many useful materials for their own elaborations. *The one* by the lines of integration and territorialization that arrest the flows, constrict them, turn them back, break them again according to the limits interior to the system, in such a way as to produce the images that come to fill the field of immanence peculiar to this system or this aggregate, *the other* by lines of escape that follow the decoded and deterritorialized flows, inventing their own nonfigurative breaks or schizzes that produce new flows, always breaching the coded wall or the territorialized limit that separates them from desiring-production. And to summarize all the preceding determinations: *the one* is defined by subjugated groups, *the other* by subject groups. (366–67)

Unconscious libidinal investments tend toward one or another pole: the paranoiac or the schizophrenic. A chain of oppositions distinguishes these two extremes: aggregates/singularities, structures/elements, territorializations/deterritorializations, limits/flows, enslavement/escape, power/overthrow, coding/decoding, molar/ molecular. Given these two interpretations, the Unconscious emerges as either primarily expressive or productive. In one instance, it establishes totalities and representations—a complete theater. In the other, it inaugurates multiplicities and flow-breaks—a megafactory. As psychological *processes* rather than clinical illnesses, paranoia and schizophrenia mark the outer limits of unconscious desire and its social investments.

Anti-Oedipus argues that schizophrenia, the process of the production of desire and of desiring-machines, constitutes the becoming of reality. This pure flow of existence is subjugated through structures, codes, systems, and axioms. It undergoes territorializations and totalizations. The continuous flow-breaks of the Unconscious, the productions of the libidinal economy, experience artificial limitations and enslavements. Social forms and illnesses result. "Each of these forms has schizophrenia as a foundation; schizophrenia as a process is the only universal" (136). As an illness or entity, schizophrenia describes a point of arrest, a formation of repression, a stop in the flux. As a process of becoming, however, schizophrenia designates the microproduction of desire, the flow-break of partial objects, the powerful investing of the social field. The real is schizophrenia—the only universal.

The stroll of the schizo, his glorious wandering, engenders a world created in the process of its tendency, its coming apart, its decoding. When his flows cross over to deterritorialization and produce a new land, it is for him a simple finding, a finished design. The schizo, a deconstructed subject, "produces himself as a free man, irresponsible, solitary, and joyous, finally able to say and do something simple in his own name, without asking permission; a desire lacking nothing, a flux that overcomes barriers and codes, a name that no longer designates any ego whatever. He has simply ceased being afraid of becoming mad" (131). The schizo holds out positive promise. He is the revolutionary, the authentic figure, for our age.

2

Anti-Oedipus promotes new understandings of desire, the Unconscious, and schizophrenia while arguing against traditional psychoanalytic notions. It criticizes relentlessly the interpretation of the Unconscious established by Freud. For Deleuze and Guattari the partial objects in the Unconscious do not represent parental figures or family relations. The molecular Unconscious is not aware of persons; it does not symbolize or represent anything or anyone. The elements of the Unconscious precede and are never reducible to Oedipal figures or myths. Freudian psychoanalysis crushes the productive Unconscious, delimiting explosive desires and schiz-flows, circumscribing all libidinous elements, imposing mythical forms that express and represent family members. Psychoanalysis orders the Unconscious, turning it into a theater, a classical Greek theater—not even a contemporary surrealistic stage. At this scene stand papa, mamma, and baby. The wild, disruptive, and powerful forces of desire are compressed into a domestic drama—the family romance. The narrowness of this formulation, the Oedipal triangle, insures potent repression of desire and of schizophrenic processes—a repression embodied in the practices of psychoanalysis.

Throughout *Anti-Oedipus* Deleuze and Guattari rage against the imperialism of the Oedipal family. As paranoiac symbol of law and order, it provokes satiric jabs. As hermeneutic counter, it inspires bitter diatribes. The Oedipal family territorializes and codes desiring productions. Oedipus, a transcendental signifier ruling over all unconscious processes, warrants analytical order and intelligibility, insuring hermeneutic meaning and significance. Psychoanalysis everywhere deploys this interpretive scene to stage truth. The cure is directed. Neurosis is managed. But psychosis, a vast uncapped energetics, refuses direction, churning beyond the tiny theater of papa-and-mamma, demonstrating the impoverished repertoire of Freudian properties.

The libido invests the social field in its economic, political, historical, and cultural determinations. "There are no desiring-machines that exist outside the social machines that they form on a large scale; and no social machines without the desiring-machines that inhabit them on a small scale" (340). Desire is constitutive of a social field; it invades and invests the forces and means of production. From the moment there is social production there is desiring production. And vice versa. Investment in the social field precedes and encompasses that in the familial. The family is determined—not determining. Thus the Unconscious, the materialist Unconscious, unlike the idealist and ideological version of Freud, suffers the family as a molar aggregate or secondary formation. Oedipus makes a late and unfortunate appearance.

The social machine produces flows of goods and services, women and children, soldiers and weapons, herds and seeds, powers and policies, information and records, production and consumption. The three social machines—primitive, barbaric, and civilized societies—exhibit different configurations of these flows. Picturing each socius as an ornamented body, Deleuze and Guattari observe:

> The first is the underlying territorial machine, which consists in coding the flows on the full body of the earth. The second is the transcendent imperial machine, which consists in overcoding the flows on the full body of the despot or his apparatus, the Urstaat. . . . The third is the modern immanent machine, which consists in decoding the flows on the full body of capital-money. . . . (261)

A fourth formation, a universal potentiality haunting each society, is named: the clinical schizophrenic cosmic "body without organs." This socius effects a complete decoding of flows and a thorough deterritorialization. To resist it, each social machine erects codes and territorializations. Limits are set. Capitalism, in particular, most nearly approaching schizophrenization, invokes archaic reterritorializations and recodings, making use, for instance, of the Urstaat and the family, the dictator and the police. The dominant axiomatic of modern capitalist societies is *exchange value*. Everything has a price so everything flows.[25] This liquefaction of reality, a delirious flowing, cuts across every barrier, threatening to decode and deterritorialize all. Reactionary forms and paranoiac practices, therefore, rise up and ward off this horrendous threat. Nevertheless, the central dynamic of the capitalist social machine drives flows beyond all codes and territories.

Capitalism and psychoanalysis. Both discover and tap an activity of production in general and without distinction. This production exceeds representation. The decoded and deterritorialized flows of labor and of libido, both conceived of as subjective and abstract, follow the processes of schizophrenia. But schiz-flows and schiz-productions mark an *absolute* limit; capitalism and psychoanalysis, as social institutions, form *relative* limits. Employing archaic and paranoiac forms, both institutions recode and reterritorialize flows and productions for the social body. Private property and the privatized family, unrelated to the processes of schizophrenia, emerge as essential repressions, as factitious reterritorializations. Constructed on the ruins of primitive and barbaric societies, both institutions invoke territorial and mythic representations in their own service. The pernicious connections between labor and private property, on the one hand, and libido and the privatized family, on the other, are artificial, though axiomatic.

Significantly, Deleuze and Guattari regard the complicity between psychoanalysis and capitalism not as a parallel formation of equal forces, but as a relationship of part to whole. Psychoanalysis belongs to capitalism; it constitutes one part of a larger social machine. Psychoanalysis serves capitalism. Rather than fostering liberation, psychoanalysis furthers the work of modern capitalist repression, employing the family as its all-encompassing framework. Flows outside this system or frame are neither acknowledged nor permitted. Asylums, coded territories, sequester exceptions. Oedipus turns the hearth into a cell. The family, privatized, brings desire into line with the requirements of the social machine.

Oedipus is a tool of the capitalist machine. The Oedipal family serves as the locus of all social determinations. Social images apply strictly to the family. Subjugated, the subject comes to the psychoanalyst already oedipalized. Oedipus assumes shape in the family, not on the analyst's couch. Psychoanalysis does not invent Oedipus. It reenforces this sociopsychic repression. Oedipus "is the ultimate private and subjugated territoriality of European man" (102). Deleuze and Guattari are vehemently anti-Oedipus.

3

In *Anti-Oedipus* Deleuze and Guattari promulgate four theses for the project of schizoanalysis. First, libidinal investment is social. Second, specific investments may be either unconscious or preconscious and class-determined. Third, libidinal investments of the social field have primacy over all familial investments. And,

fourth, social-libidinal investments approach paranoiac or schizophrenic poles. The underlying principle is that *desire* joins up
with society: the Unconscious is a psycho-*social* factory. Where
psychoanalysis avoids economic, political, and cultural factors and
where Marxism leaves out libidinal matters, schizoanalysis intervenes, demonstrating that such Freudian and Marxist omissions
aid and abet capitalist practices. *Anti-Oedipus* promotes, therefore,
a wide-reaching concept of production: all production is always
already desiring-production and social production. Anything that
circumvents or circumscribes this order of production gets taken
to task in a radical destructive operation.

The project of schizoanalysis, deconstructive in tone and character, forcefully renounces traditional psychoanalytic and Marxist
modes of interpretation. It abjures structuralism, particularly the
Lacanian variety. It openly deplores all hermeneutics. It aims to
liberate the flow-breaks of desire. It is Barthesian. To let the
libidinal schiz-flows breach all borders and barriers. It is Derridean. To unleash molecular forces so as to undo all molar formations. It is Foucaultian. To set revolution going. It is telquelian.
To celebrate the numinous energies of existence in a joyous activity
of free play. It is Nietzschean.

The inherently functionalist strategies of schizoanalysis aim at
revolution; its reading practices further this general project. "For
reading a text is never a scholarly exercise in search of what is
signified, still less a highly textual exercise in search of a signifier.
Rather it is a productive use of the literary machine, a montage
of desiring-machines, a schizoid exercise that extracts from the
text its revolutionary force" (106). Schizoanalysis ignores the
primitive signified and the despotic signifier, focusing instead on
the "civilized" *schiz-sign* (a minimal unit of desiring flow-break).
The ultimate mission of liberation supersedes both the ancient
sober search for truth and the contemporary luxurious dissemination of meaning; rather it seeks the mad exploitation of libidinal
productions for future revolutionary ends. Schizoanalysis exceeds
contemporary deconstruction. More than a textual practice, it is
a militant and dedicated political praxis. The ideal schizoanalytic
reader—who simply stops being afraid of becoming mad; who
quests after singularities, flows, overthrows, decodings, deterri-

torializations and new lands; who then remains solitary, free, ir-responsible, joyous, independent, satisfied, and nameless—this new reader is the schizo. His activity lets the revolutionary ma-chine, the literary machine and the analytical machine become parts of one another. Ravaged, the text is left behind for the revolution.

Significantly, potential *perversions* jeopardize the schizoanalytic project. Clouds loom over the new land. The dark old social body reforms and resists:

> Previously we distinguished two poles of delirium, one as the molec-ular schizophrenic line of escape, and the other as the paranoiac molar investment. But the perverted pole is equally opposed to the schizo-phrenic pole, just as the reconstitution of territorialities is opposed to the movement of deterritorialization. And if perversion in the narrowest sense of the word performs a certain very specific type of reterritorial-ization within the artifice, perversion in the broad sense comprises all the types of reterritorializations, not merely artificial, but also exotic, archaic, residual, private, etc. . . . *In short, there is no deterritorialization of the flows of schizophrenic desire that is not accompanied by global or local reterritorializations, reterritorializations that always reconstitute shores of rep-resentation.* What is more, the force and the obstinacy of a deterritorial-ization can only be evaluated through the types of reterritorialization that represent it; the one is the reverse side of the other.
>
> (315–16; my italics)

> We are all little dogs, we need circuits, and we need to be taken for walks. Even those best able to disconnect, to unplug themselves, enter into connections of desiring-machines that re-form little earths. (315)

There is no escape from aggregates, structures, codes, (re)territorializations and other such molar formations. We need such circuits, connections, and representations. We are little dogs. Any schizoid escape from such perverted or paranoiac *necessary* formations must proceed through these artificial and exotic, ar-chaic and grandiose creations. To attain deterritorialized realms, the schizoanalytic operation must work through reterritorial-ized—perverted—*representations.* The ultimate quest for schiz-flows, *trace*-like "signifying" units, molecules of libidinal and so-cial production, must proceed in an activity of reversal—a vigorous quarrying of the hidden underside of representation. But always representation. Textual work cannot be circumvented.

Despite what Deleuze and Guattari declare, the mining of the text for valuable and radiant gists—this penetration of the discursive surface for unconscious molecular materials—is an archeological and textual endeavor. The text is excavated. Below or beyond the text lies the goal: a miniscule, yet throbbing, quantum of *life*-energy! But there is no outside-the-text. The *perverse* text blocks the way. The way to where? The libido? The socius? The Unconscious? What outside? "Representation" seals the text off from the "outside."

Representation remains for schizoanalysis the essential means to its ends. Yet the problematics of (mis)reading through representations elicit little response from Deleuze and Guattari. The rhetoricity and materiality of representational language, its stickiness and its liquefaction, receive hardly any attention. In renouncing the signifier for the schiz-flow, schizoanalysis circumvents textuality and its enigmas, but they return, doglike, to pester and threaten the enterprise.

While *Anti-Oedipus* nowhere comments directly on deconstruction, it views its practice of reading the "signifier" as a late form of despotism, attached unwittingly and paradoxically to the Law and the State (the hermeneutic enterprise), a grim energetics of death, a distortion of desire onto the Law as death. Hermeneutics and deconstruction are both agents of the repressive State.

Occasionally it still happens that the young dogs will call for a return to the despotic signifier, without exegesis or interpretation, while the law, however, wants to explain what it signifies, to assert an independence of its signified. . . . For the dogs . . . want desire to be firmly wedded to the law in the pure detachment and elevation of the death instinct, rather than to hear, it is true, hypocritical doctors explain what it all means. But all that—the development of the democratic signified or the wrapping of the despotic signifier—nevertheless forms part of the same question, sometimes opened and sometimes barred, the same extended abstraction, a repressive machinery that always moves us away from the desiring-machines. For there has never been but one State. The question "What is the use of that?" fades more and more, and disappears in the fog of pessimism, of nihilism, Nada, Nada! (213–14)

Despotism, pessimism, nihilism. Law and death. The State. All repressive elements of deconstruction, which moves away from desiring-machines. The question, *the* strategic question of schizoanalytic functionalism—"What is the use of that?"—poses itself insistently. We know the answer: deconstruction inhibits the revolution; it should foment. And yet Barthes' *The Pleasure of the Text* and Derrida's *Glas*, orgasmic Gongorian texts working beyond Oedipus and the family, answer with a writing more radical than *Anti-Oedipus*—a libidinal poetics more nearly superseding representation. "*Anti-Oedipus*," admits Deleuze, "cannot be said to be rid of all the formal apparatus of knowledge: surely it still belongs to the University. . . ."[26] To the extent that it never questions its own confident metalanguage, its self-assured hierarchical set of values, its precipitous dismissal of the textual free play of the signifier, schizoanalysis falls just that short of a deconstructive project and remains caught up in a problematics of representation. The difficulties of reading and the pleasures of misreading rarely emerge amidst this headlong rush to breach the borders of cultural forms and institutions. The analytics of desire must pass through the circuits of textuality—where grammar and rhetoric, spacing and trace lie in wait. Deleuze and Guattari demonstrate more dramatically than most contemporary theorists the inevitable difficulties and pitfalls of overleaping the ensemble of problematics opened to view by deconstruction. There is no getting around text; sooner or later it comes to haunt every project.

Of Metacriticism and Creative Criticism

One tendency of deconstruction is toward a poetics of fracture. The well-made sentence, for instance, undergoes assault. Other larger units of composition and organization provoke strategies of decomposition. The coherence of the essay and the book and their logical sequences of development give way. Techniques of fragmentation and disfiguration, pioneered by modern and postmodern artists, aid the deconstructor to dismantle his own critical work and its orders. The numerous bits and aleatory conjunctions of *S/Z* and the double broken-columns and expository discontinuities of *Glas* serve as exemplars. The massive hodgepodge of "letters," arranged chronologically, of Derrida's "Envois" in *La Carte postale* and the mishmash of "figures," arranged alphabetically, of Barthes' "Fragments" of *A Lover's Discourse* (1977) offer further instances of fracture.[27] Textuality invades critical production. The free play of the signifier migrates to and decenters critical readings *and* writings. We recall Foucault's radical program, his strategy, for writing history: employ parodic exaggerations, multiply discontinuities, and institute tactical stupidities. The text of the scholar renounces order, objectivity, and truth; it denies any solid or secure, any *nontextual*, language—any metalanguage; it accepts and embraces the condition of language. De Man and Miller designate this status of critical (and literary) discourse *allegory*. The scholar's text, a production of a deconstructed subject, sometimes of a libidinous "hysteric," disseminates meaning beyond truth or totalization. It is the birth of a frolicsome "science," a playful "hermeneutics" of indeterminacy, reminiscent of Nietzsche's most visionary and aphoristic moments. Criticism catches up with and surpasses avant-garde literature. Perhaps.

If the first half or two-thirds of the twentieth century seems an Age of Criticism, then the latter part appears an Age of Metacriticism. In place of the critical scrutiny of "literary" works, we witness the exploration and production of "critical" texts as "literary" creations. Within the field of textuality, no division exists between these two orders of critical text or analysis. Thus to examine *S/Z, Glas,* or *Anti-Oedipus* is no different and no less valuable then to explore *Sarrasine, The Balcony,* or *Gradiva.* And maybe such work is now more important. In both critical operations the old matters of style, genre, theme, and content can be made to apply. More importantly, the new problematics concerning the processes of reading, the activities of free play, the effects of intertextuality and the practices of writing bear equivalent pertinence. Literature, criticism, metacriticism—all partake of language. All share the same resources.

One impulse of deconstruction is toward a practice of metacriticism. Derrida's early critique of Lévi-Strauss, an extremely influential endeavor, serves as a model. So too does his notorious work on Lacan. De Man's essays on major critics in *Blindness and Insight,* particularly his study of Derrida's *Grammatology,* exhibit this same tendency of criticism to become metacriticism. Several of Miller's most important and well-known works (his essays on Poulet, Riddel, and Abrams) confirm the impulse, as do Riddel's texts on Heidegger, Derrida, and Miller. In a curious turn, Barthes' metacritical works playfully examine his own texts and past critical notions. Parts of *The Pleasure of the Text* and *Roland Barthes* constitute special models of a metacritical endeavor. To the extent that such moments leave behind particular critical texts and take up specific issues of critical *theory,* they qualify as "theoretical metacriticism." Derrida on Lacan's reading of Poe and de Man on Derrida's analysis of Rousseau would classify here as "practical metacriticsm." Within this emerging domain or contemporary discourse, a third force, "historical metacriticism," seems likely to develop. Hayden White's works, *Metahistory* and *Tropics of Discourse,* come to mind as possible examples.

Metacriticism may focus on any number of issues and topics. Studies exist, for instance, of the epistemology of reading, the psychology of readers, the rhetoric of critical language, the forms or genres of critical writing, the history of such genres, the psychoanalysis of specific critics, and the ideology of particular critical practices. Apparently, all the old subjects and types of criticism can be carried over to a project of metacriticism.

In our time the metacritical impulse shows up in many non-deconstructive activities and fields. In literary studies, for instance, Georges Poulet's often anthologized "Phenomenology of Reading" (1969), which presents critiques of six important French critics, exhibits a version of *phenomenological* metacriticism. And Fredric Jameson's "Metacommentary" (1971), winner of the prestigious Parker Award from the Modern Language Association, displays a *Marxist* program for metacriticism. One could multiply important examples. The point, an obvious one, is that "deconstructive metacriticism" takes part in a larger, cultural enterprise. It neither initiates nor encompasses this discourse. It does, though, offer some interesting works in the field: those, for instance, by Derrida, de Man, Miller, Riddel, Barthes, and others. To suggest the interest of such work, we shall look at the project of Geoffrey Hartman, who practices a highly visible variety of contemporary metacriticism. To conclude this section, we shall suggest a possible formalization of the metacritical stance.

I

In each of his essay collections, *Beyond Formalism* (1970), *The Fate of Reading* (1975), and *Criticism in the Wilderness* (1980), Geoffrey Hartman includes a half-dozen metacritical texts. His main metacritical interests are in the status of criticism as reading and in the forms of criticism as writing. Significantly, *Glas* dominates Hartman's more recent speculations; it occupies a singular position as an extremist limit-text; it haunts him and, in part, directs his speculations. And too a phantom form of reductive New Criticism spooks and sensitizes all his metacritical theorizing.

Hartman senses two extreme tendencies in modern criticism. On the one hand, the work of the *scholar-critic* tends to restrict itself to the scrupulous elucidation of particular texts. It defines literature in reductive formal terms and limits its work to narrow fields of specialization. It becomes a trade in which the practicing critic operates as a retainer of technological society. Inevitably, this criticism overvalues the literary work as a miracle of universal truth. On the other hand, the work of the *philosopher-critic* regards the literary text as a moment on the way to absolute thinking or higher knowledge. A lover of wisdom, restless and dialectical, the philosopher-critic undervalues literature, leaving it behind in his

Faustian quest (*CW*, 214–25). Since the days of Matthew Arnold, Anglo-American criticism continuously defines and refines itself as *scholarship*. The last "philosopher-critic" in this tradition is probably Coleridge. European hermeneutics, particularly a certain French and German strain, develops and partially maintains criticism as *philosophy*. Hartman would like to see a mixing of these traditions or critical modes. An arrangement between Common Sense and Sky Writing. Like Miller, Bloom, and de Man, fellow Yale critics, Hartman is something of a "practical" critic, who aims to keep the text always at the center of critical activity, yet he deplores the timidity and adulation characteristic of the scholar-critic. For Hartman one objective of American deconstruction is to effect an historical rapprochement of the two dangerous tendencies in criticism.

The two types of critics practice different kinds of reading. The scholar-reader, using a direct approach, applies good sense and natural wit to explicate his significant texts while the philosopher-reader, using a mediated approach, employs historical or intertextual knowledge to understand all cultural constructs (*D&C*, 187). The first approach irritates Hartman, and he often debunks the humble reader:

He subdues himself to commentary on work or writer, is effusive about the *integrity of the text*, and feels exalted by exhibiting art's controlled, fully organized energy of imagination. What passion yet what objectivity! What range yet what unity! What consistency of theme and style![28]

The second approach worries Hartman, and he sometimes sketches the faults of the extremist contemporary philosopher-interpreter:

Books or pictures are but fixed explosives, moments in a process of dissemination, and comparable to winged words, legendary acts, or endless sketches, *zettel*, and *cahiers*. His own text legacy, insofar as it exists, evokes a restless and aspiring dialectic. Ideally, of course, nothing would remain, except in the form of a self-consuming labor of thought.

(*CW*, 217)

While he frequently lambastes the ahistoricism as well as the humility of the first mode (which he sometimes calls "practical criticism"), Hartman occasionally laments the atextualism and "free play" of the second type, which in its most recent form gives up its search for a supreme Dialectic in favor of a negative herme- neutics of fragmentation and parody (*CW*, 226–49). One criticism simplifies and the other indefinitizes.

No American deconstructor remains as concerned with critical *writing* as Hartman. The major goal of his critique is to undermine the plain style of Arnoldian or Anglo-American criticism. Basi- cally, Hartman condemns the separation made between creative writing, which is always highly valued, and critical writing, which is typically debased. Such partition of the creative and critical spirit denies for criticism the full resources of the literary tradition. A "creative critic," for instance, seems unthinkable. The critic must serve the master creative text. Put down, the critic pretends or believes that his writing is commentary rather than artwork. Hart- man wants criticism to effect a mutual domination or interchange- able supremacy with creative writing.[29] In particular, the cool and literate style, free of fantasy and fiction, must go and with it the bureaucratic discrimination of functions between literature and criticism.

Hartman regards the critical essay as a distinct genre that is part of the history of prose. Against the Arnoldian tendency to di- minish the creative aspects and to expand the service functions of the form, Hartman advertises the energetic advances made by contemporary critics, particularly Derrida. In a seminal essay aptly entitled "Crossing Over: Literary Commentary as Literature" (1976), Hartman sums up his goal this way:

literary commentary may cross the line and become as demanding as literature: it is an unpredictable or unstable "genre" that cannot be sub- ordinated, a priori, to its referential or commentating function. Com- mentary certainly remains one of the defining features. . . . But the perspectival power of criticism . . . must be such that the critical essay should not be considered a supplement to something else. . . . [A] re- versal must be possible whereby this "secondary" piece of writing turns out to be "primary." ("CO," 265; rpt. in *CW*, 201)

Today literary criticism is creating a *literature* of its own—without jeopardizing fiction, poetry, or drama. The potential powers of critical writing, perhaps in self-conscious reaction to repressive historical reductions, must be realized in a creative resurgence so that ultimately the work of criticism will be as much an event in the history of literature as the work of art is in the history of criticism (*CW*, 215).

Hartman subverts conventional habits of critical reading and writing, recommending more playful and creative practices for literary criticism. Fascinated by psychoanalysis, he urges self-analysis and careful examination upon the sophisticated critic. At the same time he maintains his long-standing ties with the phenomenological tradition. He refuses to sacrifice the subject and his intentionality, to accept unlimited free play and the Gongorian text, to make of history a playful and portable context. He seeks revision—not revolution.

For Hartman the Derridean deconstruction of the logocentric tradition, its substitution of undecidables for the old hierarchies, appears unacceptable. "The main achievement of the older criticism . . . is that it revives in us the sense of *hierarchy*: the tremendous effort it takes to order and subordinate, so that even if that effort (called civilization) leads to repression or to a self-disturbing rather than settled happiness, it remains . . . heroic. . . ."[30] While he wants creative criticism, Hartman still draws a line. "I am unhappy with certain, let us call them unisex, experiments in critical writing—which weaken the task of interpretation by spicing it up with parafictional devices . . ." (*CW*, 218). In the Preface to the Yale manifesto, Hartman admits that he, like Bloom, is barely a deconstructionist and that, on occasion, he writes against deconstruction. He both admires and dreads *Glas*, for it raises a fearful specter of unreadable critical texts and a dehierarchized civilization, yet it holds out the alluring promise of a new and productive creative writing and reading for criticism.

2

The metacritical speculations of Hartman present a peculiar, yet telling, scene. We witness the resources of tradition being turned against tradition. At the same time a dread of the consequences and a stubborn courage lead to revision and maintenance of tradition. A possibility of fracture is glimpsed and courted, a new interpretation and a new writing appear as apparitions, but the vision produces anxiety and moderation. The "split writing" of

Hartman refuses to renounce the old hierarchies of the logocentric epoch so that a deep split is never actually effected. Hartman emerges as a voyeur of the border, who watches or imagines crossover and warns of dangers. Still, the borders between literature and criticism and between theory and practice collapse. Poetics and hermeneutics infiltrate one another. Hierarchies get leveled, if not reversed or destroyed. Metacritical subversion is facilitated, however resisted. Hartman advances the cause of deconstruction.

Early in *The Pleasure of the Text* Roland Barthes wonders "How can we read criticism?" He answers:

Only one way: since I am here a second-degree reader, I must shift my position: instead of agreeing to be the confidant of this critical pleasure—a sure way to miss it—I can make myself its voyeur: I observe clandestinely the pleasure of others, I enter perversion; the commentary then becomes in my eyes a text, a fiction, a fissured envelope. (17)

There are two dynamics of metacriticism. First, the metacritic casts himself as voyeur, observing from a distance the activities of another critic. This distance engenders a certain generic fascination—always a function of deliberative dissociation and intimate interest. In other words, metacriticism, whether finally loving or angry, cool or hot, depends on a peculiar involvement, a hesitant intimacy and a certain hauteur, an ambivalent detachment. Second, the metacritic constitutes the primary critical work as a construct, a fragmented entity, a text. Its parts solicit his attention. Aspects, levels, and local effects generate admiration or disgust. Indifference never surfaces. Inevitably, the activity of metacriticism appears as perversion. Other guises are only covers.

In its engagements and activities, metacriticism seems no different than criticism and literature. Our description of the metacritic characterizes the critic and the poet as well. While we may detect a progressive falling-off as we move from poetry to criticism to metacriticism, this pattern depends on an initial privileging of poetry over criticism and criticism over metacriticism. Why not declare each domain equally worthy? Or proclaim metacriticism more valuable than criticism or literature? One's understanding and appreciation of criticism, literature, and life might very well be increased more by a metacritical work than by any critical text or poem. It is conceivable and quite possible that a text by Derrida can be for us more profound, profitable and enjoyable than any essay by Arnold or novel by Dickens. Perhaps *Glas* is dearer to us today than *Natural Supernaturalism* or *Gravity's Rainbow*.

Modalities of the Edge
or Summing Critical Reading/Writing

Is anyone surprised that all readers must join this visionary company of prophets and rhetoricians? The structure of interpretation repeats itself ceaselessly. We all stand precariously before the edge of the Greek encampment, fronting the spaces of error under the sign.

Who are the members of this "visionary company"? There are three answers. Taken from our first Prologue, the epigraph refers to certain figures in the *Iliad*: cautious Polydamas, reckless Hector, the Olympian narrator, and perhaps blind Homer. They appear as types of readers, suffering a common predicament. The company also includes all interpreters. You and I and the others. The careful, the courageous, the elected, the myopic. . . . Lastly, the "visionary company," cited at this strategic place in our text, incorporates the specific band of figures previously hustled into service. This ragtag group of interpreters recalls Saussure, Lacan, Lévi-Strauss, Derrida, de Man, Miller, Heidegger, Spanos, Riddel, Barthes, White, Foucault, Bloom, Hartman, and Deleuze and Guattari. All play at prophet and rhetorician.

Scattered across Parts I, II, and III, the observations on our many visionary readers and writers will be rehearsed here, as a convenient summary and conclusion to our survey of contemporary theories and practices of critical reading and writing. To start let us return to Saussure at the scene of the edge.

I

There are two Saussures: the scientist who maps out semiology and the eccentric critic who charts hidden anagrams. The one publicly lectures on linguistics; the other secretly devours ancient poetry to pieces. We move from structuralism and jump beyond it to—what? Proto-deconstruction perhaps. Suppose we do not universal human mind. In addition, we find a peculiar panoply of different forms and styles of critical writing. Predictably, there occur arguments replete with syllogisms, references to various authoritative ancients and moderns, and scientific formulas and demonstrations. Less predictably, there surfaces an inchoate style of productive omission: fragments, discontinuities, and ellipses accompany broken-off observations, partial formulas, and inexhaustible objects of study. The fact of the incomplete and of the untotalizable generates a poetics of fracture.

Just as these moderns each suggest distinctive modes of reading and writing, so too do the exemplary ancient characters out of the *Iliad*. We return to the original scene at the edge. Relying on the cultural conventions of the bird sign, Polydamas reads the awesome eagle as an omen from the gods. While he expresses reservations, he casts himself as a substitute for the absent soothsayer: his discourse then relies on inspired analogy. Like Polydamas, the narrator admits uncertainty, yet he persists in unfolding his memorial narrative of the old heroic days assured of divine guidance: his text employs the evocative powers of apostrophe. Lastly, Hector decides to interpret the eagle as a "natural sign," not an omen; his bird signifies nothing. Having received from Zeus earlier assurance, delivered by the messenger Iris, Hector grows confident that his "natural" interpretation is correct: to construct his truth he uses authoritative allusion. Implicitly or explicitly, each interpreter claims special powers and each relies on figurative language. The activity of interpretation produces prophetic reading and ornamental discourse. To interpret a sign, to venture a reading—to be on the mythical edge—is to play seer and rhetor. As they stand before the edge of the Greek encampment, the Trojan heroes reveal the structure of interpretation. Though uncertain at first, they fill a space and risk error; they read signs and inscribe tropes.

2

When Derrida offers his reading of Saussure, he focuses on the scientific program for semiology, not on the quest for anagrams. He casts himself as the visionary father of a new science—grammatology. Openly, he revises Saussure's rhetoric, substituting his own writing for the voice of the master. The sign is interpreted anew; the *grammè*, no doubt a more archaic Greek root than Saussure's *sēmeîon*, covers the spaces of the forerunner's error. The scene of the edge opens up as the enclosure of the logocentric systematics is gradually exposed. While displacing Saussure, Derrida develops an unmerciful hyperbole: the first structuralist emerges as a fall guy for the entire tradition spanning from Plato and Aristotle to Lacan and Lévi-Strauss. Like the others in our visionary company, Derrida practices prophecy and rhetoric.

Confronting the sign, Derrida initiates innovative modes of writing and interpretation. (His writing, often imitated, sometimes suggests and licenses a practice of fractured discourse, which at the moment appears to be one of the most influential new styles of critical prose of the early space-age period.) The sign in Derrida's eye is more disturbing and peculiar than any Greek eagle (omen or not) with a snake writhing in its talons, than any complex of isolated Greek or Roman syllables scattered across the grave text of an ancient poem, than any floating signifier caged in the cellar of the psyche, or than any empty mytheme, awaiting others, all tucked in the crevices of a composite myth. The *trace*, imperceptible yet primal, highly charged while negative, inhabits everything, not just visions, poems, psyches, and myths. Everything. Still, it is invisible; we may know it only by its disruptive and transgressive effects. Seemingly subatomic, the trace is generically intractable, unnatural, and untrackable. Such truth is no stranger to fiction.

As his critics unfailingly point out, Derrida's main edge in the activity of criticism is transgression, which is a way of saying that deconstruction characteristically presumes and battens on prior constructions. It is a negative enterprise. The theory of the trace, a profoundly negativizing notion, more an idea of antimatter than matter, sins against common sense and patience. But it provides Derrida continuing access to the edge. Interpretation is inherently transgressive.

In his analysis of Lacan's hermeneutics of the floating signifier, Derrida uncovers a complicity between the kernel signifier and the signification of the phallus. In Derrida's view, Lacan systematically keys his analyses of signifiers to the deeply veiled phallus.

The truth of the signifier rests in a stable signified. Because Lacan centers his interpretations on the hidden phallus, Derrida labels his project "phallocentric," which means that his work partakes of logocentrism. The phallus instances *logos* revealed. More than any other signifier, the phallus occupies a privileged position in Lacanian analysis. It is a "transcendental signifier" to which others refer and below which others float. It centers and regulates the processes of interpretation.

In Derrida's reading, Lévi-Strauss, like Lacan, relies on one transcendental signifier or another to center and organize his analyses. The potential floating or free play of the signifier, characterized as unstable and disruptive process, is domesticated and managed through application of a matchless signifier. In place of free play reigns the center. Play is limited and structures are established in deference to and harmony with a dominant signifier. Interpretation imposes centered structure to delimit the free play of signifiers. Even though he employs these logocentric procedures to unify his myths, Lévi-Strauss admits in the Overture to the *Mythologiques* that such unity "is a phenomenon of the imagination, resulting from the attempt at interpretation; and its function is to endow the myth with synthetic form and to prevent its disintegration. . . ."

For Derrida there are two interpretations of interpretation. One seeks to decipher and establish a stable center or truth, which escapes the transgressive activities of play and of the signifier. The other affirms play and the lawless signifier. It abjures transcendence. Lacan and Lévi-Strauss, caught between the two—between logocentrism and deconstruction—carry out nostalgic and guilty projects. Derrida promotes a joyous and free interpretation of the signifier, which neither demands nor provides truth or center, escape or transcendence. Where logocentric hermeneutics centers, deconstruction decenters. Instead of restricted play and filled spaces, deconstruction desires radical free play and exorbitantly overfilled spaces, aiming to subvert regulated and filtered interpretation. While traditional interpretation tries to check or hide the inescapable errors at the edge, Derridean reading attempts to draw out and cash in on this potential proliferation (*dissemination*). It wants to keep the interpretive crisis at the edge continuously on the edge. It intends, not to avoid the uncertainty, soothsaying, and troping that accompany interpretation, but to multiply and continue these operations openly and energetically. Derrida joins the visionary company with a notable vengeance.

The idea of the trace, an undecidable concept, is a match for deconstructive interpretation. Unlike Saussure's syllable, Lacan's signifier and Lévi-Strauss' mytheme, it ultimately disrupts rather than unifies, producing an ongoing decentering and free play while discrediting any transcendent meaning or structural coding. Its power source is a permanent charge of *differance*; as such, the error under the sign is permanently figured in (*spacing*) rather than filtered out. Once again, we envision interpretation as an inherently prophetic and rhetorical activity, carried out under an indefinite and threatening sign, enacted amidst unavoidable dangers at the edge. The characteristic caution of Polydamas creates a weak guess; the assurance of Hector a costly mistake; and the humble prayers of the Homeric narrator an obvious fiction. The more fully the edge is overcome, the bigger the error. Truth comes, if at all, by chance and in retrospect.

The major text of Derrida in the Yale manifesto, a severely fractured reading of a Blanchot story, superimposed upon an absent Shelley poem, linked to another Blanchot tale, and set atop a second and different, yet intertwining, text, which comments upon a peculiar array of issues, including translation, academic politics, and itself—this doubled, heterogeneous text raises the problematic, implicitly and sometimes explicitly, of the *border*. (It is the question of *differance* set in a new and restricted frame. As he examines this particular structure, Derrida explodes the narrow frame and overruns all borders.) Derrida's dominant endeavor in the main text is to perform a new type of comparative reading of two texts. To effect this interpretation, he must transgress traditional rules and beliefs of literary criticism, which prescribe relations between different texts and oeuvres and designate procedures for comparison and analysis. In effect, Derrida must breach well-defined borders. He does so in his readings, and he theorizes about it. It is a strange and difficult, gnarled text—as our syntax hints. Here as elsewhere Derrida's critical writing, like that of other contemporaries, tends toward a poetics and practice of fracture. On the level of the work, more than the isolated sentence or paragraph, he is, at his most distinctive, one of the leading practitioners of the dispersed and provocative critical discourse. The text of the Yale manifesto explodes numerous frames, and the reading of it offers a burden of dissemination.

3

His critics tell us that there are two Heideggers: the ontologist of the 1920s and the early 1930s and the poetician of the mid 1930s and after. In the early period, the days of *Being and Time*, Heidegger contributed powerfully to hermeneutic theory. In fact, his sections on interpretation in *Being and Time* probably constitute the finest material on the subject in our century. At the same time his intense readings of poetic texts now surface ever more frequently as classics, however quirky, of literary criticism. This latter mode of textual interpretation is what interests us.

Understood as destructive interpretation, Heidegger's readings work to free texts of reified perspectives and canonical commentaries so as to establish an existential intimacy with each text, which allows the truth of Being preserved there to emerge anew. The activities of interpretation and critical writing conjure and rekindle the primordial energies of Being in a process of dramatized disclosure. Such performances of unconcealing, of the happening of truth, seek to enact the original rapture and illumination of authentic poetry. Upon this operation of unconcealing, Heidegger confers the Greek word for "truth"—*aletheia*.

For Heidegger the poetic text inaugurates and incarnates Being and thinking. The sign is by nature ontological and epistemological as well as linguistic. Interpretation performs the truth of Being and thinking through, with and in the signs of discourse. At the outset the sign is filled, perhaps overfilled. And the distance between the sign and the interpreter collapses in an unparalleled mystical intimacy. The spaces of error dissolve in this double oneness. Ironically, Heidegger is widely regarded as a most visionary and prophetic interpreter, and his critical discourse is most admired for its performative rhetoric. No doubt, Heidegger is a prophet and rhetorician, but not simply for the reasons conventionally advanced.

The phenomenology of the sign, an overripe fruit, founds a whole structure of centers and unities and an entire set of restrictions on floating and free play. The merciless introduction of difference into this sealed edifice creates opening effects, which offer for view spaces for error. Some difference exists between a black mark on white paper and Being itself, and some space intervenes between what a written mark designates and the thing or idea itself. The difficulties that such differences inaugurate remain buried in Heidegger's most powerful critical readings and writings. The got-up tone of wonder and the strategy of astonishment which characterize Heidegger's exegetical works put on exhibit a transfiguring soothsayer and word-smith, who stands at an edge and in error, both transcended in Oneness, which only grandiose figuring can create. Heidegger's troping of his poet's tropes marks a doubling that mocks his Oneness. Reading takes two, which makes a difference. Such vision exacerbates, not extinguishes, the edge. The logos, the incarnated word, no longer brings transcendence—only double trouble.

In our time, Being becomes the deconstructed self; the poetic text a network of differential traces; interpretation an activity of exploding meaning beyond truth toward joyous dissemination; and critical discourse a deviating and differentiating process of troping. Stability gives way to vertigo; identities to differences; unities to multiplicities; the center to infinite centers (or to no privileged centers); ontology to philosophy of language; epistemology to rhetoric; mysticism to demystification; intimacy to space; poetry to textuality; the full to the empty; *aletheia* to free-play; the correct to the erroneous; hermeneutics to deconstruction; the One to—not the Many—the Infinite. Heidegger is defunct. Only destruction preserves him now.

Preserving the early work of Heidegger, Spanos effects a hybrid destructive hermeneutics under pressure from the deconstructive criticism of Derrida and de Man. When he reads texts, Spanos tracks the disclosures of being and thinking in an explorative and inexhaustible process conceived as inevitable misreading. Interpretation is a ceaseless yet saving activity in the openness of time and the nothingness of existence. The ground of literature and its deciphering, of its primordial saying and interested hearing, is the happening and revelation of being (truth), which unfold through the nothing of be-ing. The sign (*legein*), radically temporal, precludes any definitive manifestation of being. Where Heidegger covers over the spaces of interpretation, Spanos exposes them partially to view.

The gap between the interpreter and the sign, bridged through the existential care and interest of the reader, retains its dangers and its openness against the intimacy of reading. Under the sign the trouble at the edge is restored. Yet the sign, in the hands of Spanos' poet, maintains a univocity and purity—an absence of differences, especially intertextual ones—that repeat themselves in the anxious grips of the reader. The rhetoric of critical discourse, like that of poetry, is transparent; no spaces loom in the activity of writing. Interpreters emerge as admitted prophets, but not as proclaimed rhetoricians. Transcendence and truth, perhaps compromised yet conserved, offer unfractured meaning and consolation, a center of hope, to the anxious subject.

Managing the spaces of interpretation and surviving the anxieties at the edge require a strength of vision and rhetoric that only a Promethean subject can muster. As interpreter, Bloom displays this heroic power in himself and in his poets. The true source of such power is harnessed in the demonic theory of misprision. All interpretation is inherently misinterpretation. Hermeneutic spaces generate errors. But all can be managed by mapping.

In Bloom, there are two main strata of reading: the newcomer reads the precursor; the critic reads the poet. While he directs his speculations at the first level, Bloom employs his findings on the second. To read a poem is to confront images, which embody psychic defenses and rhetorical figures in a dialectical pattern of revisions. This structure of misprision, mapped in a six-fold process of ratios, appears in many of the best poems of the post-Enlightenment epoch. When Bloom reads such poems, he ferrets out these six phases. Each stage marks out a formation of meaning. Meaning comes in unstable moments of poetic and critical misinterpretation. The critical decipherment compounds the poetic errancy. In other words, when the sign—an amalgam of image, defense, trope, and revision—undergoes interpretation, it experiences continuing processes of distortion. The condition of the

edge attains notable status with Bloom, particularly as he system-
atizes the structure of errors that occurs there. A most curious
prophet and rhetorician, Bloom classifies the languages of error
under the sign. Yet he avoids explicitly systematizing critical errors, preferring to imply that these recapitulate poetic ones.

In place of an intimacy between reader and text, Bloom gives
us strife-ridden misprision. Behind this activity lies the affective
will of the poet and of the critic to triumph over oblivion and
enter into the canon of permanent literary figures. Misreading
comes about through psychological defense effected by the inherently abysmal structures of tropes. Significantly, misinterpretations and disseminated meanings emanate from the unconscious
will of the strong subject and his necessary distortions of the sign.
The Promethean subject's psyche, more than the sign, accounts
for the errors at the edge. The subject, though partially deconstructed, occupies a transcendental position in Bloom's theory and
practice. Everything comes from him and everything returns to
him. Signs are filled with/by his unconscious yet willful misprisions.

Destructive criticism seeks to free the text from canonical interpretations and prescribed cultural perspectives. It intends to
establish an immediate and emotional relationship between the
reader and text. Heidegger, Spanos, and Bloom (in part) work
in this antithetical mode. (In practice, the actual encrustations of
received opinions, which form part of each text's intertext, are
often "destroyed" through avoidance or implication rather than
through direct and painstaking de-struction.) As we move from
Heidegger to Spanos to Bloom, the role of the poet's and reader's
will (or intentionality) remains central, while the importance of
misreading increases. Significantly, the sign, rarely stressed, stays
overfull: it bears a fullness of meaning and truth about existence.
However dispersed through the activities of misreading, the sign
offers learning or wisdom. The playful "nihilism" of deconstruction, which renounces meaning or multiplies it toward parodic
infinity, shows in comparison the hermeneutic conservatism of
destruction, which celebrates meaning. In deconstruction, misreading results from the mechanisms of the sign, while in destruction it emerges as a function of intentional being. Critical writing
for destruction is performance—a display and staging of the ad-

vent of truth by the anxious subject; for deconstruction interpretive discourse is a fractured production of the aberration or free play of the signifier. The dispersed deconstructive reader, if reconstructed through inference, appears frenetic, sure, and playful. One finds little actual fear and trembling in Derrida or de Man, Barthes or Riddel.

4

One of the notable differences between American and French deconstruction concerns the modes of critical writing. Whereas Derrida and Barthes, for instance, sometimes present fragmented and playful discourses, particularly from 1970 on, de Man, Miller, and Riddel—by comparison—offer well-made and conventional texts. Handling the problematic of metalanguage seems much more pressing and important to the French. While proclaiming the free play of textuality, the American deconstructors practice traditional styles of discourse; the French attempt all manner of fractured styles. In the age of the *text* is it desirable or even possible to avoid or ignore the disruptive play of textuality in critical writing itself? Is there a special language (a metalanguage) of criticism, different from that of literature, free of *rhetoricity* or *textuality*? In theory, de Man, Miller, and Riddel say "No, there is only one language." But de Man would say that literary language is typically more aberrant or rhetorical than critical language. It is, for him, a matter of degree, not kind. Riddel finds this unsatisfactory. More than the others, he writes a textual or stereographic style of discourse. Nevertheless, American deconstruction keeps pretty much within the boundaries of narrowly prescribed "good taste." Hartman documents this conservatism. Of the major critics only Bloom experiments with new forms of critical writing, and his few efforts are actually quite modest, though apparently "outrageous" by the most severe of native standards. And only Hartman theorizes about alternate modes of critical writing. In the 1980s American deconstruction may begin to overrun these borders.

Given the structure of the sign, situated as it is amid unstable and divisive grammatical, rhetorical, and referential strata, interpretation with de Man tends to produce extravagant and dizzying effects of referential aberration. Linguistic predicaments and rhetorical discontinuities proliferate, powered by the relentless forces of grammar. Since referentiality is an effect of grammar and rhetoric, and since they play havoc with reference, the possibility for the emergence of meaning or truth is suspended. Strictly speaking, texts are *unreadable*. Literal interpretation is a dream. All interpretation, given the rhetoricity of language, is misreading. When a text is densely rhetorical, it will generate numerous and interesting misreadings. Necessarily, interpretations of a text exist in the mode of error. This status affects authors as well as critics. All readers misread. Language, not the subject, accounts for the phenomena of misreading.

Before Bloom's work appeared, de Man published materials on the theory of misreading. Bloom evidently got the idea from de Man. Nevertheless, their notions of misreading are quite different. With de Man, misreading is a constitutive function of language and with Bloom it is a consequence of psychological provenance. Bloom, of course, develops a remarkable typology, his Map of Misprision, to chart the varieties and mechanisms of misreading. He is the most thorough cartographer yet of this interpretive domain. His Map also offers a hermeneutic tool to decipher and delimit the extravagances of misreading. De Man shows no inclination to check or erase the exorbitant and aberrant results of misreading; he seeks primarily to produce such errors in excruciating detail.

Just as de Man positions the act of interpretation at the edge, where critical prophesying and troping generate unavoidable errors in an incomplete though inevitable closure, so too does Miller locate the reading activity amidst the dangers at the edge. Synthesizing de Man's theory of rhetoricity and Derrida's notion of differance, Miller derives a concept of the sign in which a literal/figurative polarity disrupts reference and in which every sign is differentiated, differed, and deferred from its object and itself. The sign unfolds through an uncontrollable movement of substitutions and differences. The gaps splitting the sign constitute a structure of abysmal spaces that makes room for endless interpretations (misreadings). In critical reading, the stability of language gives way to flights of meaning. Truth slips away. Or rather truth, which is illusory from the start because language is inherently rhetorical, appears pointless as an all-encompassing critical goal.

Both de Man and Miller emphasize that a deconstructive reading can itself be deconstructed. Such reversal results from the unrelenting and insistent operations of rhetoricity. No criticism escapes the disruptions created by the play of grammatical, rhetorical, and referential strata in language. Still, each demystified reading clarifies, even though the number of such potential clarifications approaches infinity. Critical writing, like literature, partakes of textuality, only less so.

Significantly, de Man and Miller find that a deconstructive reading can recover from a text evidence of pre-existent deconstruction. A text may admit its own complex crossings amid referential and figural dimensions. In this case, the author may or may not consciously anticipate the critic. Writers are frequently mystified about their own texts.

Early on Riddel finds formulations to complain about in Yale deconstruction. In particular, he regards the theory of the "self-deconstructing text" with suspicion, sensing that it restricts the open and endless, joyous interpretation early celebrated by Derrida. In addition, such a notion privileges *literary* language over critical discourse, and it restores the old function of the author (as genius). The implicit valorization of literature and devaluation of criticism divides the theory of *écriture*, assigning a higher ontological value to *literary* writing and limiting critical writing and reading to secondary status.

Working out his later deconstructive project, Riddel develops a concept of the sign indebted mostly to Derrida—not de Man. In his view, the signifier is by nature intertextual. To turn this around, intertextuality invades the text at the level of the signifier or chain of signifiers. The shifting crevices at work in the sign effectively multiply the spaces and potential errors for interpretation. Thus misreading, the necessary errancy of every reading, happens less as a singular result of clashing synchronic strata and more as a consequence of disruptive diachronic traces undermining from within the possible coherence of the sign. Under these circumstances, any interpretation is a venture in foolhardy soothsaying and redoubled rhetoric. The spaces of interpretation generate numerous errors. We return, yet again, to the troubling scene at the edge. Riddel, descended from the Old English "hriddel," pierces and perforates, shifts and separates. The interpretation of the text necessarily scatters and provisionally collects materials. Curiously, the intertextual traces, insisted upon by Riddel, install in the sign an already (mis)interpreted layer of potential signification. The irony is that this notion renders the text partially self-deconstructed. The Yale critics don't have a lock on this idea—only a first right.

5

To the extent that deconstruction celebrates dissemination over truth, explosion and fragmentation over unity and coherence, undecidable spaces over prudent closures, playfulness and hysteria over care and rationality, and misreading over reading, it opposes traditional hermeneutics. Deconstruction shows less interest in refining a rigorous method or science of interpretation than in developing strategies and tactics to subvert such secure procedures and techniques of reading. Thus "deconstructive hermeneutics" and "deconstructive interpretation," phrases used in this book, are paradoxical and misleading conjunctions. Yet, in the history of hermeneutics spanning from Talmudic and Hellenistic scholars up to our time, we can find antithetical theorists and groups, like Gnostics and Kabbalists, who serve as forerunners of deconstruction. In other words, deconstruction may be a freak offshoot *within* the long history of hermeneutics. Or it may be, as many deconstructors believe, radically opposed to all hermeneutics. Can a general hermeneutics contain deconstruction? Deconstructors think not.

As he moves from structuralism to deconstruction, Barthes renounces the search for truth and the science of codes in favor of the joys of dissemination and the free play of the signifier. Over the period of his involvement his readings and writings become ever more self-consciously rhetorical and visionary and more suggestively fractured and playful. In the initial phase, the days of the *Tel Quel* group, Barthes theorizes about textuality and dissemination, but calls for controls on ideological grounds. Rather than practice the infinite deferment of the signified, Barthes wants to operate a tactics of the slide, aiming to keep deconstruction effective for the sociopolitical battle of meanings being waged in Western bourgeois societies. To foreclose the signified and liberate the signifier totally is to refuse all meaning. Such a strategy gives up political praxis in favor of petit-bourgeois self-indulgence. The most productive reading is that which generates volumes of meanings—not the complete explosion and consequent death of meaning.

In the later phase Barthes relaxes controls, letting go for the joys and pleasures of radical dissemination. Such revolutionary reading, conceived in the early days as the long-range goal of progressive ideology, celebrates the erotic gratifications of reading acts. The inherent spaces and slips of interpretation emerge as alluring depths and edges for orgasmic bliss. And interpretation becomes hallucination and fantasy—more than mere prophecy. Readers co-write the texts they read. With the death of the author and the birth of the text comes a new age of the licentious and hysterical reader. Critical writing, formerly analytical and coherent, becomes playfully fragmented. The rhetoric of criticism undergoes the spasms of erotic vision. The dangers at the edge provide deep pleasures of liberation for the libidinous reader-writer.

Although Foucault denies that his project is interpretive, we can extrapolate out of his works a certain practice for reading texts. (Such a derivative enterprise has been underway since the mid-1970s.) Within its own era, each text is produced, distributed, and interpreted in accordance with a system of epistemic regularities. When reactivated in a later period, the text must pass through an analogous archival systematics. The interpretation of a work, like its production, is prescribed: cultural rules determine who can read with authority, what can then be said, how it can be said, what counts as true and reasonable, what constitutes falsehood and foolishness, and what is meant and what not. Just as the signifiers composing a text emerge out of, through, and back into a cultural matrix, so the reading of a text unfolds within an epistemic network. The activity of reading is tied into a controlling social machinery, which allocates and arbitrates all knowledge and power.

While Foucault may seem to recommend a historical-cultural or contextual practice of interpretation, he actually suggests an antithetical project. He is sceptical and critical of institutionalized modes of behavior because they serve in a "game" of socio-political control and manipulation. With *genealogy* Foucault recommends a radical program for critical reading and writing: exaggerate and parody conventional critical modes; collapse all boundaries and use multiple, discontinuous, and nonsynthesizable means to "read" all texts; renounce the will-to-knowledge and the passion for truth—embrace "stupidity."

Foucault's visionary project offers a "deconstructive" mode of reading that breaks open the spaces of interpretation and liberates the coded signifier. At this scene of the edge critical writing and reading become heterogeneous, parodic, and carnivalesque. Ideologically motivated, the critic, a dispersed subject, playing the clown and idiot, champions error so as to undermine the rules of the culture, which assign her a fixed role in the controlled exchanges of knowledge and power.

With the gradual acceptance and institutionalization of deconstruction, the ideological project to disrupt and subvert the machinery of Western culture—a French enterprise not generally admitted by American deconstructors—gets co-opted and diluted. We may expect more extreme plans of liberation. Wilder writing and reading. And we may anticipate growing regularization and systematization. That the writing of this book was funded by the government is evidence enough of such ongoing processes. The book itself and this section testify further to a certain program of codification and assimilation. What is to be done?

6

In an attempt to break down the particular constraints of traditional psychoanalysis and political theory, Deleuze and Guattari promote a wild program in a polished and measured prose. Their theory of the schiz-sign, which merges the sign with the libido and the social body, serves to ground a politicized project for reading aimed toward "free play" and "dissemination"—toward deterritorialization of all molar formations and structures. In the work of reading, the smooth representational (or reterritorialized) text often resists the violence and disruption of the schizoanalyst, who must then seek other texts where intensities flow for him. In this way inert texts are left behind or dismissed as the revolutionary reader moves on in search of intensities. Schizo-reading does not seek meaning or truth and does not attempt scrupulous interpretation or painstaking deconstruction; rather it celebrates and promotes reading as simultaneous libidinal, social, and political activity; and it favors textual intervention on molecular or fragmented levels and sites. Emphasizing and extending the contemporary "discovery" of unassimilable partial objects, the schizo-reader glorifies gaps, cracks, and spaces. In its most intense moments, the project of schizoanalysis wants to refuse interpretation—its coverings, closures, and tropes, its readings and writings. With a guiding commitment to revolution, schizoanalysis produces radical and prophetic texts, all the while using conventional signs and traditional grammar. As such, it is caught up in an old practice of language and interpretation, a textual systematics of signs and visions, which it ironically revives and continues as it works toward destruction.

Very much like Deleuze and Guattari, Hayden White researches a productive Unconscious where he uncovers fundamental linguistic elements, which bear an ideological and ethical as well as a narrative and aesthetic charge. For White, however, such minimal units of language already carry a specific hermeneutic potential, which is inescapably activated in textual work. Every production is highly regulated in both its molar *and* its molecular stages of formation. Since interpretation is situated in a preconscious domain, it cannot be denied or refused. But, like Deleuze and Guattari, White writes his texts in a carefully poised and balanced, classical style: the floating of the signifier is checked by a metalanguage confident of effective representation. Style does not crack.

Relying on smooth and safe language, Deleuze, Guattari, and White avoid questioning their own texts and lead us to believe in the accuracy and truthfulness of their representations. All this occurs as the whole traditional system of representation undergoes ideological inquisition, emerging in Deleuze and Guattari's work as a paranoid or perverted molar formation and in White's enterprise as a highly limited structural machine replete with specifiable political, aesthetic, and ethical components. Beneath the prophetic aspirations of their separate projects, Deleuze and Guattari and White operate a protected language, a medium of truth and accuracy. Such a procedure revives the old theatrical strategy of parabasis. The dramatic play of language is momentarily stopped so that plain and honest speaking can occur. An illusion, this classical scene, which conventionally unfolds at the edge of the stage, does not interrupt the progress of the play; it is a deliberate deceptive moment in the overall production; it happens on stage as a regular part of the dramatic presentation. Our three contemporary visionaries rely, knowingly or not, on ancient Greek rhetoric: they employ a "special language" used for the staging of plain and true speaking, within the general movement of comedy. Amidst a carnival atmosphere, the serious moment, early coded into Greek writing, aims to get our attention. Still, it never escapes the hazards of interpretive work, of language functions; it only pretends to.

7

Moving beyond the mythical scene of the edge, snipped from the center of the *Iliad*, and beyond the numerous modalities of the edge, snapped to order here from the various sections of Parts I, II, and III, we ponder the possibility that there is only always interpretation. All facts, figures, and formulas, all runes, readings, and writings, all fashions, fictions, and fantasies, all customs, conventions, and codes, and all laws, loves, and lives are interpretations. To the extent that everything is constructed and assembled, conceived and arranged, cut up and aligned—to just such an extent—everything partakes of interpretation. The writing/reading activity creeps into, contours, and creates all that we know and experience. There is nothing other than interpretation.

The term often used by deconstructors to name the impasse of interpretation, the end point of critical reading and writing, is *aporia*. To the Greeks this meant "no way out." Unable to get beyond signs, locked in language (*écriture*), the interpreter confronts the irreducible free play of differance and figure. Since there is neither an undifferentiated nor a literal bottom or ground, the activity of interpretation is endless. There is no way out. The experience of aporia takes many forms. The fact, for example, that every text lends itself to deconstruction and to further deconstruction, with nowhere any end in sight, generates a structure of aporia. So too does the insight that no escape outside the logocentric enclosure is possible since the interpreter must use the concepts and figures of the Western metaphysical tradition. And the experience of the unavailability to discourse of a literal bottom or undifferentiated ground leads to a version of aporia. There's no way out. Interpretation is endless.

We can't live with and we can't live without *borders*. Cuts and lines. We can't submit to but we must use *contexts*. Conceptions and arrangements. We can't control yet we must deploy meanings. Constructions and assemblages. Impasse. Aporia. Neither this nor that. We can't interpret (in the logocentric sense), nor can we interpret (in the cybernetic sense of totalized megareadings). We can only always endlessly misinterpret (in the deconstructive sense). Early in the day Derrida conceived endless (mis)interpretation as "joyous." A happy multiplication of cuts and arrangements toward infinity. That we are *all* continuously on edge at the edge now goes without saying; it is our whole way of being there—the modality of the edge—which concerns deconstruction. Perhaps the last ethical impulse of this criticism.

To provoke wonder, we end where much deconstruction starts. Snippets out of the piecemeal notes and aphorisms of Nietzsche's *The Will to Power*, Book Three. This mode of interpretation and of writing prefigures contemporary deconstruction.

"There are only *facts*"—I would say: No, facts is precisely what there is not, only interpretations. (# 481)

to be able to read off a text without interposing an interpretation is the last-developed form of "inner experience"—perhaps one that is hardly possible— (# 479)

"Ends and means"
"Cause and effect"
"Subject and object"
"Acting and suffering"
"Thing-in-itself and appearance"
\} as interpretations (not as facts) and to what extent perhaps *necessary* interpretations? (as required for "preservation")—all in the sense of a will to power. (# 589)

Finally, is it necessary to posit an interpreter behind the interpretation? Even this is invention, hypothesis. (# 481)

The history of Nietzsche's fundamental role in deconstruction remains to be written. As first in our line, he deserves the emphasis of last place.

Post Script

In Latin *conclūdere* means "to shut up." Peace and quiet. Constriction. Confinement. Guarded silence. *Lūdere* means "to play." Inside this final sign, then, lies a game, a finishing lure, another possibility, a further clue, a lasting con. The word admits, though disguises, the truth about conclusions: they stop textual play. Conclusions serve as guardrails—as protection. A conclusion typically promotes unified closure and ordered coherence. The end of the text either repeats the initial thesis with a difference, or repackages the main points within tight borders, or enacts a last deduction as a final supplement. A conclusion renders up results, passes judgments, reduces details, effects settlement, shuts down play.

Deconstruction regularly questions coherence, unity, order, closure. It undermines the taming of difference, the tightening of borders, and the logic of last supplements. It assaults conclusions.

Perhaps too clever and fussy, such a treatment of *conclusion* typifies a recurring strategy of deconstruction. Often deconstruction interrogates some seemingly unimportant item—a word, an isolated letter, a title, a phrase, a printing error, a piece of punctuation—in order to break down a concept, passage, or text. The deconstructor emerges as a peculiar connoisseur who stops at the insignificant, gazes erotically at its surface, and lets exaggerated wonder become everything. Through such indolent and intimate hesitation comes corrosive and ghostly understanding. The deconstructor assumes a mind of winter, an estrangement from tradition, effecting an antithetical stance and vision. Danger lies that way and the sorrow of negative knowledge. Still, to enjoy such activity, to relish its freedom, seems less a perversity now than an unexpected salvation. "I do not 'concentrate,'" says Derrida, "either exclusively or primarily on those points that appear to be the most 'important,' 'central,' 'crucial.' Rather, I deconcentrate, and it is the secondary, eccentric, lateral, marginal, parasitic, borderline cases which are 'important' to me . . ." ("Limited Inc," p. 180). This analytics of the border, of the unimportant, unsettles the traditional habits and practices of conclusion. Deconstruction creates a fuss to begin and end with.

The author, according to deconstruction, may visit his text as a guest only: this celebrated "death of the author" not only decenters the text, but defers the conclusion. A text cannot be located or stopped at the author, for the inscription of the author is neither paternal nor privileged but ludic. An author can only wonder what guest roles he plays in his text. As a reader, a voyeur, he delimits textual play: his conclusions about the text rank in potential value with any other reader's.

The demand for conclusion—a requirement of readers, a duty of authors, an oppressive expectation, a prevailing convention— works ultimately to direct, shape, and distort the heterogeneous materials of a textual production. Refined and reductive, the conclusion installs frames on writing and insures limits on dissemination. A certain drama of repression accompanies such constriction. Conclusions do homage to insistent forces of control, direction, and authority. Deliberately, deconstruction disrupts settled arrangements, protected judgments, and requisite conclusions. It confronts conventions, producing new forms of writing and reading. Without restoration, it ravages authority. It moves beyond conclusion.

How will deconstruction end up—conclude? A future (an imaginary) account of deconstruction as a movement would explore the early activities of the *Tel Quel* group, the Yale group, the *Boundary 2* group and the later French group around Derrida (Agacinski, Kofman, Lacoue-Labarthe, Nancy, and Pautrat); it would examine their focal points, politics, applications, programs, disagreements, overlaps, hostilities; it would assess the actual and mythical roles of Derrida. It would take up fundamental questions. How did the early explorative and radical impulses, the conserving and accommodating tendencies, and the drives for recognition and institutionalization coexist and interrelate? How did codification of rules and cooperation with the establishment come about and direct or inhibit further development? Which stimuli prompted periodic resurgences of the original revolutionary thrust? To what degrees were structuralism, phenomenology, Marxism, and psychoanalysis condemned, modified, and accepted? How were Lacan and Foucault filtered and excluded? Why did critiques and complaints alter so little, if at all, the early lines of formation and transformation? Why did the movement sometimes reconstitute and sometimes deny its founding concepts and programs? How did deconstruction begin, expand, and develop? What vexed it and what did it value?

Such an account of deconstruction, an analysis of its shifting grounds, would explore its philosophies of language, its concepts of the self (both of the author and the reader), its theories of the work and text, its ideas on context, its methods of reading and writing. It would consider the various receptions and formalizations of deconstruction. It would ultimately decide whether deconstruction was merely an offshoot of universal semiotics, or perhaps a branch of global hermeneutics, or a replacement for both.

This book offers no conclusion.

Appendixes

The following two texts, "Hermeneutics, Semiotics, and Deconstruction" and "Reflections on the Responsibilities of the Literary Critic," contain further discussion of some of the issues raised by this book and are included for the interest of the reader.

Hermeneutics, Semiotics, and Deconstruction

In the history of contemporary deconstruction the great year is unquestionably 1967 when Jacques Derrida, the main figure in the movement, published his *Of Grammatology, Speech and Phenomena*, and *Writing and Difference*. Among other things, these texts show Derrida unleashing powerful critiques of phenomenology and structuralism. Saussure and Lévi-Strauss, like Husserl and occasionally Heidegger, come in for subversive reassessment. At the same time Nietzsche and Freud undergo inchoate revaluation and emerge in a new and positive light. As deconstruction spreads during the late 1960s and early 1970s in France, England, and America, the Derridean critiques of structuralism and phenomenology take on canonical status while the improved stocks of psychoanalysis and Nietzsche studies continue to attract further energetic investment.

By 1972, when Derrida published *Positions, Margins—of Philosophy*, and *Dissemination*, deconstruction had attained widespread, often reluctant, recognition as the newest avant-garde intellectual movement in France and America. It remained steadfastly poststructuralist and postphenomenological. And it seemed still Freudian and decidedly Nietzschean. In France it was vaguely Marxist, although not in Derrida's hands; in America, it was non-Marxist, if not silently anti-Marxist.

As these developments unfolded, structuralism itself was being transformed into semiology or, if you prefer, semiotics. By the middle 1970s it became clear that semiotics was a global discipline, a new megascience, with ambitions Faustian enough to encompass

"Hermeneutics, Semiotics, and Deconstruction" was presented at a meeting of the Conference on Christianity and Literature held in conjunction with the Convention of the Modern Language Association in 1980.

not only the fine arts and social sciences but also several areas of the natural and physical sciences.

Meanwhile, hermeneutics, long ago cast as a minor branch of biblical studies, expanded its purview, reaching out to take in all manner and means of interpretive activity and theory. No doubt, Heidegger's dramatic shifting of hermeneutic theory from epistemological to ontological grounds (from *Verstehen* to *Verstehen* as a function of *Sein*) facilitated this transformation and expansion of hermeneutics. If one wanted to play the prophet, one could predict a new flourishing of research into general hermeneutics.

What will be interesting to see in all this "progress" is how semiotics and hermeneutics cut up and divide the ground. At certain fundamental points they, of course, share similar interests and goals. (The problematic of language is a crucial case in point.) One wonders if, in the distant future, semiotics will remain structuralist at heart while hermeneutics will preserve its methodological ties with phenomenology? We cannot know. Semiotics may encompass hermeneutics. Or vice versa. Or they may be defunct like alchemy.

In any case, deconstruction could be absorbed by either or both of these transdisciplines. Possibly a generation from now deconstruction will register as a minor, perverse offshoot of a larger enterprise.

But what is deconstruction? Does it, like semiotics and hermeneutics, possess an object or field of objects for study? Does it practice or favor identifiable methods and goals of inquiry? The answers must be *yes* and *no*. One mode of deconstruction—an apparently constricted and utilitarian one—focuses on texts, on ways of reading texts and comprehending textual signification. We might fancifully identify such a practice as "deconstructive hermeneutics." In addition, we can uncover certain instances of a "deconstructive semiotics," that is, of a practice of tracking and charting a priori modes or grounds of textual organization and signification. Yet such facile conjoinings of deconstruction with hermeneutics or with semiotics seem willfully paradoxical. After all, deconstruction, vaguely at the outset and more forcefully now, poses itself in fundamental, if opaque, opposition to the arts and sciences of hermeneutics and semiotics.

In an interview published in March 1977 in *Digraphe*, Derrida characterizes deconstruction, observing "deconstruction is not a critical operation, the critical is its object; deconstruction always bears, at one moment or another, on the confidence given the critical, critico-theoretical, that is to say, deciding authority. . . ." What strikes us here is Derrida's little phrase "at one moment or another." Sooner or later, we learn, deconstruction turns on every critical reading or theoretical construction. When a decision is made, when authority emerges, when theory or criticism operate, then deconstruction questions. . . . It looks at every or any boundary, frame, margin, inscription, border. It examines the instances of decision: it investigates deciding authority. As soon as it does so, it becomes subversive. Mainly, it exhibits over and over how all borders, rules, concepts, structures—how all creations and constructions—suppress primordial difference in favor of dubious identity. To uncover the infinite varieties of such suppressions constitutes the dominant project of Derridean deconstruction.

When deconstruction looks at semiotics, it immediately takes up the theory of the sign. It questions the self-identity of signifier and signified and the self-presence of the speaking subject and the voiced sign. Derrida's work on Saussure and Lévi-Strauss early sets this pattern.

When deconstruction considers hermeneutics, it again problematizes the concepts of the sign and of presence as well as a number of other founding notions. A deconstructive inquiry into hermeneutics or into semiotics would focus on fundamental ideas of language, self, author, reader, text, interpretation, history, meaning, context, and critical writing. Other topics could obviously be added to the list.

Ultimately, deconstruction effects revision of traditional thinking. Being (*Sein*) becomes the deconstructed self, the text becomes a field of differential traces, interpretation an activity of exploding meaning beyond truth toward dissemination, and critical discourse a deviating and differentiating process of supplemental troping. Stability gives way to vertigo; identities to differences; unities to fragmentations; the center to infinite centers (or to no privileged centers); ontology to philosophy of language; epistemology to rhetoric; presence to absence; literature to textuality; *aletheia* to free play; correctness to errancy; hermeneutics and semiotics to deconstruction. In this transformation, hermeneutics and semiotics—as self-assured sciences, as useful arts of exegesis, or as deliberate textual cartographics—appear to be approachable dreams disguising impossible wishes.

In the late 1970s American deconstruction starts to fear its "progress" and "success." There is worry that deconstruction is becoming predictable and rigid—that it is now a *method*. The recipe for Derridean deconstruction is: take any traditional concept or established formulation, invert its set of hierarchical terms, and subject them to fragmentation via an insistent principle of difference. After unhinging the elements in any structure or textual system toward radical free play, stand back and sift the rubble for hidden or unexpected formations. Tout these special findings as outlawed truths. (Hence the infamous *supplement* of the *Grammatology*.) Mix all of this work with dashes of erotic lyricism and with apocalyptic intimations. Packaged within this quick codification—this easy parody—lies a rigid formulation of deconstruction as well as an anxious realization of the present crisis of deconstruction. No longer busy being born, deconstruction is busy dying. Or so it may now seem.

On the horizon of deconstruction looms a new stage now being born. It could spread further—to semiotics and hermeneutics. Let us designate it the "Era of the Libidinous Critical Text." Up till now the textual surface of the *critical* work has been largely undisturbed. However free and speculative, the critical text comes to us nicely coherent, carefully developed, and altogether unified. Invariably, it unfolds along an orderly temporal line, which is to say it plies the narrative path. Even the most structuralist of studies, the most spatial and synchronic of inquiries, presents a chronological story. It is somehow emplotted. This undisturbed state of affairs cannot or may not continue long. The critical text is beginning to break up. Everything we have learned about "literary" textuality forces itself upon "critical" textuality. We can expect that the new essay on *Finnegans Wake* or the *Cantos* will itself be paronomasial and chaotic. (At the same time it may have a mythic understructure.) The borders between the "literary" text and the "critical" text are giving way. And provocative texts on critical texts are springing up everywhere. The critical object and its modes of analysis and style are shifting—as the "nature" and force of textuality come clearer. Significantly, the quest for "meaning," a function of desire, is erupting into or giving way to an indistinct *desiring analytics*. Faintly, criticism is becoming libidinal: a self-indulgent, yet earnest, joy of reading and *writing*.

One supposes that our orderly paradigm of the universe, the last in a succession of world pictures, is ending now. Older modes of explanation—whether providential or scientific, whether predicated on a master plan or an enriched model of cause-effect—seem at an end. Even the more recent field-theory and ecosystem paradigms appear inadequate. Randomization and chance appear the most fit maps. Our texts, literary, critical, and otherwise, proclaim a new era. Our disciplines, including semiotics and hermeneutics, seem last-ditch efforts to institute and protect order and meaning. It is no surprise that the Soviet Union continues as a leader in semiotic studies and that traditional religious scholarship still champions hermeneutics, say what you will. But the epoch of order and meaning is being forced to face an emerging era of discontinuity and desiring activity. One expects that semiotics and hermeneutics, as disciplines, will grow and grow as conditions "worsen." They represent the last "best" hope of a passing epoch. One also imagines that both disciplines will be transformed by isolated visionaries to accommodate the monstrous coming era. This way hope lies.

Reflections on the Responsibilities of the Literary Critic

Every critic like every theologian and every philosopher is a casuist in spite of himself. To escape or surmount the discontinuity of knowledge, each resorts to a particular heresy and makes it predominant and even omnivorous.

  —R. P. Blackmur, "A Critic's Job of Work," *Language as Gesture*

Medium and Master

Literary criticism, we know, is creation more than discovery, and we know that criticism is less demonstration and proof than individual insight and construction. Continually, however, the mask of critical work successfully sustains the illusion that we are actually transparent mediums for the Great Poem. Yet we know, ultimately, that the voices appear inside our writing. Just here the illusion wishes to reformulate itself to expunge, once and for all, our experience of the discontinuity of knowledge—of the fissures that separate us in difference from every object, thought and feeling.

Within the conventions of our time and place we experience limitations, yet within the confines of our texts we find transcending messages of truth. Such heresy devours our creativity, and we become, once more, servants to a sub-Olympian eternal Master. Actually, the energy from a text makes us mediums of madness. Repressing it, we are masters, maestros, great curators of omnivorous Meaning and History.

"Reflections on the Responsibilities of the Literary Critic" was delivered at a special session of the Convention of the Modern Language Association in 1978.

Portrait of the Critic

We are all acquainted with the ordinary profile. The critic is the person who analyzes or evaluates texts, who judges their merits or faults, and who is characteristically decisive (Latin—*criticus*) and discerning (Greek—*kritikos*). At bottom the critic is able to separate and choose (Greek—*krinein*). This conventional portrait is our inheritance and imprisonment.

The Indo-European root word of *critic* and its variants unfold at length a chronicle of cultural represssion and reduction. (The lexical family includes *skeri* and the permutations *skribh, krei-tro, krei-dhro, krei-men, kri-no, kri-n-yo* and *sker*.)

A. *Scribere* (Latin): to scratch, to write, to incise, to scribble, to circumscribe, to inscribe, to prescribe, to proscribe, to describe, script, scribe, scripture, manuscript, scriptorium.

Skariphos (Greek): sketch, scratch, pencil.

Sker (Indo-European and descendants): to shear, to scar, to scrape, to scrub, to excoriate, (plow) share, scissors, scabbard, score, shard, skirt, skirmish, sharp, screen.

Skrifla (Old Norse): to shrivel, to wrinkle.

B. *(Dis)crimen* (Latin): judgment, crime, recrimination, distinction, discrimination.

Cernere (Latin): to shift, to separate, to decide, to discern, certain, decree, secret.

Hridder (Old English): sieve, riddle.

Cribrum (Latin): sieve, garble.

Krinein (Greek): to separate, to judge, to decide, crisis, criterion, hypocrisy, critic.

C. *Sker* and variant *kar* (Indo-European), *caro* (Latin): flesh, carnal, carnage, carnival, charnel, incarnate, carrion.

Could we not construct from all this something approaching an infinite set of variations on the role of the literary critic? If we did, no logical or dialectical ordering of the potential roles could satisfactorily encompass the entire set: there would be *some* surplus or lack. Is it, in any case, only fanciful to see suggested before us lost possibilities for criticism? What, for instance, have we ever said directly about scarring and garbling? about hypocrisy and carnage? about recriminations and carrion?

What is a critic? *Criticus* reads and writes; he constructs texts. What are texts? Nightmares of figural networking. Garble. Separate in difference. Hypocrisy. Impenetrable cultural palimpsests. Carnage. Arguments with history. Recriminations and carrion. Is *Criticus* maestro of Meaning? Medium of Madness! What, finally, does he discern and evaluate? What is a critic?

The Responsibilities of the Critic

To make an offering, to perform a rite, to offer a libation, to pledge to give back. These are the peculiar roots of *responsibility*. In carrying out such an offering—a critical decipherment, say— we ought to be free, sane, and fearful. We should fear especially blame or punishment, moral or legal sanctions; at the same time we should desire or appreciate praise and reward. Such are the conventional imperatives of responsibility. Lacking these, responsibility is diminished, if not destroyed.

But these preconditions are neither sufficient, nor sufficiently clear. Without enduring human selves and intentions, without self-determination and reasonable motives, and without awareness of consequences and self-conscious deliberation, there can be no responsibility. This six-fold structure of responsibility, this moral algebra, yet too easily omits the cultural grounds of responsibility. For the calculus of responsibility requires, in addition, a social group, a (sub)culture, which shares standards of value.

Are these classic equations of responsibility relevant to the thoughts and deeds of literary critics? We wonder. When we go to our texts are we free, sane, and fearful? Do we desire praise and reward? Are we standard bearers of our culture's values? Do we possess enduring human selves? Are we in control of our intentions? Remote and alien, these ancient philosophical questions about responsibility seem to promise neither easy nor relevant answers. Persisting in this investigation, we must join the inglorious company of fallen angels:

> Others apart sat on a hill retired,
> In thoughts more elevate, and reasoned high
> Of providence, foreknowledge, will, and fate,

Fixt fate, free will, foreknowledge absolute,
And found no end, in wandering mazes lost. (*Paradise Lost*, 11)

In high places apart, lost in speculative mazes, we practice casuistry in spite of ourselves, till finally, having hit upon a way out, we descend to declare our heresy. Ultimately, we give back too little; we offer meager celebration. Yet we are, at least in this contingency, responsible/(irresponsible).

The Heresy of Responsibility

We have responsibility not only to the Text and to Tradition, but to Society. This heresy of responsibility, which is the predominant ideology, is omnivorous. As servants, our creativity is diminished and devoured. We must sometimes unmask the ministry of meaning, the cure of history, and the prophecy of truth. We must face, perhaps only fleetingly, utter discontinuity and difference.

Here is what we now know. We are a community of bemused acolytes to Metaphor. We are celebrants of Misreading and inheritors of an indecipherable Scripture. Our commentary is devoted, yet doubled, Writing. We write the already written poems we read. We write the history we make, the selves we are, and the criticism we publish. To produce, to write, we promote discontinuity. Mediums of metaphor and madness, we are not responsible, except perhaps for our will to power over texts and for our presumption in writing. That we justify the Text, Tradition, and Society in our work is not to be misunderstood as acceptance of responsibility. To make such a byproduct the necessary precondition of critical production is to put late before early and thereby to affirm, once more and inescapably, the madness of metaphor.

Carnivalesque, our criticism should be entertaining and colorful: we need haunted houses, rollercoaster rides, distended balloons, seductive come-ons, and promising gambles. To hustle is more compelling and more captivating than to pester.

Notes

PART I. SEMIOLOGY AND DECONSTRUCTION: MODERN THEORIES OF THE SIGN

PROLOGUE: THE GREEK EDGE

1. Homer, *Iliad*, trans. Richmond Lattimore (Chicago: University of Chicago Press, 1951). I have consulted *Iliad*, trans. E. V. Rieu (Baltimore: Penguin, 1950); Malcolm M. Willcock, *A Companion to the Iliad* (Chicago: University of Chicago Press, 1976), a useful conspectus of contemporary Homeric commentary; and the Greek original, *Iliad*, vol. 1, ed. Walter Leaf (London: Macmillan, 1886). I use the Lattimore translation throughout the Prologue.

2. Greek text from Leaf, p. 410; translation from Lattimore, p. 264.

CHAPTER 1. FOUNDATIONS: LINGUISTICS, PSYCHOANALYSIS, AND ANTHROPOLOGY

1. Ferdinand de Saussure, *Course in General Linguistics*, ed. Charles Bally and Albert Sechehaye, trans. Wade Baskin (New York: Philosophical Library, 1959), p. 16. For a helpful overview of Saussure's work see Jonathan Culler, *Ferdinand de Saussure* (New York: Penguin, 1977). The *Course* by Saussure, compiled from lecture notes by students, is doubled and mediated, for we are never exactly sure when Saussure, or a note-taker, or a group of collated notes is the "voice" overheard. (The problems of translation, as in the *Iliad*, only extend the irretrievability of the "original" text.) To contrive a reading of the Saussure text is to reenact the crisis of interpretation.

2. See Charles Morris, *Signs, Language, and Behavior* (1946; rpt. New York: Braziller, 1955). Morris is, of course, indebted to the earlier work of Charles Sanders Peirce.

3. See Jean Starobinski, *Words upon Words: The Anagrams of Ferdinand de Saussure*, trans. Olivia Emmet (New Haven: Yale University Press, 1979).

4. Sylvère Lotringer, "Le 'Complexe' de Saussure," *Semiotexte* (Spring 1975), 2:112. This special issue of *Semiotexte* is devoted to "Saussure's Anagrams."

5. Jacques Lacan, "The Insistence [or Agency] of the Letter in the Unconscious" (1957)—first English trans. by Jan Miel pub. in *Yale French Studies* (October 1966), 36/37; a different trans. is pub. in Lacan's *Écrits*, trans. Alan Sheridan (New York: Norton, 1977), pp. 146–78. Hereafter I use the latter text. For a preliminary overview of Lacan see Anika Lemaire, *Jacques Lacan*, trans. David Macey (1970 in French; London: Routledge & Kegan Paul, 1977).

6. The *Discourse of Rome*, first pub. in 1956, printed in English as *The Language of the Self: The Function of Language in Psychoanalysis*, was translated with a detailed commentary by Anthony Wilden (New York: Delta, 1968). A different trans., titled "The Function and Field of Speech and Language in Psychoanalysis," is available in Lacan's *Écrits*, trans. Alan Sheridan, pp. 30–113. Hereafter I use the latter text.

7. Sigmund Freud, *The Interpretation of Dreams*, ed. and trans. James Strachey (New York: Avon, 1965), esp. chaps. 4 and 6. This edition is a rpt. of vols. 4 and 5 of *The Standard Edition of the Complete Psychological Works of Sigmund Freud*, ed. James Strachey (London: Hogarth, 1953). Additional notes, though, have been included in this rpt.

8. For discussions of Lacan's basic concepts see Jean Laplanche and J.-B. Pontalis, *The Language of Psycho-Analysis* (1967 in French; New York: Norton, 1973).

9. Jacques Lacan, *The Four Fundamental Concepts of Psycho-Analysis*, ed. Jacques-Alain Miller, trans. Alan Sheridan (New York: Norton, 1978), p. 251. This book, pub. in France in 1973 as *Le Séminaire de Jacques Lacan, Livre XI*, contains Lacan's eleventh annual seminar, which was given in 1964. The editor tells us: "My intention here was to be as unobtrusive as possible and to obtain from Jacques Lacan's spoken word an authentic version that would stand, in the future, for the original, which does not exist. For the shorthand transcription, riddled as it is with inaccuracies, and lacking the speaker's gesture and intonation, cannot be regarded as the original" (p. xi). As in the Homeric and Saussurean texts, we encounter here again the interpretive crisis: the original text is lost; the messenger reports the text; the text, moreover, is translated.

10. Claude Lévi-Strauss, "The Structural Study of Myth" (1955) in his *Structural Anthropology*, trans. Claire Jacobson and Brooke Grundfest Schoepf (1958 in French; New York: Basic Books, 1963), p. 209. Hereafter *SA*. This seminal essay, originally written and published in English, is apparently the most reprinted of all Lévi-Strauss' works.

11. Claude Lévi-Strauss, "The Scope of Anthropology" (1960) in his *Structural Anthropology*, vol. 2, trans. Monique Layton (1973 in French; New York: Basic Books, 1976), pp. 9–10. Hereafter *SA* 2. Taking up the first chair of social anthropology in France in 1960, Lévi-Strauss delivered this manifesto at the Collège de France.

12. Claude Lévi-Strauss, "Structural Analysis in Linguistics and in Anthropology" (1945) in *SA*, pp. 31–54, where revisions of 1957 are incorporated. For an introductory survey of Lévi-Strauss' work see Edmund Leach, *Claude Lévi-Strauss*, rev. ed. (New York: Viking, 1974).

13. When, for example, he speaks of cultural systems of "cooking," Lévi-Strauss shows the same analytical preference for constituent units cast into patterns of opposition: "Like language, it seems to me, the cuisine of a society may be analyzed into constituent elements, which in this case we might call 'gustemes,' and which may be organized according to certain structures of opposition and correlation" (*SA*, p. 86).

In a now classic demonstration of structuralist method, Lévi-Strauss and Jakobson in an essay on Baudelaire's sonnet "Les Chats" culminate their analysis: "The two human categories, sensual/intellectual, oppose each other, and the mediation is achieved by the cats"— "Charles Baudelaire's 'Les Chats'" (1962), trans. F. De George in *The Structuralists: From Marx to Lévi-Strauss*, ed. Richard and Fernande De George (New York: Doubleday, 1972), p. 136.

14. For one revisionist discussion of Saussure see *SA*, pp. 90–94, where Lévi-Strauss observes "I will say that the linguistic sign is arbitrary a priori, but ceases to be arbitrary a posteriori" (91). Once it enters language system, the arbitrary sign takes on semantic values (connotations and denotations), which limit its movements and meanings in the system. It is only at the level of the phoneme (and mytheme) that semantic value is arbitrary.

15. Lévi-Strauss, Preface to Roman Jakobson's *Six Lectures on Sound and Meaning*, trans. John Mepham (1976 in French; Cambridge, Mass.: MIT Press, 1978), p. xxii. In this Preface, Lévi-Strauss says he knew almost nothing about linguistics when he first attended Jakobson's lectures during the war years 1942–43. He credits Jakobson with introducing him to structural linguistics and declares himself still, thirty-five years after the fact, a "disciple" (p. xi).

16. *The Raw and the Cooked: Introduction to a Science of Mythology*, vol. 1, trans. John and Doreen Weightman (1964 in French; New York: Harper & Row, 1969), p. 12. Hereafter *RC*.

17. See, for example, *SA* 2, p. 66; and Lévi-Strauss' *The Savage Mind* (1962 in French; Chicago: Unversity of Chicago Press, 1966), p. 252, where he observes: "Language, an unreflecting totalization, is human reason which has its reasons and of which man knows nothing." Hereafter *SM*.

CHAPTER 2. THE SUBVERSION OF FOUNDATIONS

1. Jacques Derrida, *Of Grammatology*, trans. Gayatri Chakravorty Spivak (1967 in French; Baltimore: Johns Hopkins University Press, 1976), p. 5. Hereafter *OG*. For a useful introduction to Derrida see Spivak's Preface, pp. ix–lxxxvii.

2. In 1968, a year after publication of the *Grammatology*, Derrida developed at length the concept of *difference*, which he renames *différance*, in an essay pub. in both a journal and book collection: "La Différance," *Bulletin de la société française de philosophie* (July–September 1968), 62:73–101; and *Théorie d'ensemble* (Paris: Seuil, 1968). He later republished this essay as part of his collection *Marges—de la philosophie* (Paris: Minuit, 1972), pp. 1–30. *Difference* plays a pervasive and prominent role in many of Derrida's works, including *Of Grammatology*. We shall take it up more thoroughly in chap. 3.

3. Although we are not concerned here with the status of grammatology as a "science," but rather with grammatology as a critique and displacement of Saussure's semiology, the question of its scientificity leads Derrida to say: "This is why there is no simple answer to the question of whether grammatology is a 'science.' In a word, I would say that it *inscribes* and *delimits* science; it must freely and rigorously make the norms of science function in its own writing; once again, it *marks* and at the same time *loosens* the limit which closes classical scientificity"—from Jacques Derrida, "Semiology and Grammatology" (Interview with Julia Kristeva in 1968), *Positions*, trans. Alan Bass (1972 in French; Chicago: University of Chicago Press, 1981), p. 36. Hereafter *Pos*.

4. Jacques Derrida, "Positions" (Interview with Jean-Louis Houdebine and Guy Scarpetta in 1971), *Pos*, pp. 37–96. Most of this revealing interview was first made available in English in *Diacritics* (Winter 1972), 2:35–43 and *Diacritics* (Spring 1973), 3:33–46.

5. Jacques Derrida, "Le Facteur de la vérité," *Poétique* (1975), 21:96–147. Available in English in a somewhat reduced version as ".The Purveyor of Truth," trans. Willis Domingo, James Hulbert, Moshe Ron, and M.-R. L[ogan] in *Yale French Studies* (1975), 52:31–113. Hereafter "PT." Later republished in French in Derrida's *La Carte postale: de Socrate à Freud et au-delà* (Paris: Flammarion, 1980), pp. 440–524.

6. For samples of Derrida's work on Freud see, for instance, "Freud and the Scene of Writing," *Writing and Difference*, trans. Alan Bass (1967 in French; Chicago: University of Chicago Press, 1978), pp. 196–231, (hereafter *WD*), which was first pub. in trans. by Jeffrey Mehlman in *Yale French Studies* (1972), 48:73–117; "Speculations—On Freud," trans. Ian McLeod in *Oxford Literary Review* (1978), 3:78–97; and, of course, "The Purveyor of Truth." Generally speaking, Derrida's works are permeated with references to Freud.

For samples of Derrida's work on Nicolas Abraham see, for instance, his introduction to Abraham's and Maria Torok's *Cryptonymie* (1976) pub. in English as "Fors," trans. Barbara Johnson in *Georgia Review* (Spring 1977), 31:64–116; and "Me—Psychoanalysis," trans. Richard Klein in *Diacritics* (Spring 1979), 9:4–12.

7. Lacan's "Seminar on the 'Purloined Letter,'" a psychoanalytic analysis of Edgar Allan Poe's famous story, was first delivered as a speech in 1955, then pub. in 1957 and finally collected in *Écrits* (1966). In the introduction to the 1970 edition of *Écrits*, Lacan says about the "Seminar" that it "keeps the entry post it possesses elsewhere. . . ." The "Seminar"

is available in a partial English translation, trans. Jeffrey Mehlman in *Yale French Studies* (1972), 48:39–72.

8. "This is the strict definition of the *transcendental position*: the privilege of a term within a series of terms which it makes possible and which presupposes it" ("PT," 94*n*).

Offering the "best definition of the transcendental phallus," Derrida cites Lacan's *Écrits*, p. 554: "For the phallus is a signifier, a signifier whose function, in the intrasubjective economy of the analysis, raises perhaps the veil of that which it held in mysteries. For it is the signifier destined to designate as a whole the signified-effects . . ." ("PT," 95*n*).

9. See Barbara Johnson, "The Frame of Reference: Poe, Lacan, Derrida," *Yale French Studies* (1977), 55/56:457–505. Just as Derrida deconstructs Lacan, so Johnson deconstructs Derrida's reading of Lacan. Essentially, Johnson restores Lacan as a wily poststructuralist who resists logocentric lures. On Lacan's "signifier" and Lacanian "interpretation" see esp. pp. 498–99.

10. Jacques Derrida, "Structure, Sign, and Play in the Discourse of the Human Sciences," *The Languages of Criticism and the Sciences of Man: The Structuralist Controversy*, ed. Richard Macksey and Eugenio Donato (Baltimore: Johns Hopkins Press, 1970), pp. 247–65; a different trans. in pub. in *Writing and Difference*, trans. Alan Bass, pp. 278–93. Hereafter I use the latter version designated *WD*. Derrida pub. the French version of this essay in *L'Écriture et la différence* (Paris: Seuil, 1967), pp. 409–28.

11. *OG*, pp. 97–140. The substance of Derrida's polemic first appeared in an issue on Lévi-Strauss of *Cahiers pour l'analyse* (September–October 1966), 4:1–45. In my discussions, passages by Lévi-Strauss are quoted from Derrida's critique in *OG*.

12. The issue of whether deconstruction "destroys" semiology and usurps its place or actually constitutes a radicalized version of semiology still remains an open question. On this issue see, for example, Derrida's discussion with Kristeva in *Pos*, esp. pp. 23–24, 35–36; Jonathan Culler, *The Pursuit of Signs: Semiotics, Literature, Deconstruction* (Ithaca: Cornell University Press, 1981), pp. x–xi, 42–43; and my Appendix "Hermeneutics, Semiotics, and Deconstruction."

CHAPTER 3. EXTENSIONS OF SUBVERSION

1. Available in English as *Speech and Phenomena: And Other Essays on Husserl's Theory of Signs*, trans. David B. Allison (Evanston: Northwestern University Press, 1973). Hereafter *SP*. Allison also appends a trans. of Derrida's seminal essay "La Différance" (1968) on pp. 129–60.

2. Also treated as a minor work in the project of deconstruction is Derrida's introduction to and translation of Husserl's *Die Frage nach dem Ursprung der Geometrie als intentionalhistorisches Problem* (1939)—pub. as *Edmund Husserl's L'origine de la géométrie*, 2d ed., trans. and intro. by Jacques Derrida (1962; Paris: Presses Universitaires de France, 1974). Available in English as *Edmund Husserl's Origin of Geometry: An Introduction* by Jacques Derrida, trans. John P. Leavey, Jr., ed. David B. Allison (Stony Brook, N.Y.: Nicholas Hays, 1978). Leavey provides a useful preface, a translation of Derrida's essay, an English version of Husserl's *Origin*, and a bibliography of Derrida's French and English works.

3. Paul de Man, *Blindness and Insight: Essays in the Rhetoric of Contemporary Criticism* (New York: Oxford University Press, 1971), p. viii. Hereafter *BI*. This book is a collection of essays written between 1966 and 1971. It contains the first American deconstructive reading of Jacques Derrida, pp. 102–41.

4. Paul de Man, *Allegories of Reading: Figural Language in Rousseau, Nietzsche, Rilke, and Proust* (New Haven: Yale University Press, 1979), p. 300. Hereafter *AR*. This book is a collection of essays pub. between 1972 and 1977. For an assessment of de Man's work see

Frank Lentricchia, *After the New Criticism* (Chicago: University of Chicago Press, 1980), chap. 8.

5. J. Hillis Miller, "Georges Poulet's 'Criticism of Identification,'" *The Quest for Imagination*, ed. O. B. Hardison, Jr. (Cleveland: Case Western Reserve University Press, 1971), p. 216.

6. J. Hillis Miller, "Tradition and Difference," review of M. H. Abrams' *Natural Supernaturalism*, in *Diacritics* (Winter 1972), 2:6. Hereafter "TD."

7. See J. Hillis Miller, "Williams' *Spring and All* and the Progress of Poetry," *Daedalus* (Spring 1970), 99:405–34.

8. J. Hillis Miller, "Nature and the Linguistic Moment," *Nature and the Victorian Imagination*, ed. U. C. Knoepflmacher and G. B. Tennyson (Berkeley: University of California Press, 1977), p. 450. Hereafter "NLM."

9. J. Hillis Miller, "The Linguistic Moment in 'The Wreck of the Deutschland,'" *The New Criticism and After*, ed. Thomas Daniel Young (Charlottesville, Virginia: University Press of Virginia, 1976), p. 58. Hereafter "LM."

10. J. Hillis Miller, "The Stone and the Shell: The Problem of Poetic Form in Wordsworth's Dream of the Arab," *Mouvements premiers: Études critiques offertes à Georges Poulet* (Paris: José Corti, 1972), p. 143. About the strategy of employing etymology, Miller observes "the effect of etymological retracing is not to ground the word solidly but to render it unstable, equivocal, wavering, abysmal"—J. Hillis Miller, "Ariadne's Thread: Repetition and the Narrative Line," *Critical Inquiry* (Autumn 1976), 3:70. Hereafter "AT."

11. J. Hillis Miller's earliest full-fledged rhetorical deconstructions occur in "The Fiction of Realism . . . ," *Charles Dickens and George Cruikshank*, ed. Ada Nisbet (Los Angeles: Wm. Andrews Clark Library, 1971), pp. 1–69; and in his intro. to Charles Dickens' *Bleak House*, ed. Norman Page (1971; rpt. Harmondsworth: Penguin, 1977), pp. 11–34. Derrida lays a groundwork for the practice of deconstructive rhetoric in his "White Mythology: Metaphor in the Text of Philosophy," trans. F. C. T. Moore in *New Literary History* (Autumn 1974), 6:6–74, which was first pub. in French in *Poétique* (1971), 5 and then in Derrida's collection *Marges—de la Philosophie* (1972), pp. 247–324.

12. J. Hillis Miller, "Stevens' Rock and Criticism as Cure, II," *Georgia Review* (Summer 1976), 30:345. This essay promotes the new "Yale critics." Hereafter "SR II."

PART II. VERSIONS OF TEXTUALITY AND INTERTEXTUALITY: CONTEMPORARY THEORIES OF LITERATURE AND TRADITION

CHAPTER 4. THE TRUTH OF LITERATURE

1. Martin Heidegger, "Letter on Humanism" (1947), trans. Frank A. Capuzzi and J. Glenn Gray in *Martin Heidegger, Basic Writings*, ed. David Farrell Krell (New York: Harper & Row, 1977), p. 193. Hereafter "LH" and *BW*.

2. Martin Heidegger, "Hölderlin and the Essence of Poetry" (1936), trans. Douglas Scott in *Existence and Being*, ed. Werner Brock (Chicago: Henry Regnery, 1949), pp. 283–84. Hereafter "HEP" and *EB*.

3. Martin Heidegger, *Being and Time*, trans. John Macquarrie and Edward Robinson (1927 in German; New York: Harper & Row, 1962), sec. 34. Hereafter *BT*. Some of his critics emphasize in Heidegger a turn (*Kehre*) in the late 1920s and early 1930s away from ordinary *being* (*Dasein*) toward more universalist *Being* (*Sein*) and away from ontology toward philosophy of language.

When published in German, the Complete Works of Heidegger will exceed fifty volumes. This work began in 1976 and will take perhaps two decades. The secondary literature on Heidegger approaches 5,000 items at this writing. A useful biographical treatment is Walter Biemel, *Heidegger*, trans. J. L. Mehta (1973 in German; New York: Harcourt Brace Jovanovich, 1976); a helpful introduction is William J. Richardson, *Heidegger: Through Phenomenology to Thought* (The Hague: Nijhoff, 1963); and an interesting collection of essays is Michael Murray, ed., *Heidegger and Modern Philosophy: Critical Essays* (New Haven: Yale University Press, 1978), which contains a bibliography of Heidegger's works in English translation.

4. Martin Heidegger, "Building Dwelling Thinking" (1951), *Poetry, Language, Thought*, trans. Albert Hofstadter (New York: Harper & Row, 1971), p. 146. Hereafter "BDT" and *PLT*. This book is composed, with Heidegger's consent, of seven works written between 1935 and 1951 and first published in German between 1950 and 1960.

5. Martin Heidegger, "The Origin of the Work of Art" (1935), first published in German in 1950 and again in 1960 with slight revisions—available in English as published in 1960 in *PLT*, p. 72. Hereafter "OWA."

6. "Nevertheless, the linguistic work, the poem in the narrower sense, has a privileged position in the domain of the arts"—"OWA," 73.

7. "Heidegger's thought circles about a double theme: the meaning of Being and the appropriative event (*Ereignis*) of disclosure. *Sein* and *Alētheia* remain the key words, *Sein* meaning coming to presence, and *Alētheia* the disclosedness or unconcealment implied in such presence"—Krell, "General Introduction," *BW*, p. 32.

For a discussion of *appropriation* (*Ereignis*) see, for example, Martin Heidegger, *Identity and Difference*, trans. Joan Stambaugh (1957 in German; New York: Harper & Row, 1969), pp. 31–41. Hereafter *ID*.

In a very late work, "The End of Philosophy and the Task of Thinking," first published in French in 1966 and in German in 1969, Heidegger attempts a revision of *aletheia*, which has the effect of making this "activity of unconcealing" a precondition rather than the production of truth. This essay, trans. Joan Stambaugh, is available in English in *On Time and Being* (New York: Harper & Row, 1972) and in *BW*, pp. 373–92. Hereafter "EPTT" from *BW*.

8. Martin Heidegger, "Language" (1950) in *PLT*, 199.

9. In the opening pages of his *Erläuterungen zu Hölderlins Dichtung* (Elucidations of Hölderlin's Poetry), 4th ed. (1951; Frankfurt am Main: Klostermann, 1971), Heidegger suggests that, rather than aiming for exegesis or explanation in the traditional sense, he wants to offer *elucidations* (*erläuterungen*), which illuminate poetic texts to yield insights belonging to "thinking": "Die vorliegenden *Erläuterungen* beanspruchen nicht Beiträge zur literaturhistorischen Forschung und zur Ästhetik zu sein. Sie entspringen einer Notwendigkeit des Denkens" (The present *Elucidations* don't claim to contribute to research in literary criticism or to aesthetics. They rise out of the necessity of thinking)—p. 7. See also Heidegger, *Kant and the Problem of Metaphysics*, trans. James S. Churchill (1929 in German; Bloomington: Indiana University Press, 1962), p. 207: "It is true that in order to wrest from the actual words that which these words 'intend to say,' every interpretation must necessarily resort to violence. This violence, however, should not be confused with an action that is wholly arbitrary. The interpretation must be animated and guided by the power of an illuminative idea. Only through the power of this idea can an interpretation . . . get through to the unsaid . . . to attempt to find an expression for it. The directive idea itself is confirmed by its own power of illumination."

For an extensive analysis of Heidegger's style see George Steiner, *Martin Heidegger* (New York: Viking, 1979).

10. Paul A. Bové, *Destructive Poetics: Heidegger and Modern American Poetry* (New York: Columbia University Press, 1980).

11. A "selection" of Spanos' most important essays includes: "Heidegger, Kierkegaard, and the Hermeneutic Circle: Towards a Postmodern Theory of Interpretation as Disclosure," *Boundary 2* (Winter 1976), 4, which also appeared in *Martin Heidegger and the Question of Literature* (Bloomington: Indiana University Press, 1979), pp. 115–48—hereafter "HK" and *QL*; "Breaking the Circle: Hermeneutics as Dis-closure," *Boundary 2* (Winter 1977), 5:421–57—hereafter "BC"; "Postmodern Literature and the Hermeneutic Crisis," *Union Seminary Quarterly Review* (Winter 1979), 34:119–31; "Hermeneutics and Memory: Destroying T. S. Eliot's *Four Quartets*," *Genre* (Winter 1978), 11:523–73—hereafter "HM"; and "Repetition in *The Waste Land*: A Phenomenological De-struction," *Boundary 2* (Spring 1979), 7:225–85, which serves as the concluding essay of Bové's special issue of *Boundary 2* (1979) on "Revisions of the Anglo-American Tradition"—hereafter "R."

12. Spanos' critique of the traditional philosophical understanding of time is long-standing, dating back to his existentialist works of the late 1960s. See, for example, *The Christian Tradition in Modern British Verse Drama: The Poetics of Sacramental Time* (New Brunswick: Rutgers University Press, 1967); and, among many other articles, "Modern Literary Criticism and the Spatialization of Time: An Existential Critique," *Journal of Aesthetics and Art Criticism* (1970), 29:87–104; and "The Detective and the Boundary: Some Notes on the Postmodern Literary Imagination," *Boundary 2* (Fall 1972), 1:141–68, which is revised and enlarged in *Existentialism 2: A Casebook*, ed. William V. Spanos (New York: Crowell, 1976).

13. Heidegger, *BT*, sec. 32. Among the many fine commentators on this section of *BT*, Spanos favors Hans-Georg Gadamer, *Truth and Method*, trans. unnamed (1960 and 2d ed. 1965 in German; New York: Seabury Press, 1975); and Richard Palmer, *Hermeneutics: Interpretation Theory in Schleiermacher, Dilthey, Heidegger, and Gadamer* (Evanston: Northwestern University Press, 1969).

Spanos doesn't often attend to the texts of Paul Ricoeur, who takes into account structuralism and hermeneutics in his work. See, for example, Ricoeur's *The Rule of Metaphor*, trans. Robert Czerny and others (1975 in French; Toronto: University of Toronto Press, 1977); and *The Philosophy of Paul Ricoeur: An Anthology of his Works*, ed. Charles E. Reagan and David Stewart (Boston: Beacon Press, 1978), esp. pp. 97–166. (The work of Ricoeur is contrasted with Derrida's project by Dominick LaCapra in a review essay in *Diacritics* [Winter 1980], 10:15–28.)

14. For a discussion of the growth and significance of contemporary "reader-response criticism," see, for example, Susan R. Suleiman, "Introduction: Varieties of Audience-Oriented Criticism," *The Reader in the Text: Essays on Audience and Interpretation*, ed. S. R. Suleiman and Inge Crosman (Princeton: Princeton University Press, 1980), pp. 3–45. This collection contains essays by sixteen authors and an annotated bibliography on the subject.

15. Since 1975 Spanos has shown a serious interest in "oral poetics." See, for example, "The Oral Impulse in Contemporary American Poetry," which is a special issue of *Boundary 2* (Spring 1975), 3, edited by Spanos.

16. Spanos believes that the postwar period is giving birth to a new "tradition of the sublime." In his works on Eliot and Sartre as well as on more recent writers, he uncovers a pervasive thematic: contemporary literature presents the horrible uncertainties of life and pictures human existence as thoroughly dreadful; so strong is this thematic that the imagination cannot comprehend it. As such, "negative capability" emerges continually as *the* authentic contemporary stance. See, for example, Spanos, "The Un-Naming of the Beasts: The Postmodernity of Sartre's 'La Nausée,'" *Criticism* (Summer 1978), 20:223–80, esp. 278.

A brief *destructive* critique of *deconstruction* occurs in Spanos' "Retrieving Heidegger's De-Struction," *Society for Critical Exchange Reports* (Fall 1980), no. 8:30–53. This is a special issue on deconstructive criticism, containing six essays and a lengthy bibliography on deconstruction.

CHAPTER 5. THE DISSEMINATION OF THE TEXT

1. Joseph N. Riddel, *The Inverted Bell* (Baton Rouge: Louisiana State University Press, 1974), xxvi, 308 pp.

2. J. Hillis Miller, "Deconstructing the Deconstructers," review of Joseph N. Riddel's *The Inverted Bell*, in *Diacritics* (Summer 1975), 5:24–31. Hereafter "DD."

3. Joseph N. Riddel, "A Miller's Tale," *Diacritics* (Fall 1975), 5:56–65. Hereafter "MT."

4. See, for example, Riddel, "Against Formalism," *Genre* (1970), 3:156–72; "Interpreting Stevens: An Essay on Poetry and Thinking," *Boundary 2* (1972), 1:79–97; and *The Inverted Bell* (1974).

5. This issue of *Genre* (Winter 1978), 11, contains Spanos' "Hermeneutics and Meaning: Destroying T. S. Eliot's *Four Quartets*," 523–73; and Bové's "The World and Earth of William Carlos Williams: *Paterson* as a 'Long Poem,'" 575–96, which employs the later Heidegger in a destructive reading of both Williams criticism and his *Paterson*.

6. Evidently, Riddel follows the work of Hartman and Bloom. See, for example, his review of Hartman's *Beyond Formalism* (1970) in *Comparative Literature* (Spring 1973), 25:178–81; and, among a few pieces on Bloom, his review essay on Bloom's tetralogy (1973–1976) in *Georgia Review* (Winter 1976), 30:989–1006. (We shall take up Bloom in chap. 6 and Hartman in Part III.)

7. Joseph N. Riddel, "Re-doubling the Commentary," review of Derrida's *Of Grammatology* and of Michel Foucault's *Language, Counter-Memory, Practice*, in *Contemporary Literature* (Spring 1979), 20:242. Hereafter "RC."

8. Roland Barthes, "The Struggle with the Angel" (1971), *Image – Music – Text*, ed. and trans. Stephen Heath (New York: Hill and Wang, 1977), p. 141. Hereafter *IMT*. This book contains thirteen essays, published between 1961 and 1973, selected by Heath.

"The Struggle with the Angel" shows Barthes midway or caught between structuralism and deconstruction. On the one hand, he works out a provocative structuralist reading of Genesis 32:22–32 (Jacob's Wrestling with the Angel), employing various forms of analysis modeled after Lévi-Strauss, A. J. Greimas, and Vladimir Propp. On the other hand, he modestly inserts "textual readings" here and there, pointing out that such analysis "conceives the text as taken up in an *open* network which is the very infinity of language, itself structured without closure; it tries to say no longer *from where* the text comes (historical criticism), nor even *how* it is made (structural analysis), but how it is unmade, how it explodes, disseminates—by what coded paths it *goes off*" (126–27).

9. Roland Barthes, *The Pleasure of the Text*, trans. Richard Miller (1973 in French; New York: Hill and Wang, 1975), p. 35. Hereafter *PT*. For an introduction to Barthes see John Sturrock, ed., *Structuralism and Since: From Lévi-Strauss to Derrida* (New York: Oxford University Press, 1979), pp. 52–80.

10. The turn of the *Tel Quel* group toward deconstruction is marked by the publication of the essay collection *Théorie d'ensemble* (1968). Of this group Julia Kristeva evidently exerts the most influence on Barthes. In his autobiography Barthes later complains about the group: "His friends on *Tel Quel*: their originality, their *truth* (aside from their intellectual energy, their genius for writing) insist that they must agree to speak a common, general, incorporeal language, i.e., political language, *although each of them speaks it with his own body*. . . . [But] my body cannot accommodate itself to *generality*. . . ."—Roland Barthes,

Roland Barthes, trans. Richard Howard (1975 in French; New York: Hill and Wang, 1977), p. 175. Hereafter *RB*.

For an overview of the development of *Tel Quel* from 1960 to 1980, see "Paradise Lost? An Interview with Philippe Sollers," intro. and trans. by Shuhsi Kao in *Sub-Stance* (1981), no. 30:31–50. Sollers, editor of *Tel Quel*, observes in 1980: "We have abandoned the notion that the group, the activity of each member and the review itself, has to be subordinate to an overall political view. . . . Hence *Tel Quel* called *Tel Quel* into question, an example of permanent revolution" (49).

11. Roland Barthes, *S/Z*, trans. Richard Miller (1970 in French; New York: Hill and Wang, 1974), p. 10.

In general, deconstruction turns its criticism upon the concept "self." The status of the "self," for instance, in J. Hillis Miller's project is exemplary. He sees human consciousness as "a fathomless chasm" and the (apparent) stability of the self as "an effect of language": "The self is a linguistic construction rather than being the given, the rock, a solid *point de départ*" ("SR II," 345). In short, "there is no literal language of consciousness, the self being itself a figure or effect of language" ("NLM," 440). The self is a figurative construction— a metalepsis ("LM," 60n). Just as literary texts create selves (characters) through language, so philosophical and psychological texts establish the seemingly irreducible Self in language. The self of any author as well as any literary character is, in reality, mere figurative construction. To put it succinctly, Miller undermines the "self" by textualizing it; he situates the self within the lines of force of *rhetoricity*. Ultimately, the self becomes trope (metalepsis).

For a deconstruction of Descartes' *cogito* see Jean-Luc Nancy, "Dum Scribo," trans. Ian McLeod, *Oxford Literary Review* (1978), 3:6–21.

Nietzsche observed: "The 'subject' is only a fiction: the ego of which one speaks when one censures egoism does not exist at all"—*The Will to Power*, trans. Walter Kaufmann and R. J. Hollingdale (New York: Random House, 1967), p. 199, #370.

12. Barthes observes about himself: "His relation to psychoanalysis is not scrupulous (though without his being able to pride himself on any contestation, any rejection). It is an *undecided* relation"—*RB*, 150. Indeed, Barthes' "typology of readers" is a provocation, not a developed model. He never considers, for example, sadistic, masochistic, narcissistic, voyeuristic, or schizophrenic readers. The most rigorous contemporary American psychoanalytic treatment of readers is that of Norman Holland. For an introduction to Holland's work see my "A Primer of Recent Critical Theories," *College English* (October 1977), 39:138–52.

13. For extended consideration of Barthes' typology see "Roland Barthes and the Four Pleasures of Reading," which is a special issue of the *Journal of Practical Structuralism* (July 1979), 1. For a detailed Marxist analysis of the "disintegrated subject," see Rosalind Coward and John Ellis, *Language and Materialism: Developments in Semiology and the Theory of the Subject* (London: Routledge & Kegan Paul, 1977). This book is the work of avant-garde British critics, who attend carefully to semiological and deconstructive theories. (Apparently, deconstruction came to the attention of British intellectuals in the early 1970s. We may expect a flowering of this interest and further publications during the 1980s.)

14. Harold Bloom, et al., *Deconstruction and Criticism* (New York: Seabury Press, 1979), p. ix. Hereafter *D&C*.

Derrida's contribution in *D&C* is a double text where one analysis rests upon another. A continuous borderline separates the bottom from the top text. The top one, constituting roughly seventy-five percent of the whole, is titled "Living On"—hereafter "LO." The lower text is "*Border Lines*"—hereafter "BL." "Living On: *Border Lines*" is translated by James Hulbert.

15. As Derrida indicates, the destruction of "reference" has caused much anger and many attempts at repair. For some samples see Oswald Ducrot and Tzvetan Todorov, *Encyclopedic Dictionary of the Sciences of Language*, trans. Catherine Porter (1972 in French; Baltimore: Johns Hopkins University Press, 1979), pp. 347–65; Fredric Jameson, "The Ideology of the Text," *Salmagundi* (1976) 31/32:204–46; Edward W. Said, "The Problem of Textuality: Two Exemplary Positions," *Critical Inquiry* (Summer 1978), 4:673–714; Walter Benn Michaels, "Saving the Text: Reference and Belief," *Modern Language Notes* (December 1978), 93:771–93; Thomas E. Lewis, "Notes toward a Theory of the Referent," *PMLA* (May 1979), 94:459–75; and Charles Altieri, "Presence and Reference in a Literary Text: The Example of Williams' 'This is Just to Say,'" *Critical Inquiry*, (Spring 1979) 5:489–510.

16. Derrida develops the theory of *dissemination* in *La Dissémination* (Paris: Seuil, 1972), esp. pp. 13, 31–33, 50, 245, 294, 299–300, 390. Cf. Julia Kristeva's idea of *signifiance* in *Semeiotiké: Recherches pour une sémanalyse* (Paris: Seuil, 1969), where a notion of dissemination accompanies the phenomenon of the "deconstruction of the subject": the explosion of meaning across a text joins the disintegration or loss of the reader's self. In *PT* Barthes characterizes such production as orgasmic experience. Another version of this libidinal dispersion of meaning appears in Jean-François Lyotard's *Economie libidinale* (Paris: Minuit, 1974)—where it manifests political import. (Thus far Lyotard's works have exerted little influence on American deconstructors.)

CHAPTER 6. THE (INTER)TEXTUALIZATION OF CONTEXT

1. Hayden White, *Tropics of Discourse: Essays in Cultural Criticism* (Baltimore: Johns Hopkins University Press, 1978), pp. 69–70. Hereafter *TD*. This volume collects twelve articles published between 1966 and 1976.

2. Hayden White, *Metahistory: The Historical Imagination in Nineteenth-century Europe* (Baltimore: Johns Hopkins University Press, 1973), p. 30.

3. Harold Bloom, *A Map of Misreading* (New York: Oxford University Press, 1975), p. 85. Hereafter *MM*.

4. *MM*, pp. 53–60, 115–19; and Harold Bloom, *Poetry and Repression: Revisionism from Blake to Stevens* (New Haven: Yale University Press, 1976), p. 27. Hereafter *PR*.

5. Harold Bloom, "The Breaking of Form," *Deconstruction and Criticism*, ed. H. Bloom, et al., p. 37. Hereafter *D&C*. For an evaluation of Bloom's work see Frank Lentricchia, *After the New Criticism* (1980), chap. 9.

6. Harold Bloom, *The Anxiety of Influence: A Theory of Poetry* (New York: Oxford University Press, 1973), p. 5. Hereafter *AI*.

In his semiotic theory of intertextuality, which offers a linguistic model of three types of intertextuality, Michael Riffaterre develops practical methods for interpreting intertextual elements in literary texts—see, for example, his *Semiotics of Poetry* (Bloomington: Indiana University Press, 1978), pp. 115–50; and "Syllepsis," *Critical Inquiry* (Summer 1980), 6:625–38.

7. Harold Bloom, "Coda: Poetic Crossing" in his *Wallace Stevens: The Poems of Our Climate* (Ithaca: Cornell University Press, 1977), pp. 375–406.

8. Harold Bloom, *Kabbalah and Criticism* (New York: Seabury, 1975), p. 106. My italics.

9. Michel Foucault, *The Order of Things: An Archaeology of the Human Sciences*, trans. unnamed (1966 in French; New York: Pantheon, 1970), p. xxiv. (The original French title is *Les Mots et les choses*.) The translation contains an informative "Foreword to the English Edition," pp. ix–xiv.

10. Michel Foucault, "Nietzsche, Genealogy, History" (1971) in Foucault's *Language,*

Counter-Memory, Practice: Selected Essays and Interviews, ed. Donald F. Bouchard, trans. D. F. Bouchard and Sherry Simon (Ithaca: Cornell University Press, 1977), pp. 153–54. Hereafter "NGH" and *LCP*. This book contains seven essays (published between 1962 and 1971), two interviews (1971 and 1972), and a course summary (1971).

11. Michel Foucault, "The Discourse on Language," trans. Rupert Sawyer, pp. 216–29, published as an appendix in Foucault's *The Archaeology of Knowledge*, trans. A. M. Sheridan Smith (1969 in French; New York: Harper & Row, 1972). Hereafter *AK*. "The Discourse on Language" was delivered as an inaugural lecture at the Collège de France in 1970 and published separately in 1971 as *L'Ordre du discours*.

For a useful introduction see Hayden White's essay on Foucault in *Structuralism and Since: From Lévi-Strauss to Derrida*, ed. John Sturrock (1979), pp. 81–115.

12. Michel Foucault, "History, Discourse and Discontinuity," trans. Anthony M. Nazzaro in *Salmagundi* (1972), 20:229–33. Hereafter "HDD." (Originally published in 1968 as "Réponse à une question.") In the latter part of this essay, Foucault discusses how his project relates effectively to progressive political practice.

13. In his essay "The Problem of Textuality: Two Exemplary Positions" (1978), Edward W. Said contrasts Derrida's and Foucault's theories of the text. Ultimately, Said castigates both men for not practicing engaged political and cultural criticism. Not surprisingly, Derrida comes off much worse than Foucault in this critique. For a discussion of Foucault and Said on the relations among "textuality – knowledge – power," see Josué V. Harari's "Critical Factions/Critical Fictions," which is an introduction to *Textual Strategies: Perspectives in Post-Structuralist Criticism*, ed. J. V. Harari (Ithaca: Cornell University Press, 1979), pp. 40–47; and also Michael Sprinker, "Textual Politics: Foucault and Derrida," *Boundary 2* (Spring 1980), 8:75–98.

When Foucault responds to Derrida's early critique, published in *Writing and Difference* (pp. 31–63), of his *Madness and Civilization*, he displays notable powers of debate. Foucault's response was published as an appendix to the later revised edition of *Folie et déraison* (Paris: Gallimard, 1972), pp. 583–603, which is available in English as "My Body, This Paper, This Fire," trans. Geoff Bennington in *Oxford Literary Review* (Autumn 1979), 4:9–28. For Foucault's critique of the theory of *écriture* see his "What Is an Author?" (1969), *LCP*, pp. 119–20.

The current leading critique of Foucault is Jean Baudrillard's *Oublier Foucault* (Paris: Galilée, 1977), which is translated into English by Nicole Dufresne in *Humanities in Society* (Winter 1980), 3:87–111. This special issue on Foucault contains five other essays.

14. Michel Foucault, "Theatrum Philosophicum" (1970), *LCP*, p. 185. See pp. 181–87 where Foucault develops a theory of *difference*.

15. Michel Foucault, *The History of Sexuality*, vol. 1, trans. Robert Hurley (1976 in French; New York: Pantheon, 1978), p. 96. Cf. Foucault's *Discipline and Punish: The Birth of the Prison*, trans. Alan Sheridan (1975 in French; New York: Pantheon, 1977), esp. pp. 293–308.

Foucault discusses his growing interest in "power" in a lecture delivered during January 1976—see "Two Lectures" in Foucault's *Power/Knowledge: Selected Interviews and Other Writings 1972–1977*, ed. Colin Gordon, trans. C. Gordon, et al. (New York: Pantheon, 1980), pp. 92–108; see also pp. 183–84, 198–99. This book contains six interviews, three conversations, two lectures, and one article—all published between 1972 and 1977.

16. Michel Foucault, "The History of Sexuality: Interview," trans. Geoff Bennington in *Oxford Literary Review* (1980), 4:14. (This interview with Bernard-Henri Lévy was originally published in French in 1977.)

17. Jacques Derrida, "Signature Event Context" (1971), trans. Samuel Weber and Jeffrey Mehlman in *Glyph* (1977), 1:185.

18. Jacques Derrida, "Limited Inc," trans. Samuel Weber in *Glyph* (1977), 2:220.

19. See, for example, Julia Kristeva's discussion of intertextuality in "Problèmes de la structuration du texte," *Théorie d'ensemble* (1968), pp. 311–13. (This book, published by Seuil in the "Collection 'Tel Quel,'" contains more than two dozen essays by fourteen authors, including Barthes, Derrida, Foucault, Sollers, and Kristeva. It is the closest thing in the 1960s to a manifesto of "deconstruction.") See also Roland Barthes, "Theory of the Text" (1973), trans. Ian McLeod in *Untying the Text: A Post-Structuralist Reader*, ed. Robert Young (Boston: Routledge & Kegan Paul, 1981), esp. pp. 39, 45. (This book collects thirteen poststructuralist essays by such authors as Barthes, de Man, Foucault, Johnson, Macherey and Balibar, Mehlman, Miller, and Riffaterre. After each selection the editor provides lists of texts for further reading.)

PART III. CRITICAL READING AND WRITING: STRATEGIES OF DECONSTRUCTION

1. Jacques Derrida, "The Ends of Man" (1968), trans. Edouard Morot-Sir, et al. in *Language and Human Nature*, ed. Paul Kurtz (St. Louis: Warren H. Green, 1971), p. 205. This essay was first published in translation in *Philosophy and Phenomenological Research* (1969), 30(1):31–57; published in French in Derrida's *Marges* (1972). As far as I can discover, "The Ends of Man" was the first work of Derrida rendered into English.

2. When he explains *undecidables*, Derrida says: "it has been necessary to analyze, to set to work, *within* the text of the history of philosophy, as well as *within* the so-called literary text . . . certain marks . . . that *by analogy* (I underline) I have called undecidables, that is, unities of simulacrum, 'false' verbal properties (nominal or semantic) that can no longer be included within philosophical (binary) opposition, but which, however, inhabit philosophical opposition, resisting and disorganizing it, *without ever* constituting a third term, without ever leaving room for a solution . . ." (*Pos*, 42–43).

Over the course of his oeuvre Derrida employs various names for his reading practices, including, among others, desedimentation, deconstruction, and decelebration. While this last hints at the powers of parody inherent in deconstructive repetition (a preliminary step of inversion), the first two suggestively name the tactic of staying within the intertextual enclosure, but without resolving or effacing its faults, fissures, and divisions. In addition, Derrida tosses out numerous names for *split writing*, including double science, double stratification, double register, bifocal writing, two listenings, two scenes, and paleonymy.

3. De Man's concept of *allegory* is developed at length in his "The Rhetoric of Temporality," in *Interpretation: Theory and Practice*, ed. Charles S. Singleton (Baltimore: Johns Hopkins University Press, 1969), pp. 173–209. See also "Reading," *AR*, pp. 57–78.

4. Paul de Man, Foreword, *The Dissimulating Harmony: The Image of Interpretation in Nietzsche, Rilke, Artaud, and Benjamin*, by Carol Jacobs (Baltimore: Johns Hopkins University Press, 1978), p. ix.

5. Paul de Man, "Literature and Language: A Commentary," *New Literary History* (Autumn 1972), 4:188; my italics. Hereafter "LL." On the concept of "unreadability" see *AR*, p. 245.

6. Paul de Man, "Nietzsche's Theory of Rhetoric," *Symposium* (Spring 1974), 28:49–50. Hereafter "NTR." When published in *Symposium*, this conference paper, later reprinted in *AR* (pp. 103–18), included de Man's responses to questions from the audience. This revealing (ephemeral) material is available only in *Symposium*, not in *AR*.

7. See Paul de Man, Introduction, Special Issue on "The Rhetoric of Romanticism," *Studies in Romanticism* (Winter 1979), 18:495–99. Among other things here, de Man confesses that "the writing of literary history and the reading of literary texts are not easily compatible" (497). He suggests that he himself is "in an awkward double bind, reflected in writings that are lopsided in their emphasis on textual analysis as compared to the paucity of the historical results . . ." (498).

8. J. Hillis Miller, "On Edge: The Crossways of Contemporary Criticism," *Bulletin of the American Academy of Arts and Sciences* (January 1979), 32:18–19.

9. J. Hillis Miller, "Fiction and Repetition: *Tess of the d'Urbervilles*," in *Forms of Modern British Fiction*, ed. Alan Warren Friedman (Austin: University of Texas Press, 1975), p. 68. Hereafter "FR."

10. J. Hillis Miller, "Stevens' Rock and Criticism as Cure," *Georgia Review* (Spring 1976), 30:31. Hereafter "SR."

11. J. Hillis Miller, "The Still Heart: Poetic Form in Wordsworth," *New Literary History* (Winter 1971), 2:298. Hereafter "SH."

12. J. Hillis Miller, "Ariachne's Broken Woof," *Georgia Review* (Spring 1977), 31:59. Hereafter "ABW." About the effect of such intertextuality on the individual text, Miller observes: "A literary text is not a thing in itself, 'organically unified,' but a relation to other texts which are relations in their turn. The study of literature is therefore a study of intertextuality . . ." ("SR II," 334).

13. As a rule, Miller takes pains to demonstrate that the texts he reads are already deconstructed. He regularly points out that "any literary text, with more or less explicitness or clarity, already reads or misreads itself. The 'deconstruction' which the text performs on itself and which the critic repeats is not of the superstructure of the work but of the ground on which it stands . . ." ("SR II," 333). This notion of the self-deconstructing text comes from de Man.

14. Miller, like de Man, observes of deconstructive criticism: "The boundaries between literature and criticism are broken down in this activity, not because the critic arrogates to himself some vague right to be 'poetical' in his writing, but because he recognizes it as his doom not to be able to be anything else" ("SR II," 333). Given the rhetoricity of all language, deconstruction necessarily blurs the traditional hierarchical distinction between literature and literary criticism. Metalanguage is impossible. See also *D&C*, p. 230.

15. See Barthes' *L'Empire des signes* (Geneva: Skira, 1970), pp. 58–65.

For a deconstructive reading of Barthes and Balzac, see Barbara Johnson, "The Critical Difference," *Diacritics* (Summer 1978), 8:2–9. Interestingly, Johnson argues that the text of *Sarrasine* is self-deconstructing so that "Balzac has already in a sense done Barthes' work for him" (8).

For an explicit discussion of the *fragment* as preferred critical genre, see *RB*, pp. 92–95, 147–48. And for a pointed statement on *metalanguage*, see Barthes' "Lecture," trans. Richard Howard in *October* (Spring 1979), 8:13. This lecture, given in January 1977, was delivered when Barthes assumed the Chair of Literary Semiology at the Collège de France. By 1977, of course, Barthes was no longer a semiologist—see Nadine Dormoy Savage, "Rencontre avec Roland Barthes," *French Review* (February 1979), 52:438, where Barthes states "au moment où j'accédais à cette chaire de sémiologie pratiquement je ne faisais plus de sémiologie. J'ai traversé la sémiologie . . ." (at the moment when I acceded to this chair of semiology I was no longer in actual fact dealing with semiology. I passed through semiology . . .).

16. Jacques Derrida, "Ja, ou le faux-bond," *Digraphe* (March 1977), 11:103. This is the second part of an interview; the first part was published as "Entre crochets," *Digraphe* (April 1976), 8:97–114.

17. Jacques Derrida, *Glas* (Paris: Galilée, 1974), p. 77b. To designate the left and right columns, "a" and "b," respectively, are used.

18. In her "*Glas*—Piece: A *Compte Rendu,*" *Diacritics* (Fall 1977), 7:22–43, Gayatri Chakravorty Spivak offers a preliminary readng of *Glas* as autobiography. Among other things, she relates the text to the death of Derrida's father.

19. Geoffrey H. Hartman, "Crossing Over: Literary Commentary as Literature," *Comparative Literature* (Summer 1976), 28:268. Hereafter "CO." This essay is reprinted in Hartman's *Criticism in the Wilderness: The Study of Literature Today* (New Haven: Yale University Press, 1980), pp. 189–213. Hereafter *CW.*

20. Geoffrey H. Hartman, "Monsieur Texte II: Epiphony in Echoland," *Georgia Review* (Spring 1976), 30:183. The first half of this study was originally published as "Monsieur Texte: On Jacques Derrida, His *Glas,*" *Georgia Review* (Winter 1975), 29:759–97. Both of these essays are reprinted in Hartman's *Saving the Text: Literature/Derrida/Philosophy* (Baltimore: Johns Hopkins University Press, 1981), pp. 33–66, 1–32.

21. Félix Guattari, "A Liberation of Desire: An Interview," trans. George Stambolian in *Homosexualities and French Literature,* ed. G. Stambolian and Elaine Marks (Ithaca: Cornell University Press, 1979), p. 57. See also Julia Kristeva, *Desire in Language: A Semiotic Approach to Literature and Art,* ed. Leon S. Roudiez, trans. Thomas Gora, Alice Jardine, and L. S. Roudiez (New York: Columbia University Press, 1980), esp. pp. 116–18.

22. Jacques Derrida, *La Vérité en peinture* (Paris: Flammarion, 1978), pp. 23–24.

23. See, for example, Fredric Jameson's *Fables of Aggression* (Berkeley: University of California Press, 1979), where the "molar/molecular" model of Deleuze and Guattari is put to use; and also Jameson's *The Political Unconscious: Narrative as a Socially Symbolic Act* (Ithaca: Cornell University Press, 1981), chap. 1, esp. pp. 21–23.

24. Gilles Deleuze and Félix Guattari, *Anti-Oedipus: Capitalism and Schizophrenia,* trans. Robert Hurley, Mark Seem, and Helen R. Lane (1972 in French; New York: Viking, 1977), p. 311.

25. Jean-François Lyotard, "Energumen Capitalism" (1972), trans. James Leigh in *Semiotexte* (1977), 2(3):17, 20. This number of *Semiotexte* is a special issue on *Anti-Oedipus,* containing seven articles on the book, two interviews and two essays by Guattari, two articles by Deleuze, two short pieces by Guattari and Deleuze together, and several brief poems by Artaud.

Lyotard points out that, while *Anti-Oedipus* undermines psychoanalysis raucously, it subverts Marxism silently. There is apparently a lingering reverence for Marxism, which rules out any parodic or angry attack. Thus Lyotard sets out to foreground and extend Deleuze's and Guattari's implicit destruction of Marxist formulations.

26. Gilles Deleuze, "I have nothing to admit," trans. Janis Forman in *Semiotexte* (1977), 2(3):113–14. This "Lettre à Michel Cressole" was originally published as an appendix to Cressole's *Deleuze* (1973).

See p. 114 on "two ways of reading a book." For a condensed overview of the work of Deleuze and Guattari after *Anti-Oedipus,* see Charles J. Stivale, "Gilles Deleuze & Félix Guattari: Schizoanalysis & Literary Discourse," *Sub-Stance* (1981), no. 29:51–55.

27. Roland Barthes, *A Lover's Discourse: Fragments,* trans. Richard Howard (1977 in French; New York: Hill and Wang, 1978). And Jacques Derrida, "Envois," *La Carte postale: de Socrate à Freud et au-delà,* pp. 5–273. For a suggestive "reading" of *The Post Card* see Gregory L. Ulmer, "The Post-Age," *Diacritics* (Fall 1981), 11; and on *A Lover's Discourse* see Ulmer's "The Discourse of the Imaginary," *Diacritics* (Spring 1980), 10:61–75.

28. Geoffrey H. Hartman, *The Fate of Reading and Other Essays* (Chicago: University of Chicago Press, 1975), p. 9.

29. Geoffrey H. Hartman, *CW*, pp. 253–64. See also Robert Moynihan, "Interview with Geoffrey Hartman, Yale University, March 19, 1979," *Boundary 2* (Fall 1980), 9:201–2, 206–9; and especially Geoffrey H. Hartman, "How Creative Should Literary Criticism Be?," *New York Times Book Review*, 5 April 1981, pp. 11, 24–25. The recent work of Cary Nelson, to cite another example, also explores various contemporary tendencies toward "creative criticism."

30. Geoffrey H. Hartman, Preface, *Psychoanalysis and the Question of the Text*, ed. G. H. Hartman, Selected Papers from the English Institute, 1976–77 (Baltimore: John Hopkins University Press, 1978), p. xv.

Note on Bibliography

The written materials of and about deconstruction exceed a thousand items. Books and articles on related subjects—structuralism and phenomenology, to name just two—expand the number of sources beyond ready calculation. Since a great deal of bibliographical work already exists in these areas, I shall simply record for the curious student and interested scholar several rich sources of information to complement my Notes and to facilitate preliminary research.

The two most useful bibliographies are currently those by Richard Barney, "Deconstructive Criticism: A Selected Bibliography," *Society for Critical Exchange Reports* (Fall 1980), no. 8 [Supplement], pp. 1–54; and Josué V. Harari, ed., in *Textual Strategies: Perspectives in Post-Structuralist Criticism* (Ithaca: Cornell University Press, 1979), pp. 421–63. The Barney bibliography lists works up to 1980 by Roland Barthes, Paul de Man, Jacques Derrida, Eugenio Donato, Barbara Johnson, J. Hillis Miller, Joseph N. Riddel, and William V. Spanos. In addition, this careful compilation provides a selection of 130 critiques and commentaries on deconstruction, relating these secondary materials to individual deconstructors through cross listing. The Harari bibliography gives detailed information on Roland Barthes, Gilles Deleuze, Paul de Man, Jacques Derrida, Eugenio Donato, Michel Foucault, Gérard Genette, Joseph N. Riddel, Edward Said, and Michel Serres. Moreover, Harari presents judicious selections on Structuralism, Literary Criticism, Philosophy, Psychoanalysis, Anthropology, Linguistics, and Semiotics. These supplementary lists cite materials by and about, among others, Sylviane Agacinski, Harold Bloom, Félix Guattari, Geoffrey Hartman, Sarah Kofman, Julia Kristeva, Philippe Lacoue-Labarthe, Jacques Lacan, Claude Lévi-Strauss, Jean-François Lyotard, Jeffrey Mehlman, and Jean-Luc Nancy. Finally, Harari briefly profiles the two dozen leading journals of contemporary literary and critical theory, singling out the most important issues published during the 1960s and 1970s.

The materials related to deconstruction will grow in numbers in the 1980s. As I write this note, I am aware of books in progress by John Brenkman, Jonathan Culler, Paul de Man, Eugenio Donato, J. Hillis Miller, Joseph N. Riddel, and Michael Ryan. A recent translation of essays by Julia Kristeva is to be followed by another volume of her work from Columbia University Press. There are five books by Jacques Derrida soon to be published in translation by the University of Chicago Press, as well as another from Columbia. Finally, I have heard about plans for future casebooks, anthologies, and bibliographies on deconstruction.

Index